Morality & Utility in American Antislavery Reform

Morality & Utility in American Antislavery Reform

by Louis S. Gerteis

The University of North Carolina Press
Chapel Hill and London

Library of Congress Cataloging-in-Publication Data

Gerteis, Louis S.
    Morality and utility in American antislavery reform.

    Bibliography: p.
    Includes index.
    1. Slavery—United States—Anti-slavery movements.
2. Abolitionists—United States. I. Title.
E449.G38 1987   332.4′4′0973   86-19217
ISBN 0-8078-1722-8

To
Joseph
Jessie
&
Emily

Contents ─────────────────────

Preface ————————————————————

THIS work began as an inquiry into the relationship between anti-slavery reform and the Liberal Republican opposition to President Ulysses S. Grant's reelection in 1872. At the outset I wanted to consider why so many of the prominent and radical opponents of slavery also opposed Radical Reconstruction in the late 1860s and early 1870s. The story of the Liberal break with the Stalwart Republicans did not need retelling, but the familiar charges of reformist timidity in the face of southern reaction and of a betrayal of principle seemed to me to obscure the significance of the reformers' participation in the Liberal campaign. What had been lost over time, and what I hoped to recover, were the historical links between late nineteenth-century liberalism and the antislavery cause. I did not accept the reformers' lofty professions of principle as definitions of their motives or goals, but I did believe that a close reading of the extensive and purposeful record they had created and preserved could reveal a great deal about their developing social attitudes and political expectations.

I hoped to explore the process of historical transformation. As it turned out, the reformers' self-conscious concern with consistency of principle and with their historical role as agents of progress provided a useful point of departure for a study of the relationship between the moral values of the antislavery cause and the utilitarian faith of liberal reform. Nineteenth-century reformers, as I came to appreciate, had a great deal to say about a wide range of subjects. In their public professions and private correspondence, they labored to demonstrate to their contemporaries and to posterity that their activities were guided by a reverence for republican values, for the rule of law, for the laws of political economy, and for allied standards of morality in public affairs. That the reformers contributed as well to a transformation of republican values, to the emergence of modern doctrines in law and political economy, and to new standards of public morality in the conduct of mass politics became the principal concerns of this study.

In a work such as this, which has developed over a number of years, the usual caveat that all errors of fact and interpretation are the responsibility of the author alone applies with unusual effect. It is, nevertheless, a pleasure to thank those who have offered help and encouragement throughout the project. To several of my colleagues in the History Department at the University of Missouri–St. Louis I owe particular thanks. George Rawick listened patiently and read a series of rough drafts as I tried to identify problems and pose solutions. Howard S. Miller offered useful comments on my early efforts to evaluate antislavery concerns in law. James Neal Primm offered valuable advice concerning analysis and style in my treatment of antislavery uses of political economy. To the History Department as a whole I am grateful for the opportunity to present aspects of this study for criticism and discussion in the History Colloquium series.

I wish to express my gratitude as well to Howard Temperley of the University of East Anglia for his generosity in reading the entire manuscript and in raising helpful questions regarding the intentions of antislavery reformers. I am also indebted to Stanley Engerman for his careful comments on what became Chapters 4 and 8 and to Ira Berlin, George Fredrickson, Richard Sewell, and William Wiecek for their willingness to read portions of the manuscript in its early stages of development. I owe thanks as well to Margaret Gerteis, who read several drafts and offered valuable suggestions along the way. My work has been significantly improved in the final stages of writing by the comments and criticisms provided by Harold Hyman and Richard Latner as readers for the University of North Carolina Press.

The staffs of the following libraries assisted greatly in the completion of my research: Boston Public Library, Chicago Historical Society, Columbia University Library, Dartmouth College Library, Detroit Public Library, Houghton Library of Harvard University, Library of Congress, New York Public Library, and the Historical Society of Pennsylvania. My intellectual debts to previous scholarship are substantial and, I hope, adequately acknowledged in the notes to the text. I extend my thanks to the American Philosophical Society and to the Office of Research Administration of the University of Missouri–St. Louis for financial support during several research trips. Finally, to Janice Parker I owe the greatest debt of all. Her energy, enthusiasm, and good sense are a delight and a blessing and have hastened this work to completion.

Introduction ─────────────

From the early 1830s through the abolition of slavery during the Civil War, American antislavery reformers pressed their demands for freedom with a sense of urgency that contrasted sharply with older projections of slavery's gradual decline.[1] In this new mood, the practice of slaveholding collided violently and, it seemed, unavoidably with American republican values. With remarkable suddenness, and with a sense of exhilaration that prompted determined and even heroic action, reformers shed the traditional restraints of gradualism to demand the immediate abolition of slavery as a clear and present danger to the republic.

Bolstered by the successes of British abolitionists, American antislavery reformers drew particular strength from the altruism of their cause. If, in the broadest sense, their agitations must be understood in relationship to what David Brion Davis describes as "the triumphant hegemony of a capitalist world view and particularly to capitalist views of labor," their cause also challenged capitalist complicity in slavery and disrupted profitable economic ties between slave masters and allied merchants and manufacturers. Antislavery reformers had no discernible immediate economic advantages to gain from slavery's demise. There is every reason to accept the sincerity of their concern with the plight of the slave and the despotism of slavery. As Eric Foner observes, "It will not do to defang the abolitionist crusade: it was indeed a radical impulse, challenging fundamental aspects of American life."[2]

Demands for immediate abolition during the mid-nineteenth century marked a departure from past practices but not a rejection of traditional antislavery convictions. Nineteenth-century reformers continued to insist, in the manner of Adam Smith and the American revolutionary generation, that slavery could not survive in a modern society. But the urgency of their attack on slavery reflected conditions and perceptions unique to their era. Looking on slavery through the newly mounted lens of utilitarian political economy, reformers joined with John Stuart Mill in England and Henry C. Carey in America in identifying objective forces of progress that were sweeping slavery aside and leaving the South's "peculiar institution" a relic of a barbarous past—if it managed to survive at all. The reformers' sense of urgency, then, expressed a new confidence in their own historical destiny and responsibility. These self-conscious agents of progress attacked slavery at its economic, moral, legal, and political base. By questioning the right of southern masters to hold their laborers as property, antislavery reformers rejected the traditional accommodations that associated slavery with the developing capitalist world view. The clash of interests sparked by antislavery reform and the expectations the reformers raised for the postemancipation South and nation form the central themes of this study.

Two terms receive a good deal of use in this study and require definition and discussion at the outset. The first, "utilitarianism," refers to the doctrines of political economy and the related ethical theories most directly associated with Mill and with his mentor Jeremy Bentham. My interest is not with the theory of utilitarianism but with its American applications. In any case, the term's meaning remains the same: that men act and interact in society to maximize their individual pleasure and that the greatest happiness for the greatest number in the long run (that is, the highest social good) will be achieved in the pursuit of individual self-interest. As a theory of political economy, utilitarianism offered an objective guide to moral action which challenged traditional notions of Christian philanthropy at the same time that it projected the perfectibility of human society. By the 1850s, utilitarianism subsumed older and narrower laissez-faire doctrines and became incorporated into the optimistic language of political liberalism, which invoked state powers to promote individual autonomy and the liberty to pursue material gain. It was in the aggressive pursuit of a liberal state, moreover, that the compatibility of slavery with American republican values came directly into question. In the antebellum rhetoric of antislavery reform, the fight against slavery pitted right against wrong, civilization against barbarism, liberty against despotism. The inexorable advance of freedom defined the rise and fall of nations. As a slaveholding nation, America could not advance although the path of potential progress remained clear. The Declaration of Independence proclaimed the equality of man, and antislavery reformers took it to be their historical task to advance this standard of liberty, extending the principle of equality to the enslaved laborers of the South. At the very least, utilitarianism required nominal freedom and equality for all.[3]

The second term that requires definition and discussion refers to the social basis of utilitarianism and political liberalism—that is, to a developing middle class. The formation, influence, and social function of an American middle class continues to be a matter of historical investigation and debate.[4] In the familiar consensus analysis of the 1940s and 1950s, the absence of a landed aristocracy in America and the wide distribution of property in the form of land made the vast majority of Americans independent producers and middle class in temperament. Political liberalism, bland but serene, seemed to suffuse the nation's public life.[5] More recent concerns with the social transformation of early industrial society (and particularly with the emergence of an American working class) depict a more turbulent reality. The world of the independent producer, particularly the artisan, was in turmoil during the first half of the nineteenth century. Prosperous master craftsmen emerged as employers of wage labor, and journeymen artisans (once relatively young as a group and hopeful of becoming independent producers in their own right) grew increasingly dependent as wage earners. Out of this social flux emerged a middle class, distinguished by property and social values from the workers they employed and separated by their modest wealth and uncertain social standing from the established elites whose economic and political power they challenged.[6]

The relationship between antislavery reform and developing middle-class concerns is itself a topic of historiographical debate.[7] Neither the antislavery struggle nor the multitude of moral reforms that swept across the expanding North during the 1830s and 1840s necessarily defined the interests of a new middle class of manufacturers and entrepreneurs. But in both cases—in the increasingly secular concerns of antislavery reform and in the perfectionist enthusiasms of evangelical Protestantism—reform appealed strongly to elements of the middle class and expressed itself in terms of middle-class interests and values. To speak of the antislavery movement as middle class in character is not to reduce the antislavery impulse to a pursuit of narrow economic interests. Nor does such a discussion require that antislavery reform receive universal or exclusive support from the middle class. Certainly one would expect the most fervent and in social terms the most radical expressions of antislavery sentiment (the "come-outers," for example) to raise resentments even in the absence of diverging interests. Indeed, abolitionism's capacity to outrage public opinion remains its most striking characteristic.[8] Nevertheless, using the reformers' perceptions of their own interests and goals both as a point of departure and of reference, the social concerns of antislavery reform come into focus: middle-class reformers had good reason to champion individual autonomy and self-control through temperance and other moral reforms, and they had good reason as well to grow increasingly hostile toward an expanding slaveholding interest.

The relationship between antislavery reform and antebellum workingmen's movements underlies any discussion of the social significance of the slavery issue in the industrializing North. The capacity of some antislavery reformers to identify the oppression of "wage slavery" has suggested to some historians the existence of an antislavery tradition distinct from the free labor and free market concerns of middle-class reformers.[9] Certainly the victory of Union forces over the rebellious South during the Civil War involved more than middle-class hostility to the slave power. Nor did a patriotic response to the Union call to arms necessarily subordinate workingmen's interests and goals to a middle-class pursuit of nationalism. Nevertheless, reliable evidence of an antislavery tradition independent of middle-class goals has yet to be presented. In this regard, it might prove useful to distinguish the war from antislavery reform and to recognize that the war—not antislavery reform—produced a collective experience (on both sides of the contest) that may have added new strength to postwar challenges to the consolidation of industrial capitalism.

At a time when the historical profession held abolitionists in very low esteem, Richard Hofstadter observed that "[Wendell] Phillips was in some ways more sophisticated than those who condemn him."[10] When Phillips spoke of the advancing influence of the northern middle class, he perceived himself to be allied with an emerging social order resting on equitable relations between capital and labor. He and reformers generally may have deceived themselves into thinking that they were central to the new industrial order, but their understanding of the process of historical change required neither self-deception nor cynicism. In the postwar era, it is true, utilitarian principles led most antislavery reformers toward the stern liberal orthodoxy of Edwin L. Godkin, or to the somewhat more abivalent Mugwump style of Charles Francis Adams. But utilitarianism also sustained visions of social harmony and human perfection which the dominant drift toward Social Darwinism could not entirely contain. These visions led some reformers (Phillips among them) to champion cooperativist and socialist remedies in the manner of the English Fabians to the class divisions of industrial America. Whatever individual scholars make of the character and purpose of antislavery reform, the reformers' capacity to question the foundations of social order, to oppose established interests, and (when necessary) to resist the authority of the state continue to merit study.

It is an unavoidable aspect of antislavery reform that the modern concept of race emerged as the antislavery struggle advanced. To be sure, antislavery reformers labored to overturn discriminatory laws and restrictions as they resisted slavery itself. In this struggle, they denounced all barriers of class and caste as the tyranny of past ages and identified progress in human affairs with the advancement of individual liberty and equality. Moreover, the antislavery concern with autonomous moral uplift paralleled and in some ways encouraged the self-help arguments of northern black leaders during the antebellum decades. But antislavery reform also advanced comfortably with developing doctrines of white superiority and expressions of the white man's burden among the dark-skinned peoples of the world. When Frederick Douglass concluded his autobiography in 1892, the concepts of race and of American destiny could not be separated. Douglass looked back over the era of antislavery reform with pride in the accomplishments of his active life, accomplishments which "servitude, persecution, false friends, desertion, and depreciation" could not expunge.[11]

Douglass understood that the antislavery cause in America did not wholly embrace the black struggle for freedom, although the destruction of slavery certainly altered the conditions of that struggle in the North as well as in the South. In the 1850s, when Douglass observed that immigrant laborers displaced northern blacks from traditional employments as servants and menial laborers, he witnessed the liberating and limiting character of the utilitarian view of progress. "The old employments . . . are gradually, and it may be inevitably, passing into other hands," Douglass noted. It was not entirely bad that they did.

"White men are becoming house servants, cooks and stewards, common laborers and flunkies to our gentry," he continued. The increasing numbers of the white laboring poor "proved that if we cannot rise to the whites, the whites can fall to us."[12] This, too, reflected the meaning of progress in antislavery reform.

In the distinct but interrelated spheres of political economy, law, mass politics, and moral reform, a middle-class pursuit of free labor and free market relations transformed the republican values of the Revolution. Free labor republicanism, in turn, sustained reformers in their opposition to slavery as a system of despotic class relations resting on the absorption of labor by capital. Conversely, freedom and democracy required the independence and harmony of capital and labor. In political terms, the advancement of antislavery reform demanded a substantial unity among the "producing classes" of the North, a unity of employer and wage earner which reformers hoped to forge in mass politics. Accordingly, although antislavery reformers identified overwhelmingly with the anti-Jackson sentiments of the Whig party—and with the Yankee Calvinist values Whiggery championed—the triumph of their reforms depended upon a political victory over the defenders of the traditional order, including the defenders of traditional political accommodations of slaveholding interests. Antislavery reform never entirely shed its New England Whig bias, but reformers identified sufficiently with mass politics to drive the old elite from the field or, at least, to force it to forge accommodations with the new managers of party politics. In the moral sphere, reformers combined the postmillennialist and perfectionist doctrines of the Second Great Awakening with middle-class drives to release individual energies and to promote social order and productive labor through self-restraint. Secular and spiritual visions of progress merged as morality and utility outlined a single course of human endeavor.

Morality
& Utility
in
American
Antislavery
Reform

Never, never can I be too thankful to God, that I was not born a slave; that my wife and little ones are secure from the clutches of the kidnapper; that my hearth-stone is sacred to purity and love; that it is not the horrible fate of myself and family, to be prized as goods and chattels, and herded with four-footed beasts and creeping things. O, to be free as the winds of heaven; to be restrained by nothing but love to God and love to man; to go and come, rise up or lie down, labor or rest, just as the free spirit shall elect.
—William Lloyd Garrison,
Selections from the Writings and Speeches of William Lloyd Garrison, 1852

Slavery comes to an end by the laws of trade. Hang up your Sharpe's rifle, my valorous friend! The slave does not ask the help of your musket. He only says, like old Diogenes to Alexander, "Stand out of my light!" Just take your awkward proportions, you Yankee Democrat and Republican, out of the light and heat of God's laws of political economy, and they will melt the slave's chains away!
—Wendell Phillips,
Speeches, Lectures, and Letters, 1863

The Heritage of the Revolution

1

ECHOES of the American Revolution permeated nineteenth-century antislavery reform as the enemies of slavery equated republican values with free labor and defined property in slaves as a valueless relic of a barbarous age. Evoking the memory of the Founding Fathers to refute existing accommodations of slaveholding interests, reformers attached particular significance to the liberal aspects of the revolutionary past which encompassed their own concerns. Their confident appeal to the authority of the Revolution reflected a transformation of republican values that gradually eroded the foundations of eighteenth-century equanimity toward slavery. From the first stirrings of immediate abolitionism in the early 1830s through the struggle for emancipation and the enfranchisement of southern blacks in the 1860s, antislavery reformers traced their sentiments to the Declaration of Independence and judged their own dedication to reform by the purity of principle they attributed to the Founding Fathers.

In their zeal, reformers transformed the meaning of the past they embraced. In the revolutionary generation, a liberal emphasis on individual liberty and equality did not directly challenge slavery. Rather, when writing the federal Constitution, the Founding Fathers accommodated slavery with apparent ease. Consequently, the national government they established rested as firmly on southern slavery as it did on the free labor system of the North.[1] This accommodation of slavery reflected the involvement of northern merchants in the trade of slaves and slave-produced tobacco and revealed as well the capacity of slaveholders to embrace—indeed, to encourage—a broadening democracy among yeomen and artisans. As long as slaveholders advanced the principle of democracy, the federal accommodation of slavery remained stable. In this setting, Alexander Hamilton's hostility to slavery as an unproductive labor system and his proposals for compensated emancipation (views that would become prominent and influential among Whigs and Republicans sixty years later) attracted little attention.[2]

Nineteenth-century reformers abandoned the federal accommodation of slavery amid the widening social concerns of a new middle class of manufacturers, merchants, entrepreneurs, and farmers. Suddenly, reformers insisted that slavery contradicted republican values. For the first time, they pitted the liberal heritage of the Revolution against slaveholding interests. In the reformers' view, slavery persisted only as the tyranny of a decadent social order. Antislavery reformers, knit together by bonds of commerce and an expanding marketplace, identified the ascendence of the middle class with the moral and material progress of their age. In the rhetoric of reform, slaveholders assumed the attributes of an aristocracy clinging to their human property with a tenacity akin to the European and British nobility's attachment to traditional privilege and retrograde social and economic relations. The repudiation of the slaveholders' republican values—particularly their identification of liberty and slavery—became the unifying object of liberal reform in America. As the abolitionist orator Wendell Phillips declared on the eve of the Civil War, "the merchant of the nineteenth century spurns to be a subordinate." Freed of past accommodations of slavery, Phillips predicted, "a middle class of trading, manufacturing energy . . . will soon undermine the aristocracy of the slaveholding South."[3]

With good reason, but in increasing isolation, southern slaveholders defended a conservative heritage of the Revolution. When Governor George McDuffie of South Carolina responded to abolitionist attacks in 1835 by identifying "domestic slavery" as "the cornerstone of our republican edifice," he was at least partly correct. But more was at stake in the antebellum debate over slavery than historical accuracy. Firmly rooted as it was in the revolutionary past, McDuffie's republican edifice seemed neither republican nor edifying to the middle-class enemies of slavery. By the late 1850s, moreover, a substantial majority in the North accepted the essential terms of antislavery republicanism. Northerners rejected as corrupt and corrupting McDuffie's conservative values and his reverance for established social relations.[4]

The liberal tendencies of the revolutionary era were not as dominant as nineteenth-century reformers claimed, but even in its uncertainty—in its developing liberal focus and its lingering conservative sympathies—eighteenth-century antislavery thought ensured that discussions of slavery and of American republican values could not be separated. In the remarkable and widely celebrated case of *Somerset* v. *Stewart* (1772), Britain's Lord Chief Justice, Baron Mansfield, helped to underscore this point and to provide later generations of Americans with an ambiguous but valuable precedent for antislavery action.[5]

The issue Mansfield confronted in *Somerset*—the status of a slave from Virginia in England—reflected both an advancing liberal critique of slavery and a conservative reaction against the corrupting influences of commerce. At stake were the proprietary rights of a Virginia master over his slave, James Somerset, whom he carried to England as a body servant. Once in England, Somerset left his master's service and was later seized and held for transport and future sale in the slave markets of Jamaica. Leading English abolitionists aided Somerset and successfully brought the captive before Mansfield on a writ of habeas corpus, a procedure that tested the legality of Somerset's imprisonment and, potentially, the constitutionality of slavery in England. The abolitionists' arguments in the case followed a line of legal reasoning that accompanied the decline of villeinage in England and the creation of a growing class of propertyless freemen. Although fears of idleness and crime among the English poor prompted a variety of efforts in the seventeenth and eighteenth centuries to compel work and enforce correct deportment through schemes of disciplined, involuntary labor, such efforts always avoided outright slavery. Thus though the notion of unfree labor was by no means alien to Mansfield (who dedicated himself to the defense of traditional patterns of authority and deference) the upward social mobility of an expanding middle class of artisans, small proprietors, and mechanics underlay the English abolitionists' desire to insulate English "liberties" from the colonial slave codes.[6]

A defense of tradition, then, and a pursuit of progress combined to free Somerset. Asserting Somerset's freedom before Mansfield, Francis Hargrave presented a thoroughly liberal historical analysis that traced the decline of villeinage and the rise of freed labor to argue that England had progressed beyond slavery to an age of individual liberty. Nowhere did English law recognize the status of slavery, Hargrave insisted, and such a status ought not to be introduced out of deference to the pecuniary interests of slave traders or for the convenience of visiting colonial slaveholders. Granville Sharp, a prominent abolitionist who joined in Somerset's defense, combined a recognition of the historical tendency toward freed labor with an idealistic appeal to constitutional traditions, which, he insisted, had never sanctioned slavery.[7] Mansfield, sensitive to the subversion of traditional values in an age of expanding commerce, freed Somerset in order to limit the sphere of slavery to the positive laws of Parliament and the local codes of the colonies.

Certainly the introduction of African slavery to the English colonies, together with the value of the slave trade to English merchants, raised potential conflicts between developing English standards regarding the labor of freemen and the chattel slavery flourishing in the New World. In decisions preceding *Somerset,* English jurists ruled that civil actions for the recovery of property could not be applied to servants in England.[8] Had English law followed a different course and enabled masters to hold men as property, England would necessarily have followed the American practice and admitted distinctions between slave and free peoples to its legal code or adopted slavery as the universal standard for the working poor.

Although Mansfield did not intend to discourage slavery in the Western Hemisphere or to interfere with the English slave trade to the colonies, he found the proprietary claims of slaveholders sufficiently subversive of ancient standards of liberty to rule that by English law Somerset was free. Significantly, Mansfield chose not to follow the "custom of the merchants," a course of legal reasoning that might have sanctioned Somerset's sale in Jamaica. Instead, he elevated English liberties above the potential contamination of the slave trade and the colonial slave codes. "So high an act of dominion," Mansfield reportedly said of slavery, "must be recognized by the law of the country where it is used." Mansfield did not question Somerset's status as a slave in Virginia. Rather, he recognized slavery to be a function of positive, written law, wholly isolated from English common law and repugnant to all principles of equity. The "state of slavery," Mansfield ruled, "is of such a nature that it is incapable of being introduced on any reasons, moral or political; but only by positive law."[9]

As nineteenth-century reformers recognized, *Somerset* represented a signal victory for English abolitionists. In the nineteenth-century reform view, moreover, *Somerset* erected a barrier between the universal principle of freedom and the peculiar and parochial interests of slaveholders. Northern reformers understood Mansfield's distinction between English law and colonial slave codes to apply directly to the relationship between federal powers and the prerogatives of the states. For the revolutionary generation, however, *Somerset* raised embarrassing questions. The decision reminded Americans that their struggle for liberty went hand in hand with a defense of the economic interests of slaveholders. *Somerset* suggested that if colonists wanted all of the rights of Englishmen, emancipation might be part of the bargain. Richard Wells of Philadelphia raised this issue in 1774 when he questioned Americans' willingness to sanction the law of force, which sustained slavery, when that law had been divorced from the English constitution. "I contend," said Wells, "that by the laws of the English constitution, and by our *own declarations,* the instant a negro sets his foot in America, he is as free as if he had landed in England."[10]

The implication of Wells's barb was clear enough. An American defense of colonial rights that could not be separated from a defense of slaveholders' rights to protect their property in men embarrassed the Whig opponents of British colonial policy. Believing that the same principles of law that made slavery unconstitutional in England rendered the American slave codes theoretically null and void, the English abolitionist Granville Sharp felt this conflict keenly. In practice, Sharp cautioned, the American slave codes were of long standing and had been sanctioned by several kings of England. To preserve what Sharp described as "that reciprocal faith, which is due to all solemn compacts," American slavery must be specifically repealed by the several colonial legislatures before it could be a proper subject for parliamentary action. Accordingly, when the American abolitionist Anthony Benezet corresponded with Sharp in 1772 concerning a planned antislavery petition campaign, Sharp responded with a lecture on colonial rights. "*With respect to the toleration of slavery in the colonies,*" Sharp insisted, "I apprehend the British Parliament has no right to interfere." Sharp argued that antislavery petitions in Parliament should deal solely with the slave trade and the importation of slaves into the colonies because Parliament could consider these issues without violating colonial rights.[11]

American abolitionists made little direct reference to *Somerset* in the revolutionary era. They either ignored the decision or concentrated instead on overtly liberal American precedents for abolition. As John Adams and Jeremy Belknap recalled in 1795, several Massachusetts slaves successfully sued for their freedom in the decade before *Somerset* and the Revolution. According to Belknap, the Massachusetts case of *James* v. *Lechmere* (1769) involved a successful suit by a slave against his master for illegal imprisonment as well as for assault and battery and trespass. Arguing the slave's case before the Superior Court, Massachusetts Attorney General Jonathan Sewell insisted that under the colony's royal charter all persons born or residing in Massachusetts were as free as any English subject in Great Britain. Furthermore, according to English common law, no man could be deprived of liberty without trial. Sewell acknowledged the existence of statutes in the colonies that mitigated or regulated slavery, but he insisted that no laws specifically authorized it. Several years earlier, in 1767, the lower house of the Massachusetts General Court debated a bill "to prevent the *unwarrantable & unusual* Practice . . . of inslaving Mankind in the Province." The bill never came to a vote, but its language soon shaped liberal arguments for judicial emancipation.[12]

Reflecting the declining importance of unfree labor, the new American states of the North provided for emancipation in the 1780s and 1790s. In doing so, they conspicuously avoided references to *Somerset,* although there were clear echoes of Hargrave's liberal historical analysis, if not of Mansfield's conservative decision, in the American arguments for judicial emancipation. The famous Quok Walker decision in 1783 stood as the American version of *Somerset.* In the Walker case, the Massachusetts Superior Court found slavery to be incompatible with the state's constitution, specifically with its bill of rights, which asserted that "all men are born free and equal." The decision followed the arguments presented by Levi Lincoln (later to be Thomas Jefferson's attorney general) that slavery had never been "expressly enacted" in Massachusetts and that the idea of slavery "is inconsistent with our own conduct and Constitution and there can be no such thing as perpetual servitude of a rational creature." New Hampshire followed Massachusetts's lead and abolished slavery by judicial decree. Elsewhere in the North, however, slavery came to an end through acts of gradual emancipation, which presupposed the legality of slavery while challenging the wisdom of its continuation. In Pennsylvania, abolitionists grew impatient with the progress of gradual emancipation and pressed for judicial emancipation in the manner of Quok Walker. In the resulting test case, *Flora* v. *Graisberry* (1802), abolitionists stressed the incompatibility of slavery with the natural rights of man proclaimed by the state constitution. After many delays, the Pennsylvania supreme court upheld the state's act of gradual emancipation and

ruled that the continuation of slavery did not violate the state's constitution. Judicial abolition did not prove to be as appealing as American
abolitionists had hoped, but they continued to press for emancipation
on the basis of American principles and practices.[13]

The tendency among American abolitionists of the revolutionary
era to avoid *Somerset* is explained in part by a generalized unwillingness
to be bound directly by English law and by a more specific hostility to
the conservative uses of common law interpretation. Thomas Jefferson (who ordered a copy of "Hargrave's argument in the Negro's case"
in 1787) resolved the difficulty posed by *Somerset* by ignoring the decision entirely and focusing his attention instead on the danger of judicial despotism which he perceived in Mansfield. Jefferson pressed for
codification in the new republic as a repudiation of Mansfield's eagerness to apply principles of equity to common law and as a means of
securing liberty and the legislated will of the people from the tyranny
of judges.

Without once referring to *Somerset,* Jefferson repeatedly lamented
Mansfield's influence on the bench. Good laws derived from the consent of the governed, not from the whim of judges, Jefferson insisted.
It followed that laws should be recorded clearly and unambiguously
in statutes and in written constitutions. Jefferson acknowledged that
with "progress of commerce and refinement of morality" the written
law would, from time to time, fail to offer a remedy for a new class of
cases. Judges might then legitimately resort to equitable judgments
that reached beyond the written law. But Jefferson insisted that it was
vital to the preservation of American liberty that decisions in equity be
tightly circumscribed in courts of chancery and kept distinct from
courts of common law, by which Jefferson meant *"written law."* Indeed, just as soon as courts of chancery identified a new class of cases,
Jefferson insisted that the state legislatures "should reduce these rules
to a text and transplant them into the department of the common
law." Jefferson saw in Mansfield all of the dangers of judicial excess
against which the Americans had rebelled. "Relieve the judges from
the rigor of text law," he warned in the 1780s, "and permit them, with
pretorian discretion, to wander into it's [sic] equity, and the whole
legal system become incertain." As "a man of the clearest head and
most seducing eloquence," Mansfield had managed "to persuade the
courts of Common Law to revive the practice of construing their text
equitably." The lesson for America seemed clear: written law must be

followed strictly, according to the meaning of its words; no American court should admit vague rules of ancient English common law or cite "any English decision . . . since the accession of Ld. Mansfield to the bench." Although Mansfield had made some good decisions, Jefferson concluded that "there is so much sly poison instilled into a great part of them, that it is better to proscribe the whole."[14]

Jefferson's hostility to Mansfield's use of equity did not derive simply or narrowly from an effort to protect slaveholding interests from the potential threat of the *Somerset* decision. Indeed, Jefferson ignored the slave question in this instance, perhaps because he believed it to be subsumed in a wider competition between the agrarian values he championed and the diverging commercial and manufacturing interests of the North and East. As Jefferson illustrated so clearly, American revolutionaries drew strength from a traditional republican quest for virtue as well as from an emerging liberal emphasis on self-interest. In the agrarian republic Jefferson envisioned, an abundance of western land encouraged the steady expansion of a class of independent, noncommercial farmers and thereby diluted the power and influence of the aristocratically inclined slaveholding planters of the South and the corrupting commercial and manufacturing interests of the North. In this sense, slavery raised no fundamental obstacle to the cultivation of republican virtue. Rather, Jefferson regarded an expansion of commerce and manufacturing and the accompanying growth of a dependent and subservient class of clerks and factory operatives as inimical to republican values. Codification kept judicial powers where Jefferson thought them to be safest, dependent upon legislation for the meaning of the law. Although Jefferson's advocacy of codification enjoyed a brief revival in the North during the Jacksonian era, northern jurists—representing the very forces Jefferson feared—made abundant use of equity jurisprudence throughout the early nineteenth century as they accommodated the rule of law to the interests of emerging entrepreneurs and manufacturers. Antislavery appeals to *Somerset* developed apace.[15]

Despite Jefferson's efforts to bury Mansfield and equity jurisprudence beneath the certitude of written law and a strict interpretation of the Constitution, the efforts of southern jurists to distinguish slave relations from the general application of the law introduced *Somerset* into American case law. Following the failure of legislative efforts to secure gradual emancipation in Maryland, opponents of slavery turned to the courts to assert the freedom of a slave whose mother claimed to be free by Mansfield's decision. A lower court ruled in favor of the slave, but the Maryland Court of Appeals sustained the slaveholder in *Mahoney* v. *Ashton* (1802) and overturned the judgment. Maryland's attorney general, Luther Martin, presented the slaveholder's appeal and, in reference to *Somerset,* insisted that the "positive law of this state" established slavery. Although Martin had abandoned his earlier enthusiasm for Jeffersonian democracy, he retained a Jeffersonian contempt for Mansfield and equity jurisprudence. Overlooking the conservative aspects of the decision, Martin charged Mansfield with resorting to equity to meet the libertarian temper of the times—"[John] Wilkes and Liberty; of which the young heated brain of Hargrave . . . was full." [16]

In Mississippi in 1818 and in Kentucky in 1820, state supreme courts relied on *Somerset* to free slaves who had resided with their masters in a free state or territory. And in Mississippi in 1820, the state supreme court invoked *Somerset* to rule that laws regarding murder applied to slaves. In these early southern cases, *Somerset* may have helped to rationalize slave law by isolating municipal slave codes from the more general application of the law. In time, the liberal and antislavery applications of *Somerset* also became clear to southern jurists. In the 1850s, the Georgia lawyer Thomas R. R. Cobb denounced *Somerset*'s pernicious influence in his own efforts to develop a systematic legal defense of slavery. In a similar mood, the Georgia Supreme Court dismissed the antislavery applications of *Somerset* as a "fungus" engrafted on the law "by the foul spirit of modern fanaticism." [17]

Somerset began to assume new importance for antislavery reformers in the 1820s. Mansfield's equitable interpretation of common law to restrict the proprietary claims of slaveholders held special meaning for nineteenth-century proponents of progress, who found the common law to be a useful instrument in the promotion of entrepreneurial and manufacturing interests. To be sure, as Roger B. Taney demonstrated during his tenure as chief justice of the Supreme Court, arguments favoring the "creative destruction" of property rights did not necessarily conflict with slaveholding interests. But the notion that the needs of the community superseded individual property rights advanced along a broad front in the first half of the nineteenth century, and antislavery reform drew sustenance from it. In the process, slavery assumed increasing importance in public affairs, in the shifting uses to which northern jurists put *Somerset,* and in arguments over slavery in the territories.

In the period between the debate over slavery in the Constitutional Convention of 1787 and the debates concerning Missouri in 1819–20, common republican concerns with order and harmony permitted a discussion of slaveholding interests in terms that applied broadly to relationships bewteen masters and servants or apprentices as well as masters and slaves. Thus, although the Constitution clearly accommodated slaveholding interests—particularly in the "three-fifths" clause, which specifically benefited the owners of property in slaves—the document consistently referred to "persons," not to slaves. In the much debated fugitive clause, the framers of the Constitution employed language that clearly applied to indentured or apprenticed labor as well as to slaves.[18]

Strong as these traditional republican values remained in the early national period, liberal views of individual liberty found expression as well and increasingly challenged traditional barriers of class and caste. Slavery in the territories quickly replaced older concerns with the slave trade as the principal focus in the developing struggle between antislavery interests in the North and what they eventually characterized as a consolidated slave power in the South. At issue were the direction and control of national policy in the distribution of economic benefits. The territorial debate began with the adoption of the Constitution, when leading antislavery federalists, including Benjamin Franklin and Benjamin Rush of Pennsylvania, Isaac Backus of Massachusetts, and Moses Brown of Rhode Island, urged ratification on the grounds that a strong national government could promote the cause of individual liberty. The Constitution vested Congress with "many important and salutary powers," Franklin noted, and he thought that these powers "ought rightfully to be administered without distinction of color."[19]

The first antislavery petitions before Congress—the Quaker petition from Pennsylvania and Franklin's petition from the Pennsylvania Abolition Society—sparked a brief debate and brought forth arguments that set the pattern for early discussions of the extension of slavery. The petitions called for an end to the slave trade and for a generalized antislavery stance by the national government. Supporting the petitions and arguing against efforts by fellow southerners to bury them, James Madison insisted that Congress had a clear right to regulate both the foreign and domestic slave trade. Madison cited the constitutional provision that restrained Congress from prohibiting the slave trade for twenty years as a specific acknowledgment of federal jurisdiction over that trade. The constitutional prohibition against ending importation in "existing" states directly implied that "regulations might be made in relation to the introduction of slaves into the New States to be formed out of the Western Territories." The national government had already acted to forbid slavery in the Northwest Territory, Madison noted. That Congress had the power to prohibit slavery in all the territories, he concluded, "is as clear as that we have any rights whatever."[20]

Congress chose to ignore these arguments and to interpret the constitutional restraint against congressional prohibition of the slave trade as a positive restriction against any congressional interference with slavery for the stipulated twenty years. Nevertheless, the status of slavery in the territories remained ambiguous and potentially troublesome. In 1790, the issue of slavery expansion arose in specific form with the passage of the North Carolina Cession Act. In ceding its western territories to the national government, North Carolina included a prohibition against any congressional encouragement of abolition. Because the Cession Act specifically shunned the antislavery precedent of the Northwest Ordinance, opponents of slavery feared that the national government was explicitly rejecting the liberal elements of the revolutionary past.[21] In response, opponents of slavery began to distinguish between the government's present policies and the natural law doctrine which they conceived to be at the core of the Revolution. The development of such arguments made it increasingly possible to disentangle slavery from an ever more remote and idealized revolutionary past.

This liberal idealization of the revolutionary past characterized early antislavery protests. In a 1793 pamphlet denouncing the North Carolina Cession Act, the Virginia Quaker Warner Mifflin criticized the congressional action as a rejection of America's revolutionary faith. Mifflin reached beyond the Constitution to the "self-evident truths" proclaimed in the Declaration of Independence, which he interpreted as a national covenant "with the God of heaven and the whole earth." Because of this covenant, the spirit of liberty and equality that pervaded the Declaration remained "obligatory" for any government established under the Constitution. The extension of slavery into the territory that became Tennessee proved that "our nation are revolted from the law of God, the law of reason and humanity, and the just principles of government; and with rapid strides establishing tyranny and oppression." With a similar sense of alarm, the American Convention of Abolition Societies organized in Philadelphia early in 1794. Protesting the enactment of the Fugitive Slave Law of 1793, the convention directed memorials to Congress reminding the legislators of the hallowed principles of the revolutionary Fathers. The delegates to the convention vowed their obedience to written law, but they distinguished natural rights from the slaveholders' "nominal rights of property . . . which may only be traced to our statute-books." [22]

By 1798, when the establishment of the Mississippi Territory raised a ripple of antislavery protest in Congress, opponents of slavery began to define the institution as a direct challenge to republican government. Like the North Carolina Cession Act, the Mississippi bill followed the precedent of the Northwest Ordinance with the exception that slavery was not prohibited. Albert Gallatin of Pennsylvania reminded his colleagues that "having determined slavery was a bad policy for the Northwest Territory," no sound reason existed for a different decision regarding Mississippi. Gallatin and other Republicans supported the efforts of George Thatcher, a Massachusetts Federalist, to incorporate an antislavery provision in the Mississippi bill. Thatcher argued that slavery stood "in direct hostility to the principle of our Government." Because slavery threatened national survival, the government "had the right to take all due measures to diminish and destroy the evil." [23]

As antislavery arguments relied increasingly on appeals to natural rights which transcended statute law, abolitionists perceived a conflict between what was morally right and what was legally correct. This perception underlay the moderate tone of abolitionism in the late eighteenth and early nineteenth centuries, but it also encouraged abolitionists to attack slavery as a violation of natural rights and Christian morality. Accordingly, the Maryland Abolition Society found itself "embarrassed" by a conflict between its faith in "universal liberty" and the frequently contradictory "obligations imposed by unwise and perhaps unconstitutional laws." The obligation to obey the written law tended to hold abolitionist reform sentiments in check. At the same time, however, the language of abolitionism became increasingly abstract and sweeping. To oppose the Fugitive Slave Law of 1793, for example, Maryland abolitionists turned to scripture and to principles of natural rights derived from English common law. They based their appeal not on written law (which they recognized as sustaining slavery) but on the "unmoveable foundation of justice, of 'right,' of 'the rights of man,' of 'righteousness,' of 'the law of nature.'"[24]

Similarly, the Maryland Quaker John Parrish considered slavery a violation of the natural rights proclaimed by the Declaration of Independence as the moral foundation of the republic. Parrish acknowledged that the Constitution provided for the return of fugitive slaves. "Yet," he asked, "can any labour or service be due from a person deprived of his natural rights?" In light of the Declaration's "repeated avowal of the natural rights of men," Parrish concluded that the fugitive clause of the Constitution, as it applied to slaves, was incompatible with the principles upon which the entire Constitution rested.[25]

Parrish's *Remarks on the Slavery of the Black People* (1806) focused natural rights arguments on the Constitution and on the recreant legislators who violated the already hallowed faith of the Founding Fathers. Parrish assumed as an article of faith that the revolutionary generation intended to secure the natural rights of men in a democratic republic in which slavery could have no lasting place. "Look back on the language of your predecessors," Parrish challenged the lawmakers of his day. The Founders' "reverence for our great Creator," together with the "principles of humanity, and the dictates of common sense," led them to establish a government "to promote the welfare of mankind." Parrish concluded that viewed in this light, slavery opposed "the essence of the Constitution." "The preamble to the constitution is plain," he insisted. "Equal liberty and impartial justice" underlay "all good government." Accordingly, politicians ought to enforce the Constitution in keeping with its fundamental meaning and draft laws in "unequivocal terms as not to be misunderstood, or admit of a double meaning."[26]

The idealized discussion of the revolutionary past which Parrish's argument illustrates ultimately divorced antislavery from any accommodation of the political and economic interests of slaveholders. In the tradition of Franklin's and Madison's antislavery appeals, Rufus King expressed the transformed meaning of slavery with particular clarity during the debate over slavery in Missouri. As a member of the Confederation Congress, King had urged that slavery be excluded from the Northwest Territory; as a delegate to the Constitutional Convention, he had argued against counting slaves for purposes of representation. Now, in the midst of the Missouri debates, King rested his antislavery argument entirely on natural rights, which transcended existing statutes and the Constitution itself: "I hold that all laws or compacts imposing slavery . . . upon any human being are absolutely void because contrary to the law of nature, which is the law of God, by which he makes his way known to man and is paramount to all human control." [27]

Although the Missouri debates began cautiously, with New York representative John W. Taylor reiterating Madison's argument that Congress possessed the authority to exclude slavery from the territories, opponents of slavery quickly ranged beyond the limits inherited from the revolutionary era. Thus Timothy Fuller of Massachusetts argued that the Constitution's guarantee to the states of a republican form of government derived directly from the Declaration's natural rights principles. This, said Fuller, was "the predominant principle" of the Constitution, and it prohibited Congress from creating other than free states. Fuller admitted that the Constitution permitted slavery in existing states, but he considered that to be a concession to slaveholding interests and not an implied constitutional recognition of the institution's legitimacy. Arthur Livermore of New Hampshire extended the point. "Slavery," he insisted, "is not established by our Constitution." Rather, "a part of the States are indulged in the commission of a sin from which they could not at once be restrained, and which they would not consent to abandon." Let slavery continue where it existed, concluded Livermore, "for our boasted Constitution connives at it." But "liberty and equal rights are the end and aim of all our institutions, and . . . to tolerate slavery beyond the Constitution, is a perversion of them all." [28]

In the Missouri debates, for the first time, the opponents of slavery identified natural rights with national purpose. For the next two decades, this identification linked antislavery efforts to constitutional arguments that claimed broad authority for the federal government in the area of economic development. John Taylor of Caroline County, Virginia, had been quick to point out that these fervent nationalist arguments, uniting Calvinist piety with individual liberty, threatened to advance the commercial interests of the Northeast at the expense of what he depicted as the agrarian interests of the South and West. Taylor also appeared to perceive a distinction in northern society between established commercial and manufacturing interests and an expanding and increasingly aggressive middle class. As the followers of Andrew Jackson shortly demonstrated, slaveholders' hostility to economic nationalism—particularly in its organized expression in banks and other chartered corporations—could be linked politically to self-styled workingmen's hostility to monopolistic privilege. In the wake of the Missouri Compromise, the emerging Jacksonians moved to unite the agrarian interests identified by Taylor with northern middle-class demands for equal rights.[29] Defenders of economic nationalism, in turn, began to define—in the manner of *Somerset*—the municipal limits of slavery.

For a time, antislavery sentiments largely coincided with northern Whiggery. "I have no doubt," wrote the Whig jurist William Jay during the Missouri crisis, "that the laws of God, and, as a necessary and inevitable consequence, the true interests of our country, forbid the extension of slavery." At the same time Supreme Court Justice Joseph Story, a consistent defender of economic nationalism, characterized slavery as "so repugnant to the natural rights of man and the dictates of justice, that it seems difficult to find for it any adequate justification." Similarly, the champion of New England Whiggery, Daniel Webster, concluded that although political exigencies prevented immediate abolition in existing slave states, "we have a strong feeling of the injustice of any toleration of slavery," and the system ought not to be extended. Justice Story's circuit decision in *Le Jeune Eugene* (1822) presented a sweeping denunciation of the international slave trade and of slavery itself as "repugnant to the great principles of Christian duty, the dictates of natural religion, the obligations of good faith and morality, and the external maxims of social justice." So, too, President John Quincy Adams's attorney general, William Wirt, argued for the freedom of the *Antelope* captives in 1825, citing Hargrave's argument in *Somerset* and asserting that the Africans stood before the Supreme Court as Somerset stood before Mansfield "as if brought up before it upon a habeas corpus." Wirt admitted that Americans were "compelled to tolerate the existence of domestic slavery under our own municipal law," but the "calamity" of American slavery ought not to excuse the international slave trade.[30]

As the Whig party coalesced in opposition to Jackson, the enemies of slavery tended to unite antislavery reform with anti-Democratic sentiments and to equate the Democracy with the slave power. William Birney—whose father, James G. Birney, opposed Jackson and slavery with equal vigor—described Jackson's elevation to the presidency as the beginning of the ascendance of the slave power in its campaign "to overthrow the freedom of speech, of the press, and of the mails, the right of trial by jury, the right of petition, and every other bulwark of civil liberty to extend slavery . . . and gain undisputed political supremacy in the nation." Even those politically minded abolitionists who would later identify themselves with the Democracy (notably Charles Sumner, Salmon P. Chase, John P. Hale, and Henry Wilson) opposed Jackson and his followers until the late 1830s. Deeply influenced by Joseph Story, Sumner remained in the ranks of conservative Boston Whiggery throughout the 1830s. Chase, who studied law with Attorney General William Wirt during the last years of Adams's administration, saw in Jackson's victory the defeat and humiliation of the nation's legitimate political order. In Chase's mind, Jackson represented the victory of southern "vice," "stupidity," and "ignorance" over the "virtue," "talent," and "learning" of New England. Moreover, Jacksonians perverted traditional republican virtue: "Patriotism means selflove, violence means energy, cruelty magnanimity, and reform the removal of an honorable opponent and the substitution of a servile tool."[31]

The link between antislavery reform and Whig politics contributed to the new uses of *Somerset* and to the early "moral suasion" tactics of nineteenth-century abolitionism. In *Somerset*, Mansfield distinguished between positive municipal law and the broad principles of natural law. The former could sustain slavery (however unjustly) whereas the latter always favored liberty. This distinction merged nicely with the Whig emphasis on broad national powers in the encouragement and direction of economic development. The adaptation of *Somerset* to the American situation underscored the local and restricted character of slavery and proclaimed the supremacy of a national commitment to freedom and to the principles of equal rights associated with the Whig concept of progress. It was in this context that the American Anti-Slavery Society launched its attack on slavery as the "Monster Sin." The tactic of moral suasion complemented both natural rights arguments to contain slavery and the Whig drive for an active state. At the formative meeting of the American Anti-Slavery Society in 1833, William Lloyd Garrison, John Greenleaf Whittier, and Samuel J. May drafted a declaration of principles that combined natural rights and Calvinist moral arguments for immediate abolition with a call for the national government to abolish the domestic slave trade and end slavery "in those portions of our territory which the Constitution has placed under its exclusive jurisdiction."[32]

Moral suasion, the unifying theme of the immediate abolitionist movement, joined Calvinist doctrines of individual piety and salvation with natural rights doctrines of individual liberty. By tying a moral assault against slavery with Whig notions of the proper role of the state in the regulation and direction of economic activity, abolitionists in the early 1830s overcame the "embarrassed" and restrained character of earlier antislavery efforts. Moral suasion granted all of the constraints which law and the Constitution imposed on the state's power to act against slavery. Abolitionists acknowledged that a citizen could do no more than petition the government to exercise state powers against slavery wherever the Constitution clearly permitted it. Moral suasion, however, reached beyond the limits of civil government and beyond the Constitution to permit an absolute renunciation of slavery as sin. Into the new moral reform sphere spilled all of the religious enthusiasm and radical individualism of the Second Great Awakening. These new energies fueled immediate abolitionism and produced political tensions which Whiggery could not contain. *Somerset* both provided a vehicle for Whig antislavery interests and became the impetus for the collapse of antislavery Whig unity.

During the early 1830s, the American Anti-Slavery Society pursued its moral reform goals in a manner consistent with a Whig accommodation of slaveholding interests. The tactics of moral suasion and the society's declaration of principles maintained the traditional recognition that a moral condemnation of slavery ought not to impinge upon the legal and constitutional rights of slaveholders. For a time, moral hostility to slavery did not disturb the federal accommodation of slavery and even acknowledged the right of existing slave states to maintain their peculiar institution. Nevertheless, the moral assault against slavery unleashed forces that soon pressed beyond the traditional accommodation of slaveholding interests. The 1840 schism in the American Anti-Slavery Society, the organization of the Liberty party, and the related enunciation of Garrisonian disunionism marked a radical break with traditional antislavery protest. After 1840, antislavery reformers took ever sharper aim not simply at slavery but at its extraterritorial effects, at what they described as the usurpations of a tyrannical slave power.[33]

Slavery and Republican Values

2

DURING the 1830s reformers attacked not slavery alone but the tyranny upon which it rested. The abolitionists' moral condemnation of slaveholding provided a focus for an intense scrutiny of the proper foundations of social order applicable to the northern communities from which reform emanated as well as to the slaveholding communities of the South. When William Lloyd Garrison used the occasion of his thirty-sixth birthday in December 1840 to reaffirm his commitment to reform, his perception of tyranny encompassed a universal field of labor:

> O! not for Afric's sons alone I plead,
> Or her descendants; but for all who sigh
> In servile chains, whate'er their caste or creed:
> They not in vain to Heaven send up their cry;
> For all mankind from bondage shall be freed,
> And from the earth be chased all forms of tyranny.[1]

Garrison's commitment to universal reform coincided with a widening attack on the corrupting effects of the slave power. As reformist discussions broke free from past accommodations of slavery, reform ranks divided on questions of constitutional interpretation and modes of political action. These divisions assumed considerable importance in the antislavery movement and at times overshadowed the reformers' broader common goals. Nevertheless, two fundamental points tied these distinctive antislavery concerns to a wider liberal pursuit of liberty in economic and social relations. Casting aside older preoccupations with republican liberty (which had promoted an accommodation with slavery in the revolutionary era), antislavery reformers defined free labor as the foundation of republican virtue. Because slavery corrupted republican values, antislavery reformers insisted as well that a republican state could recognize only free men and that state powers could not properly be employed to protect or recognize slaveholding interests.

Although the free labor republicanism advanced by antislavery reformers ultimately won a wide following across the North, the old compromises with slavery continued to command respect even as the conditions for their abandonment took root. In this sense, antislavery reformers correctly claimed that they placed principle—by which they meant their faith in the unity of moral and material progress— above any immediate political or economic interests. It was the reformers' pursuit of a transcendent truth, together with a romantic penchant for the sublime, that permitted them to set aside traditional legal restraints and political accommodations. Freed of slavery's corrupting effects, these reformers distinguished republican values from slavery and embraced an idealized liberal heritage of the Revolution as the foundation for the nation's development in an industrial age.[2]

The principle of utility, identifying moral action with the promotion of happiness for the greatest number, underlay the moral appeal of antislavery reform and the sensitivity of its advocates to the corrupting character of slavery. Antislavery reformers understood that the free labor republicanism they aggressively championed unsettled the political consensus of their day and threatened to disrupt established economic ties with the South. But they also understood that the utilitarian values they advanced expressed the ethical and economic interests of a developing middle class. Utilitarian values advanced first in the area of moral reform (initially removed from politics) and in abstract discussions of law and political economy. In time, the political implications of moral reform became clear, as did the instrumental uses of law and doctrines of political economy. When the new Republican party made the supremacy of free labor relations its central political principle, it also proclaimed itself the party of an ascendant middle class. As Wendell Phillips explained in 1863, "the conscience of the middle classes" had secured emancipation in America as it had thirty years earlier in the British Parliament.[3] That conscience did not emerge fully formed, of course, and its capacity to overcome established political and economic ties between North and South did not develop without a struggle. If, with the destruction of slavery, the triumph of liberty over despotism (of virtue over evil) seemed inevitable, it was because the meaning of liberty and the nature of virtue had been redefined in the preceding era as antislavery reformers rejected conservative definitions of republican virtue and identified liberty with free labor.

In the reformist perception, slavery corrupted republican values because it fundamentally denied the principle of utility. In this view, free men willingly exchanged leisure for labor because the rewards of productive labor improved the moral and material conditions of life. One labored to secure greater happiness for oneself and one's family. An individual pursuit of happiness promoted the greatest happiness of all. Tyranny rested on the denial of this freedom and on the moral and material degradation of those to whom it was denied. To speak of liberty in terms that sanctioned a denial of freedom to any individual was to corrupt republican values. Thus Garrison responded to those "gentlemen of property and standing" who assembled in Boston's Faneuil Hall in 1835 to denounce abolitionist agitation:

> Enslave but a single human being, and the liberty of the world is put in peril. Nay, all the slavery that exists—all the tyranny of past ages—originated from a single act of oppression, committed upon some helpless and degraded being. Hence it is, that, whether I contemplate slavery singly or in the aggregate, my soul kindles within me—the entire man is moved with indignation and abhorrence—I cannot pause, I cannot slumber—I am ready for attack, and will admit of no truce, and of no compromise. The war is a war of extermination; and I will perish before an inch shall be surrendered, seeing that the liberties of mankind, the happiness and harmony of the universe, and the authority and majesty of Almighty God, are involved in the issue.[4]

Garrison's sensitivity on this point stood in sharp contrast to the conventional expressions of patriotism voiced at the antiabolitionist meeting he denounced and from the antiabolitionist mob that shortly dragged him through the streets of Boston. And the sensitivity of reformers generally conflicted with the boisterous and self-congratulatory celebrations of liberty that marked patriotic celebrations in Jacksonian America. An idea of liberty that sustained (or ignored) slavery, a patriotism untroubled by slavery's blighting effect on the republic, exposed a corruption of republican values and revealed America for what it threatened to become—a sham democracy disguising a hideous despotism. Antislavery reformers appealed to a higher patriotism, to a notion of liberty consistent with the principle of utility.

Reformers saw the corrupting influence of slavery all about them in the declining authority of traditional social relations and in disturbing new expressions of popular politics that animated the Jacksonian Democracy. The ills of society were myriad but interrelated. "The Dangers of the Nation," as Garrison explained to a Boston audience on Independence Day 1829, arose most immediately from the raucous and militaristic displays of patriotism that attended Fourth of July celebrations. "Patriotism," Garrison protested, "has degenerated into mere animal indulgence; or, rather, into the most offensive personalities. . . . The love of country has been tested by the exact number of libations poured forth, the most guns fired, the greatest number of toasts swallowed, and the loudest professions of loyalty to the Union, uttered over the wine-cup."[5] Garrison deplored the "torrent of flattery, artfully sweetened and spiced, which poured out for the thirsty multitude to swallow." Men boasted of their freedom, he said, who "go shackled to the polls." "We are governed not by our sober judgments, but by our passions . . . we are led by our ears, not by our understandings." Underlying and sustaining this fatuous patriotism lay a deeper evil. Slavery ("a gangrene preying upon our vitals") rendered meaningless all "declamation in praise of liberty and equality" and "the unalienable rights of man." Conversely, hostility to slavery expressed the purest patriotic sentiments and a continuation of the great moral struggle against "the worst passions of human nature." The temperance crusade had already demonstrated the effectiveness of such a struggle: "We have seen how readily, and with what ease, that horrid gorgon, Intemperance, has been checked in its ravages." A moral assault on slavery must produce even better results because "moral influence, when in vigorous exercise, is irresistible."[6]

Garrison's call for a higher patriotism expressed distaste for the vulgarities of mass political behavior in Jacksonian America. Yet more was involved in the antislavery concern with patriotism than questions of taste. The drinking and shooting which Garrison deplored were not the spontaneous activities of high-spirited and boorish patriots. They represented a legacy of traditional social intercourse which reformers now identified with a corruption of public morals. The remnants of the old militia system together with newer forms of military display became objects of reform concern. The militia, once the model of American republican virtue, steadily declined in the early decades of the nineteenth century to become little more than perfunctory military displays by the time Garrison leveled his attack on vulgar patriotism. Militia musters became notable primarily as occasions for those who continued to serve as militia officers (once the representatives of the social elite of their communities) to drink and socialize with the militiamen, the common farmers and artisans who continued to respond to the traditional call to arms.

As the militia's military significance waned, its social function changed as well. Elite volunteer units, handsomely uniformed and proudly aloof from the mass of citizen soldiers, emerged independently of the state militia system. Adding to the patriotic array, volunteer corps composed of clerks and artisans, such as the Mechanic Phalanx of Lowell, Massachusetts, organized in 1825, followed the example of the elite units. After 1840, units of Irish and German immigrants joined in as well. Acknowledging the strength of the volunteer organizations, state governments tried to incorporate them into the surviving structure of the moribund militia system. In 1840, for example, the Massachusetts legislature passed an act requiring all able-bodied white men to enroll in the traditional manner in the state militia, but the state no longer required these men to arm and equip themselves or to submit to training. Instead, the Massachusetts act provided for an "active militia" of ten thousand men drawn from the volunteer units.[7]

Popular military displays seemed to reformers to celebrate coercion. The reformist desire to attach love of country to the principle of utility (that is, to measure national strength and virtue in terms of moral and material progress) illustrated an interrelationship between abolitionism and the antebellum peace movement, both of which expressed a moral repugnance for coercion, whether it be war or slavery. At the same time, however, the developing class and ethnic identities revealed by the revived militia system disturbed reformers as they identified patriotism with utilitarian standards of moral deportment, individual autonomy, and self-restraint. Charles Sumner developed this point in 1845 in his Independence Day address in Boston's Faneuil Hall, an event which Sumner's conservative Whig patrons expected to convey conventional patriotic sentiments. Instead, Sumner used the occasion to launch his reform career and, to the delight of Garrison and reformers generally, castigated the corrupting influence of popular patriotism. Sumner described the martial spirit in America as a "contagion," which, through the militia system, "spreads beyond those subject to positive [military] obligations" to prompt men to organize voluntary units. "Peaceful citizens," Sumner protested, "volunteer to appear as soldiers and effect in dress, arms, and deportment, what is called the 'pride, pomp, and circumstance of glorious war.'" This enthusiasm for military display desecrated the "National Sabbath," as "the ear piercing fife . . . the thump of drum and . . . the parade of bristling bayonets" identified patriotism with war.[8]

When Sumner joined the reformist appeal to a higher love of country, he embraced a cause already well advanced. Dozens of reformers—including the Garrisonian radicals Ellis Gray Loring and Wendell Phillips, Liberty party moderates James G. Birney and Joshua Leavitt, antislavery Whigs William Jay and Joshua R. Giddings, and antislavery Democrats William Leggett and George Opdyke—contributed to the reinterpretation of republican values upon which reformers rested their vision of social order and human progress. Their arguments demanded and received historical justification in pamphlets, newspapers, speeches, and legal briefs; in discussions of morality, law, politics, and economics—in short, wherever reformers appealed to history to identify republican values with the principle of utility. Antislavery reformers were not alone in their appeal to history; a faith in the classical republican heritage served slaveholding interests throughout the antebellum era. Nevertheless, historical interpretations developing themes of progress exerted a dominant public influence over the American sense of historical destiny.

The principal historical writers of the antebellum era sustained the unifying conviction of antislavery reformers that an expanding sphere of individual liberty defined progress in human affairs. George Bancroft's *History of the United States* (10 volumes, 1834–74); John L. Motley's *The Rise of the Dutch Republic* (3 volumes, 1856); and William H. Prescott's *The History of the Reign of Ferdinand and Isabella* (1837), *History of the Conquest of Mexico* (1843), and *The Conquest of Peru* (1847) all saw the early ascendance and later decline of Spain and the Spanish empire as an instructive example of the relationship between individual liberty and historical progress, a relationship that illuminated the fate of nations. America could not safely ignore this historical record. As Motley observed privately to Senator Charles Sumner in 1861, "I had always done what I could to uphold in my writing, the great principles on which the pure American government is founded." Spain's virtue in the Age of Exploration—its political and religious independence, its effective and just government, its vigorous nationalism, and its wealth—all derived from adherence to the laws of Providence, which marked the path of human progress. By contrast, the greed, indolence, and pride that characterized Spain and its empire in the mid-sixteenth century accounted for that nation's increasing weakness and gradual decline. Thereafter, it was the struggle for independence in the Netherlands, the expansion of individual liberty in England, and the emergence of a democratic republic in America that illustrated what Motley referred to as "the inexorable law of Freedom and Progress." In most respects, the United States stood at the forefront of historical progress. Slavery, however, remained an uncomfortable, indeed a dangerous anomaly. To Motley slavery was the only decadent American institution, "more accursed than the Spanish Inquisition."[9]

The advancement of principles of pure government in America rested on a public triumph of the liberal tendencies explored in these historical writings. The more immediate and political task of applying liberal principles to public policy in America fell to antislavery politicians, particularly those who forged the coalitions that preceded the Republican party. Of these reformers, none was more effective than the Ohio antislavery leader Salmon P. Chase. Chase's systematic concern with the history of slavery as a political issue sustained an interpretation of the Constitution that severed the national government from any connection with slavery. Chase's central theme, that the principle of freedom guided national policy and action and that slavery persisted only through local, municipal regulations, appeared in much of the era's reformist discourse. But the freedom national doctrine (proclaimed in the slogan "FREEDOM NATIONAL—SLAVERY SECTIONAL") received its fullest development in Chase's legal arguments and political speeches. Chase's energy in this area expressed his commitment to reform as well as a particular sense of mission that followed him as a son of New England removed to Cincinnati. In this expanding center of commerce, as Chase repeatedly observed, the free institutions of the North advanced moral and material progress within sight of slavery.

Although Chase's arguments against slavery were shaped by the competition between slavery and free labor in the West, his New England origins and his strong ties to the Northeast underlay and sustained his antislavery views. Born in western New Hampshire in 1808, Chase first moved west after his father's death in 1817 and lived for several years as the ward of his uncle Philander Chase, bishop of the Protestant Episcopal church of Ohio. After returning to New Hampshire to attend Dartmouth College, Chase graduated in 1826 and moved to Washington, D.C., where another uncle—Dudley Chase, senator from Vermont—provided him entrée to official Washington during the last years of John Quincy Adams's administration. Under the guidance of Attorney General William Wirt, Chase studied law and was admitted to the bar in Wirt's home state of Maryland in 1829.

Disgruntled by Andrew Jackson's presidential victory and discouraged about his professional prospects in Washington, Chase returned to Ohio and settled in Cincinnati. His attitudes and connections attracted the attention of the merchant-abolitionist Lewis Tappan in seeking representation for the far-flung interests of his New York mercantile firm. Tappan extended credit in Cincinnati based, in part, on information collected by Chase, to whom Tappan also paid commissions for overdue accounts collected. Chase thus came to represent the economic expansion of New York and New England. As an organizer of the Cincinnati Lyceum and an active lecturer and essayist, Chase represented the cultural expansion of northeastern influence as well. Moreover, most New Englanders in Ohio settled on the Western Reserve along the Lake Erie shore, but Chase made his home far to the south, in the Ohio Valley, where his liberal values quickly came into conflict with the influence of slavery.[10]

Two events in the mid-1830s brought Chase's antislavery views into focus and prompted his concern with the legal and constitutional principles that governed the interaction of slave and free communities. The Cincinnati antiabolitionist riot in the summer of 1836 first confronted Chase with what he thereafter regarded as the threat slavery posed for "private rights and public morals" in the free states. Following the pattern of similar riots elsewhere in the North, the Cincinnati mob focused its attention on the converted slaveowner James G. Birney and his recently established abolitionist paper, the *Cincinnati Philanthropist*. After destroying the press and type of the paper's abolitionist printer, and before turning its fury on "amalgamationist" elements on the fringes of Cincinnati's black community, the mob sacked the office of Chase's brother-in-law, Dr. Isaac Colby, a prominent physician and abolitionist and a supporter of Birney's new journal. During the turmoil, Colby's wife (Chase's sister) took refuge in Chase's house while Chase, although careful to distinguish his own antislavery views from those of Colby and his fellow abolitionists, defended Birney and his supporters. In public and in print, Chase stood in opposition to the respected citizens who directed the mob. The mob, in turn, followed the leadership of prominent and wealthy citizens, professional and commercial men for the most part, who, as members of Cincinnati's established elite, rose in opposition to the intrusion of new men—the merchants, artisans, and manufacturers recently arrived from England, New York, and New England—who threatened the established order with their independent commercial ties and their aggressive free labor and antislavery faith. It was not by accident that Chase (and later Birney's son) represented the commercial interests of Arthur Tappan. It was among these new men in Cincinnati that Birney's *Philanthropist* found an audience, and it was to them that Chase offered his talents as a lawyer as he began to shape a political course that appealed to their interests.[11]

Chase denounced the Cincinnati mob for its violation of freedom of speech and press and for its willful destruction of property. Like William Leggett in New York, Wendell Phillips in Boston, and Elijah Lovejoy in St. Louis, Chase viewed the antiabolitionist actions in Cincinnati as alarming expressions of the despotism and violence spawned by slavery. Chase and antislavery reformers generally responded to this threat by attaching the liberal principles of the Revolution to their vision of moral and material progress and thereby elevating republican values above the corrupting influence of slavery.

In the wake of the antiabolitionist riot, Chase soon had an opportunity to give legal expression to his antislavery views. In 1837, the sheriff of Cincinnati arrested a fugitive slave named Matilda and subsequently prosecuted her benefactor and employer, Birney. Serving as Matilda's and Birney's attorney, Chase seized upon a recent decision by Justice Lemuel Shaw of Massachusetts in *Commonwealth* v. *Aves* (1836) to argue that the local law of slavery could not extend into the free state of Ohio.

Shaw's decision involved the status of a slave girl, Med, brought to Massachusetts by her Louisiana mistress for an extended visit. The details of the case, including the elaborate historical argument of Med's attorney, Ellis Gray Loring, appeared in the *Philanthropist*, and

Loring's brief, which drew heavily on Francis Hargrave's argument in *Somerset,* together with Shaw's decision that the slave laws of Louisiana could not extend into Massachusetts, suggested to Chase the manner in which a correct reading of history and law confined slavery within the narrow limits of the municipal laws of slave states. *Comonwealth* v. *Aves* came closer than any other American court decision to embracing Mansfield's dictum in *Somerset* that slavery depended legally on positive municipal law. Yet the decision was significant to Chase's thinking for other reasons as well. At work in the case involving Med was a good deal of righteous indignation over the immorality of slavery, particularly as it applied to a helpless child. Yet in the context of Shaw's career as one of the creators of modern contract law, the case represented part of a continuum in the eroding legal standard of paternal obligation which led to Shaw's famous decision six years later in *Farwell* v. *Boston and Worchester Railroad* (1842).[12]

In the Med case, Shaw ruled that slavery could not enter Massachusetts under the guise of traditional paternal obligations. Significantly, the defendant (Thomas Aves) did not claim to own Med, nor did he contend that the girl's slave status necessarily attached to her in Massachusetts. Rather, he argued that "if this child is, by force of the laws of Massachusetts, now emancipated," her legal guardian remained Samuel Slater of New Orleans (the owner of the six-year-old girl's mother) or, in his absence, Slater's wife, who had brought Med to Massachusetts for a visit of several months. Aves, as the father of Mrs. Slater and the head of the household in which Med resided, claimed guardianship over the child while she remained in Massachusetts. The child, Aves argued, is "wholly incapable of taking care of itself." Therefore, the child should be restrained of its "liberty" only "as is necessary for its safety and health." But Shaw ruled against the traditional paternal responsibilities that Aves invoked. Because Aves claimed guardianship over Med so as to return her to a state of slavery in Louisiana, Shaw determined that he had no "proper and lawful custody." Shaw "freed" Med by insisting that the legal relationship between guardian and ward must be divorced from the relationship between master and slave. The latter relationship, he ruled, in the manner or *Somerset,* could not be extended beyond the authority of the municipal law that sustained it. Med was "of too tender years to have any will" and therefore could not freely consent to be moved back to Louisiana. And because Med's mother was a slave and had "no power to act for the child," Med "is necessarily left to the custody of the law." A committee of Boston women, drawn from the Boston Female Anti-Slavery Society, which originally sought a writ of habeas corpus in Med's behalf, took responsibility for the child's care and education.[13]

In *Farwell*, Shaw similarly rejected as antiquated and obsolete the common law tradition of paternal responsibility for the safety of workers in favor of the modern principle of freedom of contract. In this case, an employee of the Worchester railroad sought compensation for injuries sustained while working for the road. The employee based his claim on the fellow servant rule, derived from a common law principle that viewed the master as standing *in loco parentis* to his servant or apprentice and therefore as liable for injuries sustained by an apprentice resulting from the negligence or mischief of a fellow servant in the master's service. Shaw rejected this claim, insisting that the employee had freely contracted to work for wages for the railroad and that by entering into that contract had acknowledged the risk associated with the labor and assumed responsibility for his own well-being.[14]

As Chase noted in 1831, in an essay honoring the English abolitionist and liberal reformer Henry Brougham, antislavery reform went hand in hand with the modernization of law. English common law, observed Chase, originated "in a barbarous age, in a state of society when commerce and manufactures were unknown, and when men were divided into the despised tillers of the ground and the fierce wielders of the sword." Without reform, ancient rules in common law "could not be expected to be adapted to the exigencies of a civilized, manufacturing, and commercial community." Chase placed himself and his fellow antislavery reformers in this modern tradition and adopted Loring's argument in the Med case to draw a sharp distinction in his defense of Matilda between the narrow rights of slaveholders in the South and the broad free labor principles of the nation as a whole.[15]

At the core of Chase's defense of Matilda was the insistence that the national Constitution neither sanctioned slavery nor recognized the right to hold property in men. Chase acknowledged that the Constitution "takes up and deals with the broad and general relation between master and servants," but he insisted that "it has nothing whatever to do with the relation of owner and property." The Constitution "leaves this whole matter of property in human beings, precisely where the articles of confederation left it, with the states." The Constitution did not prohibit slavery in the original states, Chase conceded, but by offering it no special recognition the national compact effectively contained slavery in the existing states. Citing Mansfield in *Somerset,* Chase described slavery as a function of municipal law. Citing James Kent and Joseph Story on comity between nations, Chase insisted that "it is also certain that the municipal regulations of no state have . . . any extra territorial force." Finally, citing Justice Shaw in the Med case, Chase argued that the fugitive clause of the Constitution was simply a "clause of compact," applying equally to white apprentices and to black slaves and relying on interstate comity for enforcement. Chase then reviewed the history of the country since the adoption of the Constitution to buttress his claim that the national compact rested on liberal principles that could offer slavery no recognition or protection.[16]

In his historical analysis, Chase attributed a fervent liberalism to the Founding Fathers, who acted in harmony with "human nature and the code of heaven" to advance the principle of freedom, which Chase described as "the original, permanent truth, written upon the hearts of all men by the finger of God" and "proclaimed by our fathers, in the declaration of independence." Accordingly, in 1787, when the Framers drafted the Northwest Ordinance and the Constitution, they understood that in the northern states "institutions existed so incompatible with slavery, that the slave who escaped into them would become a free man the moment he should enter their territory." It was with this understanding as well that the Framers shaped the fugitive clause of the Constitution. "It was cautiously framed," Chase insisted, "so as to avoid all recognition of the condition of slavery, or the relationship of ownership between man and man." The fugitive clause referred to *persons,* white and black, who fled from justice or service. As for Matilda, she had entered Ohio in the company of the man who claimed her as his property and could not be captured as a fugitive in the meaning of the federal Constitution. Chase insisted that as soon as her master brought her to Ohio, she became free under the laws of that state. Similarly, Birney could not be fined for harboring Matilda because she had been free to leave her master and to seek employment wherever she chose. Chase's argument on behalf of Matilda did not persuade the Ohio courts to embrace the modernized *Somerset* principle or Shaw's ruling in the Med case. Although Chase's efforts failed to free Matilda, whose master shipped her to New Orleans for sale, his defense of Birney met with some success. Convicted by the Court of Common Pleas in Hamilton County for harboring a fugitive slave, Birney faced fines and imprisonment under Ohio law. While Chase was preparing his appeal, however, the Ohio Supreme Court overturned Birney's conviction on a technicality. The decision exonerated Birney by holding that color was no presumption of slave status. Although Matilda cannot be ranked with Med as an abolitionist victory, Birney's and Chase's efforts had not been wholly wasted. The arguments in the case of Matilda, as in that of Med, revealed the degree to which the nineteenth-century enthusiasm for free labor eroded the eighteenth-century understanding that slavery could be (and, indeed, should be) accommodated in the political structure of a republican nation.[17]

The freedom national doctrine, which Chase first advanced in *Matilda,* expressed a growing northern sensitivity to slave power "aggressions" and to the need to defend the liberties of the free states. Specifically, freedom national arguments denied the extraterritorial claims of the slaveholders and restricted slavery to the limits of the municipal laws of the slave states. This doctrine required a strict construction of those portions of the Constitution that applied to slaves, particularly the fugitive clause, and rested as well on notions of limited federal powers. Here reformers found themselves sympathetic to the Jeffersonian principles of limited government and correspondingly hostile to the positive state arguments of Alexander Hamilton and his Whig descendants. Confident that the laws of political economy, in harmony with God's moral law, governed men's actions as individual, rational economic beings, antislavery reformers projected as a single process the steady advancement of democracy and the destruction of slavery.

Richard Hildreth, whom Wendell Phillips credited with having "analyzed this passage in our history" best, developed a penetrating analysis of this democratic principle in his 1854 essay *Despotism in America.* Phillips cited Hildreth as his authority when he declared that "slavery will drop to pieces by the very influence of the competition of the nineteenth century." Hildreth had traced the origins of this competition to the destruction of New England's political elite (what Phillips called the "aristocracy of classes") at the hands of the Jeffersonian Democracy. Phillips later quipped that the essential elements of

"Massachusetts decency" during the declining years of Federalism included the ability "to trace your lineage to the Mayflower, graduate at Harvard College . . . pay your debts, and frighten your child to sleep by saying 'Thomas Jefferson.'" Hildreth tied these New England fears to Jeffersonian Democracy because southerners, secure in the enslavement of their working class, made a "theoretical democracy their passion." Once the Jeffersonians took the reins of national power in 1801, they "emancipated the working-classes of New England" from the thralldom of paternal restraint. Thereafter, democracy advanced steadily across the North, spurred on by what Phillips hailed as the "vigor and industry" of free labor. In succeeding decades, northern energies transformed Jefferson's democratic theory into practice and finally confronted southern slaveholders with the consequences of the democratic promise. For Phillips, the murder of Elijah Lovejoy in 1837 and the execution of John Brown in 1859 delineated the duration and radical dimensions of this transformation: "The Democratic principle, crumbling classes into men, has been working down from pulpits and judges seats through the shop-boards and shoe-benches, to Irish hodmen, and reached the negro at last. . . . For this [William] Leggett labored and [Elijah] Lovejoy died. For this, the bravest soul of the century [John Brown] went up to God from a Virginia scaffold." "Soon," Phillips argued, "throughout all America, there shall be neither power nor wish to hold a slave."[18]

The democratic principle, but not the Jacksonian Democracy, advanced the cause of liberty. Nevertheless, it was the separation of voting rights from property holding, a political reform generally associated with the rise of Jacksonian Democracy, that most clearly defined the slave power. As states in the West and North (and ultimately in most of the South as well) embraced the principle of white manhood suffrage, the three-fifths clause of the Constitution—the gem of eighteenth-century republican equanimity regarding slavery—stood isolated in the minds of antislavery reformers as a special privilege acquired by monopolistic slaveholding interests. Sectional rumblings in New England against the three-fifths clause dated from the Federalists' ill-fated Hartford Convention, but the eradication of property qualifications for voting meant a fundamental change in the idea of representation. Thereafter, the three-fifths clause provided the enemies of slavery with a means of delineating the slave power. By 1848, for example, it seemed "self evident" to Ohio's abolitionist politician

Joshua R. Giddings that northern rights were violated when an owner of one hundred slaves possessed as much political power in the House of Representatives as "sixty one of the intelligent freemen in Ohio."[19] By demanding a radical break with the slave power, the enemies of slavery identified the principles of the Revolution with a utilitarian faith in individual freedom which distinguished the moral and material progress of the North from the degrading effects of slavery in the South.

In the minds of most reformers, the Jacksonian Democracy had emerged as the political voice of the slave power. In considering constitutional interpretation, reformers pointed to the inconsistency of Democratic strict construction principles when they confronted the extraterritorial claims of the slave power. In regard to slavery, and to the relationship between capital and labor generally, the champions of free labor staunchly opposed the intrusion of federal powers. Here they distinguished themselves from the leadership both of the Whig and Democratic parties. Thus John Quincy Adams, in his support of Loring's argument in Med's case, joined those (including Chase) who insisted on a narrow reading of the fugitive clause of the Constitution to defend northern liberties against the extraterritorial claims of the slave power. "It is true," Adams wrote Loring, "that by the Constitution . . . it is stipulated that *persons held to labour* by the Laws of one State, escaping into another shall be delivered up," when proper claim was made. But the fugitive clause did not grant positive powers to the national government. Instead it placed a specific and limited restriction on the free states. "The very existence of that stipulation proves," Adams concluded, "that without it, no such delivery . . . would ever be made."[20]

After 1840, by contrast, leading Whigs and Democrats tended to advocate broadened federal jurisdiction to protect the extraterritorial claims of slaveholders. Although Supreme Court Justices Joseph Story and John McLean (both Whigs) received praise from antislavery reformers for their insistence in *Groves* v. *Slaughter* (1841) that the municipal limits of slave law sustained a Mississippi act prohibiting the importation of slaves, the majority of the Court followed the line of reasoning presented by the Whig leaders Daniel Webster and Henry Clay, who acted as private counsel for the defendant in the case. Citing *Gibbons* v. *Ogden* (1824), Webster insisted that "the whole subject of commercial regulation was taken from the states and placed in the hands of Congress." Consequently, "nothing, which is a regulation of commerce, can be affected by the state laws." Webster added that although Congress had exclusive authority over commercial regulations among the states, it also had a constitutional obligation to protect the slaveowners' right to maintain an interstate slave trade. "This right of property in the intercourse between states," Webster argued, should be beyond the reach of unfriendly legislation by state or national governments. A year later in *Prigg* v. *Pennsylvania* (1842) Justices Story and McLean abandoned the municipal limits principle and themselves invoked arguments of exclusive federal jurisdiction to strike down Pennsylvania's personal liberty law and place the matter of the rendition of fugitives exclusively in the federal sphere.[21]

Increasingly, Democrats followed the Whig lead and used federal jurisdiction to protect slaveholding interests. "It is rather a remarkable sign of the times," remarked Chase early in 1851, "that the late latitudinarian construction of Story and such as he, should now be resorted to by democrats to justify usurpations of power by Congress." The usurpations Chase had in mind were those associated with the passage of the Fugitive Slave Law of 1850, which, following Story's decision in *Prigg,* placed the full burden of capturing and returning fugitive slaves with the federal government. The *Prigg* decision illustrated for Chase "the facility with which federal judges reach conclusions adverse to freedom over obstacles apparently unsurmountable." Chase concluded that the issue of slavery had given rise to two fundamentally antagonistic interpretations of the Constitution. The antislavery construction held that "all men are persons" and that the Constitution must be "strictly interpreted in favor of freedom." The proslavery construction rested on the "opposite idea that men may be property" and that the Constitution "may be liberally interpreted so as to aid the slaveholders." *Prigg* simply underscored this conviction.[22]

The freedom national doctrine provided opponents of slavery with a legal and constitutional perspective that transcended the Whig-Democratic debate over states rights, federal jurisdiction, and congressional authority. In both the moral and political spheres, antislavery reformers labored to define what Chase called the "Northern Institution of Freedom" and to identify it with the very nature of the American republic. Even as the enemies of slavery pursued divergent constitutional interpretations during the 1840s, they broadly agreed that the principles of the Revolution rendered freedom synonymous with the nation. A national government proclaiming "Equality before the Law," as Charles Sumner insisted throughout his career, would accomplish "the final fulfillment of the promise of the Declaration." And Garrison, who denounced the Constitution as a compromise with slavery, embraced the Declaration as "the most radical political instrument in the world." In a similar vein, Chase extolled the Northwest Ordinance. "By a single sublime act," he insisted, the Founding Fathers made slavery illegal "and impressed upon the soil itself an incapacity to bear up other than freemen." [23]

Within this common liberal republican perspective, the purely moral concerns of abolitionism contributed directly to a broader utilitarian struggle against the slave power. By denouncing as immoral the master-slave relationship, abolitionists helped to define the conditions of freedom which the freedom national doctrine proclaimed to be the bedrock of the republic. When in 1837 Lewis Tappan listed six categories that identified the "disabilities of the slaves," he defined liberty in terms of individual autonomy and security and the freedom to pursue material gain. Tappan's categories deserve attention here because they point directly to the moral elements of liberty that linked free labor as a utilitarian principle to the postmillennial notions of human perfectibility that reshaped Calvinist views of social responsibility in the early nineteenth century and animated antebellum moral reform.

At the head of Tappan's list of disabilities, he noted that slaves were not free to move about as they wished. Here he echoed Garrison's celebration of liberty—"to go and come, rise up or lie down, labor or rest, just as the free spirit shall elect." In utilitarian terms, it was the universal desire of individuals to make themselves and their families comfortable that prompted men to exchange leisure for labor. Coercion of all forms (including traditional forms of masterdom) and slavery in particular stifled this incentive and degraded all labor. That slaves were also not free to accumulate property (Tappan's second category of disabilities) locked them into a life of material dependency, unable to look forward to the prospect of bettering themselves through diligent labor, thrift, and morally correct deportment. Here, Tappan's concern with the disabilities of the slaves reinforced the political economists' lesson for free workingmen—property secured independence: therefore, a fundamental respect for all property and the right to accumulate it underlay the interests of workingmen as it did for all classes. The slaves' inability to improve themselves through education or to follow the dictates of their own conscience (Tappan's third and fourth categories) produced a similar dependence in the moral sphere.[24]

These concerns, together with Tappan's final two categories—that slaves could not preserve the security of their own persons and that they could not develop satisfactory domestic relations—lay at the heart of the abolitionist moral crusade. These disabilities of the slaves were of particular significance in identifying the benefits of freedom. School, church, and family (each of which reformers insisted was denied to the slave) provided vehicles for moral progress wherever free labor relations flourished. These institutions also provided effective instruments of social control, binding free laborers to the values, beliefs, and patterns of behavior of the reformers themselves. As Tappan's categories illustrate, abolitionists looked to the downtrodden slave to delineate the benefits of freedom and the dangers of the slave power. It was not the long hours of hard labor that Tappan deplored when he considered the slave's plight. Nor did he find fault with the drudgery and regimentation of plantation labor. Rather, slavery suppressed utilitarian incentives for material gain and stifled the related elements of moral progress.

The freedom national doctrine lent political effect to the moral and economic elements of the antislavery reformers' utilitarian concerns. It was an essential ingredient in the utilitarian faith that moral and material progress developed apace and that this progress found expression in modern principles of law. Moral sentiments, however, could not be translated directly into economic policy, political organization, or legal doctrine. These latter concerns comprised a public sphere of action related to, but necessarily distinct from, the private sphere of moral sentiment. Moral sentiment led one to embrace temperance, abolitionism, and other reform enthusiasms. The expanding influence of moral sentiment (which itself reflected material progress) permitted advancements in economic relations, in political policy, and in legal doctrines. But moral sentiment could not dictate public policy. In the view of antislavery politicians such as Chase and of abolitionists such as Garrison, this was the error of the New York Liberty group, which confused morality with law. "In a country like ours," as Chase explained, there must always be a close relationship between "moral revolutions and political revolutions." Moral awakenings necessarily came first, sparked by the outrage of "the most ardent, the most zealous and the most determined." Only in the sphere of moral reform,

free from mundane considerations of profit and politics, could abolitionists "set up standards to which it is *worth while* that the people shall
be brought." But moral principles should not be confused with political efforts to isolate slavery. In their moral sentiments, abolitionists
"may go further than discretion may warrant," Chase cautioned; they
"may set up standards to which the masses cannot be brought." In
Chase's view, "Abolition is not properly speaking a political object,
anti-slavery is. Antislavery, I understand to be hostility to slavery as
a power antagonistic to free labor, as an influence perverting our
Government."[25]

For those followers of the New York abolitionist Gerrit Smith, who
wanted the Liberty party to wed morality with law, this and similar
freedom national pronouncements seemed to mark a retreat from
principle. James G. Birney, the Liberty party's presidential candidate
in 1840, expressed alarm at Chase's departure from what he, Birney,
thought to be the morally correct position that the "infamous and
bloody" fugitive clause of the Constitution was null and void for anyone who held a "greater fear of God than of man."[26] But Birney's mor-
alistic blast missed the underlying point. By isolating slavery from all
other forms of service and labor, antislavery reformers ultimately denied slavery any basis in law. Two years after *Prigg,* Chase offered a
particularly clear explanation of the expected result of his finely
honed distinction between "labor due" and "labor owed." "Slavery and
the Constitution are incompatible," he wrote Lewis Tappan in April
1844. If Chase were a judge in Ohio "and a fugitive slave . . . should
bring an action against his *pursuing master* in Ohio for wages during
the whole time of his servitude, he should have judgement." Likewise,
"if I were a U.S. Judge and a Virginia Slave should bring an action
before me against a Va. master the result would be the same."[27] The
Constitution did not directly touch slave relations in the slave states,
where the ancient law of force held sway. Everywhere else, however,
the modern principle of freedom must obtain. This was the logic of
the freedom national doctrine, which demanded the divorce of slavery from the national government.

By the 1850s, as the internal abolitionist debate over the constitutionality of slavery subsided, it seemed clear to antislavery reformers,
as Pennsylvania's antislavery Congressman Thaddeus Stevens put it,
that "by the *general* law man is not the subject of property." This being
so, Stevens insisted that "by the *common law,*" a slave escaping from a

slave to a free state became free. Still loyal to the Whig party, Stevens conceded that the Constitution's fugitive clause prevented "that principle of the common law . . . from operating in the States." But in the absence of positive local legislation, as in the western territories, the common law principle (which "has never been doubted since the celebrated decision by Lord Mansfield") obtained. Chase argued repeatedly from the Matilda case in 1837 through the Washington Peace Conference on the eve of the Civil War that the fugitive clause made no reference to *property* in men; that it provided no constitutional basis for federal legislation; and that its enforcement rested solely on interstate comity. Other reformers, notably the New York abolitionist and life insurance reformer Elizur Wright, Jr., the Unitarian abolitionist and Transcendentalist Theodore Parker, and the educational reformer and antislavery congressman Horace Mann, advanced similar arguments and also found special meaning in the fugitive clause's use of the word "due." Wright argued that the only way a person could be said to be "held to Service or Labour" in the meaning of the Constitution was through a contractual agreement or a judicial proceeding that deprived one of liberty. Mann concluded that a fugitive slave's service could not be legally due to a master. Theodore Parker concurred: "The Rendition clause must be interpreted to include only such as *partly* owe service or labor who owe it or contract for a good and sufficient consideration, and accordingly slaves do not come under the clause at all." [28]

Prigg, followed by the passage of the Fugitive Slave Law of 1850, gradually brought an end to efforts to secure a decision against slavery based on *Somerset* in the United States. Gerrit Smith and the New York Liberty group continued for a time to equate law and morality and to look for judicially decreed emancipation based on a direct application of the principles of natural law, but their efforts were overwhelmed by more powerful forces determined to separate law from morality and to divorce the slave power from the national government. As legal arguments against slavery entered their final phase in the 1850s, they were characteristically technical and aimed at constitutional reform in contrast to earlier arguments, which looked for sweeping judicial action. As Chase assured Gerrit Smith in 1856, he would "never question" the principle that "legislative acts irreconcilable with fundamental morality are void." Yet in "suits between man and man," the principle had no direct applications that Chase could perceive. With Smith, Chase looked forward to the day when the courts would denounce slavery as "so contrary to the law of nature that no legislative enactment can entitle it to recognition." But such a declaration would come only after slavery had disappeared. Before the nation reached "this state of progress," slavery would have been destroyed by "Constitutional legislation national and State."[29]

The freedom national doctrine, proclaiming freedom to be a national blessing and slavery a local curse, pointed the way to the legal isolation and eventual abolition of slavery. In his 1850 Senate speech opposing Henry Clay's compromise resolutions, Chase spoke for two days painstakingly retracing the historical arguments which he and other reformers had developed over the past decade and adding new layers of detail and illustration.[30] On one level, Chase spoke to admonish his southern colleagues, to correct "a tone of complaint, by Southern gentlemen, that this Government is rapidly becoming a mere Government of the majority—becoming a great consolidated democracy." With such complaints, southerners posed as the champions of republican liberty, and Chase intended to prove them wrong. Republican government, he said, required "Equality of natural rights, guaranteed and secured to all, by the laws of a just popular government." In addition, an allegiance to democratic principles obliged the national government "to condemn, to castigate, to abolish slavery, wherever we can constitutionally do so." Although the Constitution required the national government to act on the side of freedom, it likewise restrained interference with purely local aspects of slavery. Chase insisted that the full force of the nation's history supported freedom over despotism, yet the usurpations and aggressions of the slave power now stood in the path of the full development of American democracy.

Chase traced the history of progress in America to a fundamental conflict between slavery and freedom. The very year that the first slaves arrived on Virginia's shores, the "Pilgrim founders" landed in New England: "Slavery was introduced into Virginia. Freedom was planted in New England. The contest between the despotic principle—the element and guaranty of slavery—and the democratic principle—the element and guaranty of liberty—commenced." Chase did not blame the Virginians for introducing slavery, nor did he ignore the existence of slavery in the prerevolutionary North. He argued in the Jeffersonian manner that the colonial traffic in slaves had been encouraged and expanded by the commercial policy of Great Britain. The important point, however, was not that slavery had existed in each of the thirteen colonies but that the revolutionary fathers embarked on an antislavery course, "with a view to the ultimate extinction of slavery itself." Chase cited Jefferson's "Rights of British America" and the Articles of Association of 1774 to buttress his argument that "the earliest action of the associated colonies was antislavery action." He insisted that this antislavery spirit remained in the Declaration of Independence despite the omission of Jefferson's denunciation of slavery and the slave trade. When the Declaration "announced to the world as self-evident the truth that 'all men are created equal,'" Chase believed that Americans had embraced "the great fundamental truth, which constitutes the basis of all just government, and which condemns equally every form of oppression." Accordingly, Americans fought the Revolution "not to vindicate privileges, but the rights of all men—the rights of human nature."

Upon this historical foundation, Chase concluded that the original "national policy in respect to slavery was one of restriction, limitation, and discouragement." Furthermore, the Founders had acted with the expectation "that under the action of the State Governments slavery would gradually disappear from the States." Most important, it seemed clear to Chase that the Constitution's framers took extreme care to exclude from the document any recognition of property in men. Whenever the Constitution touched slavery it spoke not of "persons held to property" but of "persons held to service . . . under State laws." Moreover, the Constitution conferred on Congress no power "to establish or sustain" property in men. Even without the Fifth Amendment's specific guarantee of personal liberty, the general government could claim no constitutional power to institute, sustain, or protect property in men. From the origins of the American government in the Articles of Association to the adoption of the Constitution, the actions of the Founders consistently expressed "a spirit of profound reverence for the rights of man as man—the principle of perfect equality of men before the law." If that policy had been pursued, and if the principles the Founders established had been faithfully carried out by the national government, "there would have been now no slave anywhere under exclusive national jurisdiction—probably no slave within the Boundaries of the Republic."

Chase never denied that postrevolutionary Americans deviated from the Founders' "plighted faith." Indeed, the unfortunate "concession of political power" granted by the three-fifths clause of the Constitution produced a unity of slaveholding interests that by 1850 had grown to threaten the very existence of republican government in America. Chase saw the initial effects of thè fatal decision to grant special representation for those who claimed property in men in the first federal Congress, when representatives from South Carolina and Georgia angrily denounced Benjamin Franklin and others who petitioned for the abolition of slavery. Here Chase saw the beginning of a cycle of "intimidation on the one side, and concession and compromise on the other." Gradually, an aggressive slave power weakened popular sentiment against slavery and altered the nation's original antislavery policy.

Congressional acceptance of the North Carolina cession in 1790 with its proslavery proviso reversed the original antislavery policy. "It was a mischievous and almost fatal error," Chase charged. It was followed by congressional acceptance of the Maryland and Virginia slave codes in the cession of the District of Columbia and by the Georgia cession of 1802, which preceded the creation of the Mississippi Territory. With the purchase of the Louisiana Territory in 1803, the national government failed once more "to establish freedom as the fundamental law of the new acquisition." A similar failure occurred with the purchase of Florida in 1820. Only the wisdom of including a positive prohibition of slavery in the Northwest Ordinance kept some of the western territory free of slavery's blight. Gradually, an aggressive, usurping slave power came to dominate the national government and pervert its republican principles. Out of all the territories acquired by the national government since the adoption of the Constitution, only one state, Iowa, had been admitted as a free state. The others—Tennessee, Alabama, Mississippi, Louisiana, Missouri, Arkansas, Florida, and finally Texas—were admitted or annexed as slave states. Relentlessly, and on a large scale, the slave power worked "the subversion of the original policy of slavery restriction and discouragement." A nation that had once regarded slavery as "a curse, a reproach, a blight, an evil, a wrong, a sin," now heard southerners extol human bondage as "the most stable foundation of our republican institutions; the happiest relation that labor can sustain to capital; a blessing to both races." This represented a "great change" for the nation and a "sad change." If it continued, America would decline: "The spirit of liberty must at length become extinct, and a despotism will be established under the forms of free institutions." Patriotism as well as Christian duty compelled the enemies of slavery to seize the reins of federal power to prevent such a catastrophe.

Morality
and
Law

3

ANTISLAVERY reform expressed developing middle-class values in the most general sense. To be sure, the disruptive impact of antislavery agitation frequently brought reformers into conflict with clergymen and politicians who otherwise represented middle-class sentiments and interests. Certainly not all who came to identify themselves as middle class were equally or even primarily concerned with slavery. But ultimately, the central importance of the slavery issue could not be denied, and even the sternest foes of antislavery reform, the "Cotton Whigs," who considered their economic ties to the South to be essential to the economic development of the North, eventually joined the liberal assault on the slave power. The intensity of the reformers' sensitivity to slavery clearly set them apart. Nevertheless, reformers waged their battle against slavery in the same aggressive manner that entrepreneurs and newer manufacturing interests pressed for the "creative destruction" of monopolistic privilege. In this sense, the antislavery appeal demanded radical change at the same time that it promoted the consolidation of emerging middle-class interests. Antislavery reformers extolled the unity of "liberty" and "business," confident that the advancing democratic principle (which, as Wendell Phillips put it, crumbled classes into men) released individual creative and productive energies from the tyranny of past ages.

In the legal sphere, courts of chancery and a revived common law tradition of substantive justice provided a powerful instrument in the first half of the nineteenth century for the advancement of middle-class notions of progress. In the pursuit of equal rights and economic development, equitable remedies—including the American uses of *Somerset*—served the interests of those who expected to profit from widening economic opportunities. Accordingly, the champions of creative destruction pitted community progress against private interests and, as in the illustrious *Charles River Bridge* case (1837), prevailed with notable effects across the North. Antislavery efforts to circumscribe slavery within the narrow limits of municipal law and to equate free labor with the purpose and destiny of the nation carried these middle-class values beyond the free states to the federal government. Antislavery efforts in behalf of fugitive slaves and related efforts to divorce the national government from the slave power raised a number of questions regarding the proper relationship between moral reform and political action. Although it was clear to all reformers that slavery had no place in a progressive society and nation, the manner in which the advocates of progress severed the legal and constitutional bonds that had traditionally accommodated slaveholding interests assumed central importance in reformist discussions of the proper role of the state in the definition of property rights and in the direction of economic activity.[1]

For the better part of a decade, from the late 1830s until the formation of the Free Soil party in 1848, antislavery reformers engaged in a fervent and divisive debate over the relationship between morality and law and the constitutionality of slavery. The 1840 schism in the American Anti-Slavery Society over the issue (among others) of an individual's moral responsibilities as a citizen, and the publication in 1840 of James Madison's notes on the Constitutional Convention (which gave Americans their first glimpse of the Founders' discussion of slaveholding interests) contributed measurably to the intensity of the constitutional debate. William Lloyd Garrison, Wendell Phillips, and others in the Boston-centered disunionist camp found in Madison's notes confirmation of their view that the Constitution—in violation of the principles of the Declaration of Independence—compromised with the sin of slavery. Moral principle, they concluded, required citizens to withdraw from a union with slaveholders. The Constitution was "a covenant with death and an agreement with hell" that required fundamental reform. To organize politically under the Constitution or to vote for candidates sworn to uphold it were immoral acts. In the Garrisonian view, abolitionists should agitate for the dissolution of the proslavery union as the necessary precondition for the destruction of slavery and the reformation of the republic. As northerners withdrew from the Constitution, Garrison insisted, they withdrew from southern masters "all those resources and instrumentalities now furnished to them by the North, without which they are powerless."[2]

At the opposite pole of the antislavery debate, William Goodell, Gerrit Smith, and other abolitionists in the "burned-over" district of upstate New York declared voting to be a moral duty and vowed to vote for none but confirmed abolitionists. Out of their activities—first in questioning political candidates on slavery issues and later in nominating independent abolitionist candidates for office—emerged the Liberty party in 1840. Deeply influenced by Lysander Spooner's libertarian fusion of morality and law, the Liberty abolitionists insisted that the Constitution could be—and therefore *ought* to be—interpreted as an antislavery document. Insisting that the Constitution itself contained the "only authentic evidence" of the Founders' intentions regarding slavery, Spooner dismissed Madison's notes as hearsay. Of what significance, he asked, were "a few meagre snatches of argument, intent or opinion, uttered by a few only of the members; jotted down by one of them (Mr. Madison) . . . and reported to us fifty years afterwards by a posthumous publication of his papers?" All human enactments rested on principles of morality and higher law, Spooner argued, and the Constitution must be read as an expression of God's law.[3]

Upstate New York and Boston formed the main axis of the abolitionists' constitutional debate, but antislavery groups in two other areas affected its course and outcome. Leading New York City abolitionists, including the wealthy merchant and philanthropist Lewis Tappan and the socially prominent jurist William Jay, expressed alarm at the efforts of both the Liberty abolitionists and their Garrisonian opponents to impose perfectionist principles on the civil activities of citizens. Tappan and Jay labored for a time to hold antislavery reform within the established limits of Whiggish propriety. Their American and Foreign Anti-Slavery Society, although never very successful, offered reformers an alternative organization to the Liberty party and to the Garrisonian-controlled American Anti-Slavery Society. Tappan and Jay looked with initial favor on the emergence of a group of western reformers, led by the antislavery editor Gamaliel Bailey and attorney Salmon Chase, who planted the seeds that in 1848 emerged as the Free Soil party. The westerners argued in the manner of Ellis Gray Loring in the Med case that slavery could not exist in the absence of positive municipal laws. As Chase insisted, Madison's notes made it clear that the Founders recognized slavery only as a function of state law. The westerners avoided the perfectionist extreme of the Garrisonians and the New York Liberty abolitionists and adopted, to Tappan's and Jay's initial satisfaction, the traditional distinction between moral reform and political action to demand the divorce of the national government from all involvement with slavery.[4]

To an extent, the antislavery constitutional debate expressed differing perceptions of what constituted an effective formula for direct action against slavery. Beyond questions of tactics and effectiveness, however, the 1840 schism in antislavery ranks and the debate over the constitutionality of slavery reflected a wider struggle—between an advancing legal formalism and the remnants of the Jeffersonian codification tradition—over the uses and meaning of law. Important as instrumental uses of common law and equity were to the advancing interests of entrepreneurs and small manufacturers, the consolidation of their interests required legal protection in formal rules of legal interpretation, as well as a transformation of law. As a consequence, instrumental uses of law gave way steadily to the emerging barriers of legal formalism, which by the 1850s invested the law with "scientific" objectivity and precision. Jeffersonian hostility to judge-made law revived in the Jacksonian era as a challenge to this advancing formalism. At the same time, formal legal writers—notably Chancellor James Kent of New York and Supreme Court Justice Joseph Story of Massachusetts—labored to distinguish law from morality and politics and to protect the interpretation of the law from the codifiers, who, as opponents of chancery, tied the meaning of law to the ordinary notions of republican citizens.[5]

Spooner's influence among the Liberty group of abolitionists represented a subtle but potentially powerful threat to the liberal goals of antislavery reform. Spooner appealed to the perfectionist tendencies generated by the Second Great Awakening and specifically to the postmillennial optimism that sustained reformers in their faith that individual moral acts prepared the way for Christ's reign on earth. Although this perfectionist spirit eventualy harmonized with the utilitarian definition of progress, the union of the two required a careful distinction between God's higher law and the civil functions of the state. It was just this distinction which Spooner denied as he wedded morality with law and thereby challenged the subtleties of legal formalism and the utilitarian principles it secured. Spooner's influence raised the possibility—however briefly and tenuously—that antislavery reform might promote a radical individualism that could not be contained within a liberal definition of individual liberty.[6]

By 1850, Spooner's influence had largely waned and the goals of legal formalism meshed smoothly with the pursuit of antislavery re-

form. As the antislavery constitutional debate of the 1840s demonstrated, however, this result was not accomplished without a fight. As
long as some reformers viewed the perfection of human society as a
fusion of morality and law, an essentially anarchistic vision of individual obedience to God's law resisted the triumph of formalism and with
it the liberal character of antislavery reform. For a time, Spooner
found willing allies in the reformers' ranks, most importantly in Alvan
Stewart, whose 1837 argument before the New York State Anti-Slavery
Society marked the beginning of the abolitionists' constitutional debate. Stewart, a successful Utica lawyer and soon a prominent spokes-
man for the New York Liberty party, applied perfectionist principles
to the Constitution and argued that the due process clause of the Fifth
Amendment provided constitutional sanction for the immediate and
universal abolition of slavery in the United States. He based this interpretation on the view that political activity ought to be moral in character. "Voting is reaping and securing the crop planted and sowed by
moral and religious persuasion," he argued. "Voting is the Legislation
of the chosen. Each man is to vote and act, each election, as though he
alone were responsible for the entire government." In this manner,
Stewart carried the perfectionist principle into politics. Because the
government of God ultimately supplanted all human governments,
Stewart insisted that progress toward the millennium would be hastened by moral political behavior. When a "good man" voted and encouraged others to vote, he helped to "introduce this Heavenly form
of government and abolish that of human origin."[7]

God's law was the only source of human law and provided the only
means of interpreting and applying human law, and it followed from
Stewart's point of view that abolitionists "should never make a single
admission, in relation to the construction of the Constitution, which
might tell against the slave." Stewart argued that the property rights
claimed by the slaveholders were "carved out of the natural ones of
the slave." Therefore, laws claiming to enforce slavery were "clearly
null and void in the court of conscience." This argument, elaborated
upon by William Goodell and appealed to by Spooner, became the
creed of Gerrit Smith's Liberty group. Liberty party abolitionists insisted that the Constitution positively forbade slavery everywhere in
the Union. As one of Smith's supporters summarized the argument,
"the 'rights of *man*' according to the law of God and the Declaration of
Independence constitute our one idealism."[8]

Spooner, who delivered what Perry Miller described as "a last short blast against Chancery," tied the political perfectionism of the Liberty party to the codifiers' struggle against legal formalism. Spooner and the Liberty group argued simply and powerfully that law expressed Christian benevolence, that law and morality were one. It followed that the Constitution sustained abolitionism and that interpretations of law required no technical expertise and need not be constrained by formal rules. In addition to his antislavery interpretation of the Constitution, Spooner published an essay proclaiming the jury, not the judge, to be the arbiter of fact and law. From the formalists' perspective, as Wendell Phillips soon insisted, Spooner's ideas threatened anarchy. Likewise, the Liberty group, by linking the perfectionism of enthusiastic Protestantism with Spooner's assault on legal formalism, alarmed the bulk of antislavery reformers (Garrisonians included) who associated moral progress and the final destruction of slavery with northern economic expansion and the triumph of liberal values.[9]

During the 1840s, the popularity of Spooner's ideas among the Liberty party abolitionists threatened to enlist a significant portion of abolitionist sentiment in a potentially popular crusade against the consolidation of legal formalism. In the two years between the publication of Spooner's antislavery analysis of the Constitution and Phillips's response to it, the New York Liberty party officially adopted Spooner's doctrine. Moreover, the fusion of morality and law proved to be appealing to abolitionists such as Lewis Tappan who rejected Garrisonian disunionism.[10] As Phillips argued, Spooner threatened to redirect antislavery sentiments. Although Spooner expressed sympathy for abolitionist goals, he never joined the Liberty party or any other antislavery group. Phillips singled out Spooner as a nonabilitionist with dangerous ideas about law and the Constitution for systematic criticism, intending to discredit him in reform circles. Responding point by point to Spooner's argument, Phillips portrayed him as shallow in his thinking, mistaken in his terminology, and in flagrant contradiction to formal rules of legal interpretation.

Phillips opened his attack on a practical note. "The Constitution will never be amended," he argued, "by persuading men that it does not need amendment." The nation's ills, Phillips continued, "are only cured by holding men's eyes open, and forcing them to gaze on the hideous reality." But as Phillips's argument proceeded, it became clear that his disagreement with Spooner went deeper than questions of tactics or expediency in antislavery reform. Two aspects of Spooner's argument attracted Phillips's attention. First, by insisting that law was synonymous with the requirements of natural justice, and by asserting that "government can have no power except such as individuals may *rightfully* delegate to it," Spooner elevated individual autonomy over the authority of civil government. Phillips insisted that this view was anarchistic. Second, Spooner described the Constitution as a contract that could be valid and binding only to the extent that it did not violate the natural rights of any of the parties involved. Immoral contracts were void, said Spooner, reinforcing an earlier argument advanced by Alvan Stewart that laws to uphold slavery "are of themselves evidence of the most stupendous fraud which can be committed through the instrumentality of one class of men upon another." Defining slave law as fraud, Stewart turned "to the civil law, the law of nations, the common law" to establish that "*fraud* avoids all contracts and all proceedings . . . even acts of parliament when procured by *fraud*, are null and void." Stewart characterized slavery as "always stamped with fraud" because it proclaimed it to be right "for the strong to rob the weak" and because it dismissed "morality and honesty in the transactions of man . . . as exploded truisims belonging to an obsolete age." Building on this point, Spooner went on to argue in direct conflict with legal formalists that judges were morally bound to reject as null and void all laws that contradicted natural justice.[11]

Phillips demanded a clear distinction between morality and law. He countered Spooner first by asserting that civil government derived its authority from the general will, not from principles of natural rights. "We say," wrote Phillips, "that *for the purpose of the civil government of any nation,* the majority of the nation is to decide what is just and right, and that their decision is final, and constitutes, for the nation, LAW." If judges—"as men, as simple individuals, units in the sight of God"— found themselves confronted with a choice between following the dictates of their conscience or carrying out their duty to enforce an unjust or immoral law as established by the majority, it was their moral duty to resign, not to violate their oath of office and declare the bad law null and void. Citing James Kent and Joseph Story on the need to contain equity jurisprudence in formal rules of interpretation, Phillips observed that "the wisest men in all ages have held, that relying on the conscience or discretion of Judges is but another name for tyranny." Following Kent, Phillips insisted that the natural rights foundation of

English common law had no further effect in America save to permit judges to insist upon a "reasonable" construction of statutes when more than one construction was permissible. Like Kent, Phillips subordinated the tradition of equity jurisprudence to the new rules of legal formalism. By all tests of reasonable construction, Phillips insisted, the Constitution established a contract that recognized the interests of slaveholders. American civil government derived its authority from a "specific, definite, limited, *written* Constitution. It contains All the principles which the people, the nation, have agreed shall form the foundation of our *national* law." The only test of a law's legitimacy was its constitutionality. And if the justices of the Supreme Court deemed a law constitutional, it was binding to all "no matter how unjust." [12]

Phillips's subordination of common law to written law echoed the rhetoric of the codifiers at the same time that it illustrated the manner in which the formal principles of legal interpretation developed by Kent and Story triumphed over the traditional codification principles championed by Spooner. In the same fashion, the adoption in New York in 1848 of David Dudley Field's code marked the triumph of formalism over what remained of traditional standards of equity jurisprudence. In the name of codification, Field accomplished in fact what Jefferson had feared and what Spooner persisted in resisting. By abolishing the distinction between law and equity, Field brought the remnants of equity jurisprudence under the authority of formal legal rules that bore no relationship to traditional standards of morality. For Field—a Free Soil Democrat and future Republican leader—the goal of divorcing law from morality went hand in hand with the task of divorcing the national government from slavery. Both reforms aimed to free men from the tyranny of the past and to raise new barriers against a revival of the paternalistic restraints and obligations embedded in the common law tradition. "After having struggled for several years," Field wrote Charles Sumner shortly before the adoption of his code, "I think I see the means approach in this state of the reform which you and I have so much at heart—the abolition of the forms of action and of the distinction between law and equity." [13] For Field and Sumner, as for Phillips, the final subordination of equity jurisprudence to legal formalism represented an advance in the wider liberal agenda of which abolitionism was an essential part.

Adin Ballou, the communitarian leader of the Hopedale Fraternal

Community, joined those reformers who applauded Phillips's denunciation of Spooner. "You have fairly shown," Ballou wrote Phillips, "that if it were granted the Federal Constitution is Anti Slavery, the *union* is helpless for freedom to the slave under it, because all departments of the administrative government . . . have ever been proslavery in spite of it." More broadly, Ballou commended Phillips for exploding "the sophism that *natural justice and legality* are identical." If judges ever acted as Spooner said they should toward the law, "anarchy, downright no-governmentism, must be the inevitable result." Ballou found Phillips's response particularly important because Spooner's ideas had proved influential "to a certain class of minds" in the reform community. By equating law and morality, Spooner had given an appealingly "deep and exclusive meaning to the term *legal*." Phillips helped to set matters straight.[14]

Although Phillips focused particular attention on Spooner, he and the Garrisonians generally expressed alarm at the ease with which Stewart, Goodell, Gerrit Smith, and others of the New York Liberty party wedded moral principle with law. In the Garrisonian view, avowed reverence for the law and the Constitution, and the expression of a citizen's moral obligation to vote, masked intentions to subvert the supremacy of law. When the Boston abolitionist John Pierpont argued that "I am bound to act in behalf of morality through political instrumentalities," Phillips countered that though Pierpont might "swear support of the Const." he meant "all the while *not* to support it." Phillips charged that Stewart's insistence that Congress had the power under the Constitution "to abolish slavery *in the several States*" could only mean "that the Cartrage Box shall follow the ballot box." In either case, the Liberty group's expressed reverence for law and the Constitution seemed dishonest and dangerous to Phillips and to the Garrisonians. "Holding that honesty and truth are more important than even freeing slaves," Phillips concluded, the "'Garrisonites'" opposed the dissembling doctrines of the Liberty group.[15]

For many of the reasons explored by Phillips, the western wing of the Liberty group—led by Salmon Chase and Gamaliel Bailey—also opposed the constitutional doctrine of the New York Liberty group. Chase carefully drafted the early policy statements of the Liberty party in 1842 and 1844 to conform with the *Somerset* principle as enunciated in the Med case. With as much intensity as Phillips, Chase insisted on the importance of maintaining a sharp distinction between morality and law, between the principles of natural justice which sustained freedom and the law of force which maintained slavery. In this view, the legality of slavery in existing states was not a legitimate constitutional question. "Slavery in the States is no more constitutional or unconstitutional than Slavery in Brazil," Chase wrote Gerrit Smith. "It is extra-constitutional in every sense." The legitimate goal of the Liberty party, he argued, should be "to abolish slavery wherever it exists within reach of the constitutional action of Congress . . . and to deliver the Government from the control of the slave power." It was wrong and dangerous to equate abolitionism's moral goals with politics. Abolitionism, Chase argued, was moral reform and "cannot be effected by political power." At the same time, a wide range of issues involving the distribution of economic benefits impinged upon slavery and the slave power and directly involved the natural rights of man with questions of political power. Slavery, Chase explained, "has reference to subjects on which the political power of the country . . . must be brought to bear." By divorcing morality from both law and politics, reformers could hasten the day when the national government could be claimed by the forces of progress and divorced from the slave power.[16]

In organization as well as in theory, the western Liberty party worked to maintain a distinction between moral reform and political action. "In Ohio," Bailey informed Phillips, "the abolitionists are *one* in *fact*, though *two* in *form*." Aware of Phillips's views about political action and eager for the antislavery cause in the West to benefit from an address by the great orator, Bailey assured Phillips that "in the west, we have kept up faithfully the distinction between the Liberty party, and the antislavery societies." Although "nine tenths of all of our abolitionists are Liberty men and women, yet, we have nothing of the machinery of politics in our *Society* meetings."[17] The New York Liberty group stood alone in its fusion of morality and law.

The freedom national doctrine defined what most antislavery reformers understood to be the proper relationship between sentiments of moral reform and the public world of politics and law. In the Garrisonian view, reformers ought to divorce northern society and ultimately the national government from slavery and the slave power. As Phillips insisted in his reply to Spooner, civil government derived from the will of the majority, and until the majority altered existing laws, northern advocates of freedom were morally obliged to remove themselves and their free institutions from the corrupt union with slaveholders. Chase and the emerging free-soil reformers, believing that they could mobilize such an antislavery majority, argued that slavery could have no effect beyond the municipal limits of the states that recognized it. The goal of antislavery politics was to divorce the national government from the slave power. In politics, antislavery reformers ought to disentangle the state from the corrupting influences they identified in civil society. Here, too, the New York Liberty group's desire to maintain a party of pure moral reform deviated from the liberal antislavery reform agenda. Not only could the New Yorkers never garner a political majority to defeat the slave power, but their insistence that politics could be the agency of moral reform potentially gave a great deal more power to political procedures than most antislavery reformers thought wise or healthy.

Increasingly, reformers saw law and politics as barriers against corruption, not as agencies of reform. As reformers struggled against what they perceived to be the tyranny of past ages, they sought to replace archaic paternal restraints with a firmer order imposed by free economic relations and individual self-control. In politics, they were suspicious of all of the familiar mechanisms of vote gathering, including public drinking and militaristic display. Moral reform called on men to resist the popular tide, to restrain their baser instincts, and through self-control to reject the appeal of demagogues. Moral reform required individuals to purge themselves of sin and to police their own behavior. The goal of all reform, as the Garrisonian J. Miller McKim explained, was to prompt men to correct the errors of their ways. McKim explained the reforming effect of Garrisonian disunionism with the example of a drunkard whose wife initially bore his abuse and did all she could to comfort him in his turmoil. This misplaced sympathy, insisted McKim, confirmed the drunkard in his vice. But once the wife left her husband and "dissolved the union," the sinner accepted reform. Thus, contrary to the New York Liberty group's argument that by refusing to vote, the Garrisonians simply added to the political strength of the slaveholders, McKim insisted that disunionism advanced reform: "The *universal* effect of the withdrawal of fellowship by the good from the evil, is—not to confirm the evil in their ways—but *to make them better.* . . . To continue in fellowship with the wicked is to make them easy in their crimes; to withdraw from them is *one* of the steps to reform them. *Secession, is in itself, a reformatory movement.*"[18]

It is clear that Garrisonian opposition to abolitionist political action did not mean that Garrison and his followers took no interest in politics or that they would not involve themselves in political affairs. On the contrary, Garrisonians eagerly awaited the political success of antislavery principles. Yet they did insist on distinguishing between political action and moral reform, and this distinction promoted a mutual respect between them and antislavery politicians. As Henry Wilson explained, the Garrisonians complemented the efforts of antislavery politicians. As one of the architects of the Free Soil–Democratic coalition in Massachusetts that elected Charles Sumner to the Senate, Wilson understood that those who would divorce themselves from the slaveholders shared a common reform goal with those who would divorce the national government from the slave power. Moral reform accomplished the former; the latter was the task of antislavery politics.[19]

Garrisonians reciprocated this goodwill by offering antislavery politicians occasional public praise and frequent private advice. Of the latter, none was more extensive than Wendell Phillips's continuous effort to keep Charles Sumner at the radical edge of antislavery reform and free of any tendency to confuse morality with law. Sumner understood and agreed with the Garrisonian position that the Constitution sanctioned injustice and wrong, but he did not accept the disunionist conclusion. The Constitution, as Sumner observed, gave citizens the authority as well as the means to alter it. Phillips did not quarrel with this position. Indeed, once Sumner reached the Senate, Phillips continually urged him to carry the modernized *Somerset* principle to its logical conclusion and to denationalize slavery. Phillips also corrected the senator when he appeared to deviate from this course. When Sumner proposed to restore the federal government to the position it occupied in 1789, "without a slave under the Nat.[ional] flag," Phillips cautioned him not to fall victim to the notion that the Constitution rested on abolitionist principles. If the national government had been free of slavery's blight in 1789, Phillips asked, "why did it not stay so?" The champions of freedom needed more security for the future than the presumed purity of the original Constitution. Even if Congress and the courts "recognized and limited" slavery in the states, as Sumner insisted had been done in 1789, there was no reason to think that the slave power "will behave any better" than it had in the first half of the nineteenth century. The only remedy lay in confronting the constitutionally recognized power of slaveholders. But when Sumner protested that he could do no more *"under the Constitution"* than seek to restore the federal government to its original relationship to the slaveholding states, Phillips reminded him to distinguish between moral agitation and legislation. "We can *agitate for anything* under the Constitution," Phillips argued. Nothing in Sumner's *"civil* capacity" as a senator prevented him from speaking in favor of abolition. "We have always repudiated all right to legislate on slavery in the states," Phillips continued. Accordingly, Sumner "could not constitutionally vote a law in the Senate . . . to touch S. Carolina slavery, but you could agitate on that floor or on the *free soil* of Mass. as much as you chose." Again, when Sumner deviated briefly from the distinction between morality and law to suggest that each state could define for itself in its own courts the meaning of the Constitution's fugitive clause, Phillips reminded him that the Constitution gave the Supreme Court exclusive national jurisdiction.[20]

Even though Garrisonians and antislavery politicians joined forces to isolate the New York Liberty group, that group's arguments enjoyed a radical simplicity which the formalists denounced but could not entirely dislodge. "The Constitution was framed to secure the blessings of liberty," one of the Liberty abolitionists argued to Senator Sumner. Wherever the Constitution applied, "slavery is illegal and void." The more complex antislavery argument derived from *Somerset* made no sense to the followers of Gerrit Smith. Either "slavery . . . is unknown and repugnant to the constitution" or the slaveowners were correct to argue that if slaves could be held in the South they could "be held every where, wherever the constitution goes." As slaveowners pressed their constitutional claims more aggressively in the 1850s, the simplicity of the Liberty group's argument suggested that northern radicalism might match southern radicalism. The slave power knew no middle ground, William Goodell insisted in the wake of the Dred Scott decision in 1857, "so *we* know no middle ground." Southerners claimed the whole nation for slavery, "so we claim the whole country for freedom." Moreover, if one understood the law to be God's instrument for the moral reformation of the republic, it followed that civil government could not sustain slavery. Those who scorned the instrument God created to do his work "cannot remain innocent." As the struggle with the slave power intensified, the Liberty abolitionists girded themselves for Armageddon. The slave power might impose its will like "a gang of highwaymen," observed the veteran abolitionist Beriah Green in 1859, but "I owe allegiancy only & ever to Truth, Order, justice—to the sovereign Ideas, thro' which the Father reveals himself to my consciousness."[21]

As the Liberty abolitionists looked hopefully toward a final struggle between slavery and freedom, John Quincy Adams's well-known reference to the vulnerability of slavery in times of insurrection or war assumed particular importance. Adams originally made his remarks in 1842 following the congressional censure of antislavery Congressman Joshua R. Giddings. Angered by Congress's action, Adams warned his southern colleagues that they might one day desire and need the North's goodwill. In time of war, Adams noted, slavery became a distinct burden, and "the commanders of both armies have power to emancipate all the slaves in the invaded territory." Furthermore, in the case of domestic insurrection, the power to abolish slavery rested upon Congress: "If they [the slaveholders] came to the free States and say to them, you must help us to keep down our slaves, you must aid us in an insurrection and a civil war; then I say that with the call comes a full and plenary power to this House and to the Senate over the whole subject. It is a war power."[22]

Abolitionists of all stripes noted and praised Adams's argument. For Liberty abolitionists, however, the war powers argument seemed to sustain a fusion of morality and law. Whatever was right necessarily became a part of the government's function and duty. "The Constitution demands a Federal Abolition of Slavery," William Goodell argued with characteristic simplicity, "because it declares its object to be 'to establish justice and secure the blessings of liberty.'" In the same spirit, Gerrit Smith pressed Salmon Chase to adopt the slogan "'no law for slavery'" (because law and slavery were fundamentally incompatible), and to look forward to the day when "a revolutionary Judge . . . will declare it to be *no law*." As one of Smith's followers put it, with the advent of the millennium, the government of God would destroy all evil— "Slavery" and the "Slave Power" as well as "every other form of oppression found in the U.S. government and also in the State government."[23]

The logic of legal formalism eluded the Liberty group as did much of the new "science" of political economy that accompanied it. Their notions of right and wrong were simple and free of the subtle distinctions between moral sentiment and utilitarian values that shaped the arguments of Garrisonians and Free Soilers. The Liberty abolitionists viewed the fight against slavery as part of an eternal struggle between good and evil, a struggle that required men to subordinate all worldly considerations and loyalties to God's immutable laws. Thus Alvan Stewart reduced the history of the world to a series of struggles "between right and wrong, liberty and slavery." Although the Garrisonians and Free Soilers conceived themselves to be at the vanguard of historical progress, Stewart saw not progress but cyclical struggles between right and wrong: "That which was right . . . will never be wrong in the revolving circles of eternity. *Right* is a straight line running through time and eternity. Man can never crook it. It is a line surveyed by the Almighty."[24] Refusing to accept the notion that civil government must operate by rules distinct from traditional principles of morality, the Liberty group ignored and to a degree challenged the utilitarian ethic that sustained the idea of progress. As progressive-minded reformers searched for a balance between state action for the common good and the free operation of the marketplace, the New York Liberty group tended toward agrarianism and expressed hostility to all forms of concentrated wealth.[25]

Despite continued Liberty League protest, the intensity of the antislavery constitutional debate waned in the late 1840s amid the rise of the free-soil movement. By 1850, the distinction between morality and law no longer required advocates. Spooner's blast against chancery had been both short and final. In the end, progressive reformers had nothing to fear from the Liberty group's fusion of Christian benevolence with law and politics. As New York's antislavery Senator William H. Seward demonstrated in his famous "higher law" speech in 1850, formal expositions of law and political economy easily subsumed the Liberty group's higher law appeals. Seward understood his constituents in the burned-over district well and received extensive praise for his higher law address. But the substance of his speech—a Whiggish defense of northern economic interests against the aggressions of the slave power—demonstrated that appeals to the government of God could be synchronized with economic expansion in agriculture, commerce, and manufacturing, with what Seward liked to call the three wheels of material progress.[26]

During the 1850s, in the rush of events that propelled the nation toward war, constitutional positions that had once divided abolitionists began to merge into a single defense of the Union and constitutional order against the aggressions of the slave power. The responses of Lewis Tappan and William Jay to the constitutional debate illustrate the process by which the formal requirements of law and political economy gradually subsumed moral appeals for reform. As prominent members of the American Anti-Slavery Society in the 1830s, Tappan and Jay initially resisted identifying either with the Garrisonians or with the Liberty group. Their independence did not last long, however, and by the mid-1840s Tappan supported the arguments of Spooner, Goodell, and Stewart. "American Slavery," Tappan insisted, "is sinful, illegal and unconstitutional." Just men were morally obliged to read the Constitution as an antislavery document. "What is the Constitution?" Tappan asked Chase. "Is it not what a majority of the Congress say it is? What a majority of the Justices of the Sup. Court decide it is?" Ought not reformers make the Constitution say what *they* wished it to say? [27]

By contrast, William Jay, the son of the first chief justice, John Jay, and himself a respected judge in Westchester, New York, regarded the Liberty group's constitutional position with alarm. Jay compared the looseness with which Tappan approached questions of law and constitutional authority with the arrogance that emboldened slaveholders "in lynching Abolitionists." He thought Alvan Stewart's "revelation" about the war power to be about as reliable as "Joe Smith's about the golden Bible." John Quincy Adams's original reference to congressional war powers in 1842 projected imagined circumstances, not established law. If extraordinary circumstances occurred, Congress might assert its right to abolish slavery. As Jay explained, "We may imagine circumstances both in peace & war such as famine, pestilence, earthquakes, sedition, invasion &c which might justify congress in assuming for the time, powers not given, or even expressly prohibited by the constitution. Necessity we are told knows no laws; but surely we are not to interpret existing laws by imaginary cases of necessity." [28]

Abolitionist sentiments, as Jay understood them, sprang from a sense of "religious obligation," but he resisted Tappan's tendency to allow religion to spill over into politics. Jay insisted that "Constitutional restraints forbid all other than moral interference with slavery in the Southern states." Were he a member of Congress, he said, "I should think myself no more authorized to legislate for the slaves of Virginia than for the serfs of Russia." On this point Jay never wavered although Tappan encouraged him, with some success, to view the New York Liberty group's position with tolerance. Many in the Liberty party thought Stewart's arguments were too extreme, Tappan told Jay. But Tappan also saw significant advancement in the public's perception of the constitutionality of slavery, and he thought it unwise to make "concessions unnecessarily on the Constitutional question." In the 1830s Tappan thought that the public had generally believed that the Constitution "guaranteed slavery." By the 1840s he thought that "most men believe it merely *permits* it, while an increasing number are persuaded that the constitution is altogether an anti-slavery document, and will put an end to American slavery." If popular opinion continued to advance in this way, the Constitution and the nation could be won for freedom. Jay did not alter his constitutional views, but for the time being he lent his support to the Liberty party cause.[29]

In 1843, with the prospect of the annexation of Texas before the nation, Jay joined with Tappan to support the Liberty party and its presidential candidate, James G. Birney. For the next decade, Chase and others working to broaden the political appeal of the Liberty party looked to Jay as a potential presidential candidate. Jay accepted a Liberty party Senate nomination in 1845, but he remained deeply hostile to Gerrit Smith's constitutional doctrine and avoided any active role in the party. Instead, the expansive spirit of the slave power turned Jay to disunionism. Viewing the Constitution as a contract that could not be violated by declaring void those portions of it which protected slaveholding interests, Jay nevertheless insisted after the annexation of Texas that "a mutual compact cannot be binding on one party." Jay believed that when the drafters of the Constitution refused to give the federal government direct power over slavery in existing states, they had struck a bargain with slaveholders. Because slavery had been allowed to expand into the territories, however, Jay declared that "this compromise is now terminated." The Constitution had become "an instrument of cruelty, oppression, and wickedness." The North must divorce itself from the corrupted Union, "and the sooner the better."[30]

Disunionism notwithstanding, Jay remained closer than most antislavery reformers to the Whig antislavery tradition. In 1840 he had hoped that the antislavery elements of the Whig party would carry the nation for freedom; a decade later, after the Conscience Whigs united with the Democrats in the Free Soil party, he saw little hope from political organizations. "Free Soil democracy is now much like the sow that was washed," he wrote Charles Sumner, who was then about to win election to the Senate as the result of a Free Soil–Democratic coalition in Massachusetts. "Free Soil Whigism," lamented Jay, "is sorely tempted and in great danger of falling." Jay protested in vain that his disunionist views expressed Whig principles, not Garrisionian radicalism. "I have advanced no ultra fanatical doctrines in politics or religion," he complained late in 1850. "On the subject of slavery I have but reiterated the opinions of many of the best and greatest men in England and in our own country." Jay stood with conservative Whigs to oppose forcible resistance to the Fugitive Slave Law. But disunionism branded him a radical whether he liked it or not. "Solely on account of my anti slavery efforts," he complained, "I find myself nearly insulated in Society."[31]

The passage of the Fugitive Slave Law in 1850 and the Kansas-Nebraska Act in 1854 forged a new antislavery unity across the North, and the old constitutional debate became progressively less intense. The conviction that the South through its aggressions had broken its constitutional obligations to the North attracted wide antislavery support. Garrisonians phrased the issue somewhat differently, but they too arrived at the same conclusion. When in 1853 Wendell Phillips learned that Horace Mann intended to speak in Congress against the Fugitive Slave Law (arguing in the manner of Senator Chase that "the word 'due' cannot cover the relation of slavery and that the fugitive's service is not legally due to any one"), Phillips added a marginal comment on a private letter expressing his conviction that the North should disengage entirely from its contractual ties to the South. "The remedy is to back out of the whole contract," wrote Phillips, "not to sneak in and fail to keep it." Similarly, although the New York Liberty group continued to insist that the Constitution demanded abolition, they had no difficulty insisting as well that, in Lewis Tappan's words, southerners had "yielded all of the rights they ever had (if they ever had any) in the protection of slavery." Even Chase, whose version of the divorce doctrine held fast to traditional disclaimers concerning slavery in the states, insisted that interstate comity (which alone, in his view, could carry the fugitive clause of the Constitution into effect) had been irrevocably destroyed by the aggressions of the slave power.[32]

This new antislavery consensus provided the foundation for northern sectional unity. As Chase told a Cincinnati audience in 1855, the freedom national doctrine would secure "a perpetual majority of free States in the Union." Slavery might continue to exist "within the States," but northerners would not permit it to extend beyond the limits of the slave states. With slavery clearly distinguished from all other forms of service and labor, antislavery forces closed ranks behind the Union and the Constitution. "The original policy of the fathers of the Republic has been subverted," Chase intoned. "We simply demand its restoration. We want 'indemnity for the past and security for the future.'" [33]

Morality and Utility

4

THE transcendental and romantic character of early nineteenth-century reform was not a uniquely American phenomenon. Appeals to higher law and a faith in human perfectibility characterized liberal nationalist movements in Britain and Europe as well. Viewing themselves as part of a broad struggle for human liberty and celebrating the nineteenth century as an age of progress, American reformers found heroes in the English abolitionists, of course, but also in the Hungarian republican Louis Kossuth and in the Irish nationalist Daniel O'Connell, both of whom exemplified aspects of the progressive spirit of the age. Some reformers actively expressed their sympathy for liberal movements abroad. For six years, Samuel Gridley Howe offered his services as a physician to Greek patriots in their struggle against Turkish rule; William Birney, son of the Liberty party standard-bearer James G. Birney, fought as a student in Paris with the republican forces in the revolution of 1848; and New England's romantic heroine Margaret Fuller cast her lot with the Italian republicans in 1849. Reversing the process, the German liberals who emigrated to America after their abortive revolution of 1848 characterized the developing struggle between free labor republicanism and the slave power as the "American 1848."[1]

To a significant extent, the struggle against slavery did constitute the American 1848. Yet there was a peculiarly American character to antebellum reform stemming from the strong Calvinist tradition from which the reforming impulse first emerged. Indeed, appeals to the memory of the Puritan "fathers" accompanied references to the Founding Fathers with enough frequency in antislavery rhetoric to suggest that reformers felt the need to enlist Puritanism as well as republicanism in the struggle against slavery and other relics of barbarism. The distinctive imprint of Calvinism in antebellum reform is particularly significant in changing attitudes toward benevolence and good works. In the same fashion that an identification with the revolutionary past sustained new free labor doctrines, an identification with the Puritan fathers reinforced the individual austerity and abnegation of antebellum reformers and helped to transform their antislavery concerns from the single-minded moral focus of the early 1830s to a broader utilitarian assault on the evils of pauperism, vice, and ignorance in industrializing America.

Expressed as a Yankee Calvinist value, abolitionism advanced middle-class social goals. At the same time, the abolitionists' advocacy of individual autonomy and the liberty to pursue moral and material progress merged with broader middle-class appeals in the areas of law and political economy and thereby reached beyond the confines of Calvinist New England. As a result, the Calvinist tone of the early abolitionist movement merged with a broader utilitarian analysis of the proper relationship between labor and capital and the proper role of the state in the direction of economic activity.

Throughout the 1830s, abolitionists held before themselves and their communities an image of the downtrodden slave, portrayed on bended knee with manacled arms uplifted, pleading for liberty as a man and for equality as a brother. In this image, abolitionists saw the reflected essence of freedom. Abolitionism defined freedom through its opposite, the brutishness of the southern slave. It was against such a backdrop, for example, that Garrison evoked his ethereal image of freedom—"to be free as the winds of heaven"—an image temporarily free of all material considerations.[2]

"Poverty Is Not Slavery," Garrison instructed disgruntled northern workingmen and labor reformers in the first number of the *Liberator* in 1831. Garrison delivered this censure in an effort to distinguish abolitionist moral concern from the mundane problems of poverty and social alienation that troubled labor reformers. The Jacksonian tendencies of the labor reformers, together with the intense party rivalry of the 1830s, added to the importance of Garrison's distinction. As native-born Yankee Calvinists, abolitionists fell so fully within Whig ranks that throughout the antebellum era Democrats appealed effectively to immigrant fears of a Yankee cultural hegemony prominently represented by abolitionism and temperance reform.[3] Despite Garrison's efforts to insulate abolitionist moral reform from the broader utilitarian concerns of the labor reformers, the middle-class social goals upon which abolitionism rested encouraged an interaction of abolitionist moral precepts and utilitarian explorations in political economy.

The advancement of middle-class interests required a substantial unity among the "producing classes" of the North to displace an established elite in the North and the slave power in the South. For a time, progress in this direction required broadened popular participation in politics and active middle-class political involvement. In their most optimistic assertions, reformers insisted that the struggle for free labor advanced what Wendell Phillips called the "democratic principle" and in so doing harmonized the interests of capital and labor. It was in this optimistic spirit that the leading Jacksonian labor reformers—William Leggett and the elder Theodore Sedgwick—broke with the antiabolitionist stance of the Democratic party. In the same spirit, growing numbers of antislavery reformers, frustrated with the narrow appeal of New England Calvinist values, pressed beyond the abolitionists' image of the suffering slave to contrast the nobility of free labor with the poverty and degradation slavery produced. For a time, until middle-class goals required the insulation of politics from popular enthusiams, antislavery reformers conceived themselves to be at the forefront of the uprising mass of society.[4]

In 1840, Lewis Tappan confided to fellow abolitionist and Whig politician Joshua R. Giddings that "the late Wm. Leggett told me, Loco Foco as he was, that he considered the abolitionist cause of more importance than 50 Sub Treasury schemes." A few years later, the younger Theodore Sedgwick—associated with Leggett in the Locofoco legacy of the New York workingmen's movement—commented that he regarded the Massachusetts Conscience Whig leader Charles Sumner as one of the "respectable whigs," who were really "old federalists," the followers of "Washington and Jay's Party." Sedgwick distinguished these Whigs, with whom he could cooperate on antislavery issues, from the rest of "these modern mongrel Whigs," whom he denounced as "adventurers—united for plunder."[5]

As these leaders of the workingmen's movement opposed the Democrats' antiabolitionist appeal, some abolitionists began to look favorably on the goals of labor reformers. The volatile economic conditions of the mid-nineteenth century encouraged them in this direction. Like all Americans, Yankee moral reformers could feel but could neither see nor entirely comprehend the economic winds that buffeted them. Moreover, the depressions that punctuated the nation's economic expansion did not fit well with the moral reformers' perfectionist system of beliefs. What caused hard times? Who or what was to blame for the general financial embarrassment and the very real suffering that accompanied these financial reversals? The Jacksonians blamed the banks (particularly the Second Bank of the United States) for the crash in 1819, but Jackson's Specie Circular served the Whig opposition as a handy explanation of the Panic of 1837.[6] During the late 1820s and early 1830s—in the midst of the Second Great Awakening—Yankee reformers focused on the evils of strong drink as the cause of poverty. Having thereafter abstained from drinking, however, these reformers necessarily looked beyond temperance to explain why, as sober men of steady habits, they also experienced hard times after the 1837 crash. A utilitarian critique of slavery provided a satisfactory answer. The works of two of the era's leading political economists—the elder Theodore Sedgwick, a Democrat, and Henry C. Carey, a Whig—illustrate the connection between slavery and hard times which moral reformers found increasingly persuasive.[7]

Insisting upon the fundamental incompatibility of slavery and progress, Sedgwick wrote his *Public and Private Economy* (1836) as a reform tract to instruct workingmen in their true economic and political interests. The book, he wrote the Massachusetts educator Horace Mann, ought to be adopted as a primer for use in the common schools. "The object of this Book," he declared in the preface, "is to show the value of property, or wealth, and how it may be acquired." Specifically, Sedgwick endeavored to demonstrate (to what he hoped would be an audience of workingmen) that acts of social alienation—violence generally and the destruction of property in particular—worked against the interests of labor as well as capital. "Property," said Sedgwick, "is the life of the people," and its destruction was suicide. No matter that the property belonged to the rich. The man who would destroy property acted with the same perversity as a man "breaking the windows of his own house." On these fundamental points, the interests of rich and poor, of capital and labor, were identical. "The poor" had as much interest in "making property grow, whether it belongs to them or another." Similarly, labor was necessarily "interested in saving and increasing capital, by which alone their wages are paid."[8]

Sedgwick's central concern was with the laboring poor and the means by which they could improve their condition in a free and competitive economy. The existence of poverty among those who labored for wages raised difficult problems for utilitarian theorists such as

Sedgwick. The suffering of the poor in the free states also raised problems for middle-class moral reformers. Garrison's refusal to equate poverty with slavery revealed the problem without resolving it. A number of reformers (notably the Liberty abolitionists Beriah Green and Gerrit Smith) openly worried about contradictions between self-interest and competition and traditional notions of Christian brotherhood. Some, including the progressive-minded Wendell Phillips and Nathaniel P. Rogers, joined with secular labor reformers to embrace cooperation as an antidote to the unfair aspects of competition in America. Sedgwick, for his part, outlined the utilitarian analysis of poverty and its remedy to demonstrate that conditions for workingmen improved over time in the same manner that older dependent relationships (including villeinage, indenture, and slavery) gave way to free labor—that is, as the accumulation of capital increased the demand for labor and enlarged the "fund" from which wages could be paid.

Significantly, Sedgwick's analysis of the relationship between historical progress and the advancement of liberty—between prosperity and equality of opportunity—led directly to an assault on southern slavery. He defined the condition of slavery as the inability to acquire property, particularly land. Conversely, property widely and equitably distributed was essential to "liberty and happiness." Wherever the vast majority of those who "labour with their hands" were without property in the form of land or other "reasonable possessions," workingmen have "either been slaves, or nearly as wretched as slaves." Thus the "first dawn of liberty" arose as the "slave peasants" of Europe acquired property and purchased their freedom. Liberty advanced not by the "influence of religion and philanthropy alone" but because liberty rendered the peasants' labor more productive and more "profitable . . . to their former masters."[9]

Utility, then, became the engine of progress, and Sedgwick criticized the well-meaning but misguided moral reformers who would obstruct progress through philanthropy. Those whose sentimental concerns caused them to give bread to the poor neglected to see that it was better for the poor to earn their bread. The poor required not philanthropy but equal access to the acquisition of property. "The first duty of the rich to the poor," concluded Sedgwick, was to give to all men "the same legal advantages of getting bread that they themselves have." This was the core of the Jacksonian equal rights doctrine and the focus for the assault on monopolies, which Sedgwick defined as "*legal privileges given to some, and denied to others.*" Although distinctions of class—between "merchants, farmers, mechanics, manufacturers, or professional men"—struck Sedgwick as natural and inevitable, class legislation seemed unnatural and inherently monopolistic. "The true plan of free government," he wrote, was to ensure "that in the laws all are equal, and that there shall be no institutions *by law* that shall make men unequal." [10]

Sedgwick tied moral and material progress to an increasingly equal distribution of property, which constituted the "cardinal point" in true economy—to do "good" with property being the "*one* great end of our existence." The moral and material spheres were inseparable. "The Christian religion," Sedgwick declared, "lies at the foundation of all wholesome and permanent increases of wealth." An equal distribution of property corresponded to the "perfection of the Christian character." Conversely, the forces of evil pursued "ill-gotten, *disproportioned* wealth . . . wealth obtained by unfair dealing, by fraud, by oppression, by monopoly." The triumph of virtue over evil required freedom from all oppressive legislation. All laws that attempted to regulate "the wages, the business, the diet, the religion, the morals, of the people" hindered progress by denying liberty and encouraging conditions of slavery. True economy required freedom from unequal laws and oppressive regulations. Beyond this, those who wished to improve their station in life "must put their own shoulders to the wheel." Improvidence generally and lack of thrift in particular seemed to Sedgwick to be the principal causes of poverty among the laboring population. "They must work out their own salvation," he insisted, and they could do so by developing a proper regard for the value and sanctity of property. Sedgwick recognized that the introduction of the factory system created "a new world" for laborers who were required to "live upon small wages." But the salvation of the wage earner did not differ from the farmer's, the merchant's, or the professional's. The great majority of those who worked for wages "can and must lay up yearly *one-half of their wages at least.*" In this way the laboring poor could accumulate capital and acquire property as farmers in the new states of the West or become members of the expanding propertied class in the existing states. The laboring poor, in short, could and should become part of the middle class. As Wendell Phillips later observed, "poverty is no evil." Poverty by itself did not produce degradation. Quite to the contrary: "Poverty, wholesome poverty, is . . . the motive power that throws a man up to guide and control the community; it is the spur that often wins the race."[11] Although Sedgwick did not join with Phillips and other abolitionists to agitate the slavery issue as a moral question, he concluded his primer with a thorough denunciation of slavery as a barrier to progress and a threat to republican government. Slavery, resting on blatant class legislation, violated basic principles of political economy and threatened to destroy America's republican institutions. "This just democratic government will put an end to slavery," concluded Sedgwick, "or slavery will put an end to it." It was "impossible" for a system of forced labor to exist harmoniously with the free, prosperous, and progressive economy of the North. Sedgwick did not intend to embrace the black man as an equal, but that the "*white man* stands at the head" of the various families of man whereas the black man, by a "long course of degradation," had been rendered inferior did not alter the underlying truth that slavery "is the natural enemy of every man who performs labor, of every workingman in the United States." The solution, wrote Sedgwick, was "*gradual emancipation* and the *gradual removal* of the coloured people."[12]

Sedgwick regarded poverty and slavery as related problems. His sanguine view of the steady improvement in the conditions and rewards of free labor confronted him with the despotism of slaveholding interests. It was not the plight of the slave that concerned him but the threat slaveholding posed for the moral and material progress of free labor. On this point, Sedgwick's concerns were the same as those of his Whig counterpart, Hency C. Carey of Philadelphia. Both men believed that the forces of progress must eradicate poverty regardless of race or caste. Sedgwick counseled thrift among white workers and colonization abroad for black slaves, and Carey championed protection in foreign trade as the necessary palliative for both. Essays by Carey defending protectionism as the highest interest of capital and labor appeared with some frequency in Horace Greeley's *New York Tribune*. Carey's three-volume work, *Principles of Political Economy* (1837–40), developed in considerable detail his perception of a direct relationship between the natural laws of political economy and the progressive character of American economic development. Like Sedgwick, Carey found the issue of slavery unavoidable, although Sedgwick (the champion of laissez-faire) demanded government action to end slavery and Carey (the advocate of an active state) insisted until the 1850s that any direct effort by government to abolish slavery would prove "positively injurious."[13]

In Carey's description, slavery represented a transitory stage of development. As the value of a slave's labor increased, the utility of holding that labor in the status of slavery decreased. Thus "the surest way to promote the freedom of the slave is to increase his value." With every increase in the productivity of slave labor, the slave "must obtain an increasing proportion of the product, in the form of provisions, clothing, and shelter." Carey saw this process at work in the South and insisted that the increasing *"wages"* the slave obtained permitted him—like laborers in general—"to improve his physical and moral condition." The cities of the South offered the clearest indication of this ameliorating process. There, "in great number," slaves paid their masters for the privilege of hiring out their labor. "Such is the form in which the early steps to improvement are observed," Carey concluded, referring to the decline of villeinage in England. Slavery, then, was a stage through which the South must inevitably pass: "The man who really desires to benefit the African race, must retain his control over them, seeking constantly the means to improve *their condition and his own*." Carey suggested that slaveowners could encourage this mutual improvement by allowing "a few of the best slaves" to cultivate a few acres for their own use *"under the control of the master."* In this manner, by "gradual, sure, and safe" steps, slavery would disappear.[14]

Although Carey's principles of political economy denied slavery any place in a mature society, he remained steadfast throughout the antebellum era in his opposition to any direct interference with the South's labor system. "There is but one way to free the negroes," he insisted to Charles Sumner on several occasions, "and that is to produce competition for the purchase of his labour." The black man remained a slave in the South because "he is allowed but one market in which to sell his labour." As soon as there was competition for his labor, he would be free. A protective tariff would increase production and increase competition for all native labor and raise their wages. "Protection," Carey concluded, "is the real and the only road to freedom of trade and freedom in the sale of labour."[15]

Carey would draw no absolute distinction between northern freedom and southern slavery, nor would he set a timetable for the inevitable triumph of freedom. Nevertheless, a depiction of the superiority of the North and a corresponding condemnation of the slave South ran through his work. Carey identified security of person and property, together with the incentives of free enterprise and free labor, as the basic components of moral and material progress. "The wages of labour and the profits of capital are high," he wrote, "where security is accompanied by freedom, and where the certainty of enjoying the fruits of labor prompts its exertion." When Carey applied this rule to the United States, he found the highest level of development in New England and in the Northeast and a steady decline along an axis leading to the South and West. He did not identify slavery as the single cause of this unevenness in economic development. Instead, he noted that individual security barely existed in the new communities of the West and that progress there must be measured by growth in population and the establishment of law and order. At the same time, it was clear that "Security is affected by the existence of privileges confined to certain classes." In Great Britain, the aristocratic practice of protecting game preserves from poachers by employing armed keepers and "man-traps" underscored to Carey's satisfaction the means by which a privileged class endangered the security of an entire community. "In the southern States of the Union," he noted, "the existence of slavery produces effects precisely similar." [16]

Years later, in a memoir of Carey, the political economist and abolitionist William Elder acknowledged that his mentor preferred to denounce class oppression abroad, particularly in Britain, but that his arguments against the oppressive character of American slavery remained oblique. On occasion, as Elder explained, Carey contrasted American slavery favorably with the European and British evils of "famine, pestilence, or exile." Yet embedded in Carey's political economy Elder discerned "an abhorrence" of slavery as strong as "the most rabid of the Abolitionists." Carey, Elder insisted, had "conceded neither toleration nor respect to the . . . spirit of masterdom . . . which is but the wild-beast phase of human character." Elder, whose earlier labors as a Liberty party organizer gave weight to his remarks, credited Carey with going beyond the abolitionists in his critique of slavery. Carey had been a "reformer," in Elder's view, whose influence had been "revolutionary" precisely because he equated southern slavery with British oppression in Ireland. "Work without wages and with the deprivation of social and political liberty," in Elder's words, had seemed to Carey only a more blatant form of the English policy in Ireland, which "offers nominal freedom but withholds its practical benefits." [17]

Carey resisted the moral reformers' call for immediate abolition because he believed that slavery followed the same law of wages which determined the rewards of labor in more advanced and more equitable free labor systems. The maintenance slaves received in the form of food, clothing, and shelter represented wages and, like all wages, could rise only as the total supply of capital increased. The condition of the slaves would improve just as the condition of labor generally improved, with the expansion of the nation's economy. Government existed to stimulate that expansion, and Carey did not hesitate to support the forceful suppression of slaveholding interests when nullification and, ultimately, secession threatened the national government's ability to promote the general welfare. As he explained to a skeptical British audience at the outset of the Civil War, the free states represented civilization, "manifested by a strict regard for the rights of persons and property," in a struggle against barbarism, sustained by "those who look with contempt upon all who labour." [18]

Sedgwick and Carey offered prominent expressions of a growing northern preoccupation with the moral dimensions of economic development. The principles of political economy which they popularized enjoyed an increasing appeal in antislavery circles after 1840 and, together with the constitutional assault against the consolidated slave power, formed the intellectual core of the antislavery movement.

Joshua Leavitt—one of the original abolitionist organizers of the Liberty party, who, with Salmon Chase and Gamaliel Bailey, carried the bulk of the party into the free-soil movement—developed an early example of this new economic concern among antislavery reformers. Leavitt himself demonstrated the interelationship between moral reform and utilitarian values. The faith in moral progress that underlay his antislavery agitation also spurred him to write a half dozen reading primers for use in the common schools. A tireless advocate of free trade, he linked the prosperity of western farmers to tariff reform and to what he believed would be the related success of the anti–Corn Law movement in England.[19] Leavitt devoted prodigious energies as well to the cause of cheap postage, a "moral" reform in his view, which promoted the free expression and circulation of ideas. The dissemination of information and the broadened public intercourse resulting from cheap postage would render "innocuous" all of the "agitations of controversy, the measures of reform, and even the machinations of the malcontents of every description." America would remain "stable and secure" in contrast to Europe, which had been "tossed upon the billows of revolution and civil strife." Leavitt concluded that "it is the glory of the government of God to accomplish numerous and complicated results, by few and simple means." With cheap postage "human government seems to approach this glorious model."[20]

Popular education, free trade, cheap postage, and the abolition of slavery were all components of progress. If cheap postage could help secure the nation from disorder, antislavery reform suggested the means by which the nation's productive energies could be freed from slavery's powerful but artificial restraints. In two antislavery speeches delivered in Ohio during the Liberty party campaign of 1840, Leavitt developed an analysis of slavery that revealed the growing importance of economic issues in the slavery debate. Leavitt's arguments were not entirely new. As early as 1835, William Goodell had suggested a free labor critique of slavery. "The struggle is between the antagonistic principles of free and slave labor," Goodell wrote in the *Boston Emancipator* (soon to be edited by Leavitt). The panic of 1837 and the depression that followed, however, provided a vivid backdrop for Leavitt's elaboration of this argument. Leavitt himself had been hurt by the crash—the *Evangelist,* which he had edited with considerable success in New York, had been sold—and like Americans generally he responded to the financial crisis with frustration.[21]

Leavitt saw slavery as the "chief source of the commercial and financial evils under which the country is groaning." Northern voters would look in vain for relief from the presidential candidates of the Whig and Democratic parties. Neither Martin Van Buren's subtreasury scheme nor the undefined system of credit which William Henry Harrison offered voters in 1840 could restore the capital northerners had lost during the "hard times." Eventually the lost capital would be regenerated by the North's "free industry, enterprise, and economy." But as long as the slave power successfully divided antislavery interests "by fomenting the strife of party at the North," slave interests would hold the balance of power and "keep the North in subjection." How could a hardworking, sober, and thrifty people—who had enjoyed real prosperity so recently—suddenly find themselves with little money and less credit? Slavery, insisted Leavitt, was the root cause: "*Slavery absorbs the available capital of the North, and thus creates periodical revulsions, each one more severe than the last.*" Since the recovery from the Panic of 1819, advancements in the North in "religion and morals, and the glorious temperance society" had promoted the "accumulation of wealth." The productive energies of the North had increased, not declined. In this sense, the Panic of 1819 had had a beneficial effect—it alerted northerners to the need for moral improvement in their own communities. The temperance crusade, in which Leavitt had taken a leading role, had contributed to the North's productive capacities "by lessening the enormous waste of property which used to be occasioned by strong drink." Although a degree of "extravagance" persisted in the North, Leavitt insisted that the cause of the "deep and protracted embarrassment" which northerners suffered after the Panic of 1837 could be traced to slavery.[22]

In his enthusiasm for the "vast savings" generated by temperance reform, Leavitt confessed that he had "deceived" himself concerning the underlying cause for the nation's recurring financial crises: "I overlooked the drain, which was silently and rapidly carrying these accumulations of industry and economy where they can never be recovered." In flush times, Leavitt explained, northerners were anxious to do business with slaveholders. The master class enjoyed extravagance and, in prosperous times, northern merchants found the southern trade "always a great deal more profitable than the northern trade." During their northern trips, slaveowners preferred the theater or the race course to the mundane concerns of business. They refused to "haggle over the half cent . . . like the mere Yankee." Northern merchants could realize handsome profits in such a trade and, to secure them, they eagerly extended credit to the slaveowners. Thus northern capital flowed South and hard times began as soon as the Yankee merchants discovered that their southern customers would not pay their debts. "It is the Southern Debt which hangs like a millstone upon our backs and our individual merchants and manufacturers," Leavitt declared. Slaveowners did not share the northerners' "sense of obligation to pay debts." Yankees "have nothing but what they have earned by their own industry," but slaveowners "always live on the earnings of the poor." As "a free and moral people" dedicated to "industry and economy," northerners regarded their debts as a moral obligation. Southerners had no respect for northern industry or for the morality that sustained it. As long as northern capital drained into the South in the form of credit, it would be lost periodically, and economic depressions would become for northerners "as natural as the tides."[23]

Slave labor and free labor could not prosper under the same system: "No course of policy has ever yet been devised, under which slavery can be made profitable, or can support itself without draining, in some way, the resources of the free." When too much capital flowed South, the North experienced hard times. Unable to increase production—Leavitt insisted that slaves were always pressed to the limit—and unwilling to tighten their own belts, slaveowners preferred to see their debts "wiped off by periodical bankruptcies." Salvation for the North lay "at the ballot box." In the existing political order, slave interests maintained and manipulated a powerful alliance with northern commerce. "Commerce and slavery" had become so "intimately mixed up with politics" that northern politicians—always eager to advance their own careers—helped to perpetuate the "commercial delusion" that prosperity required an accommodation of slaveholding interests. On the contrary, prosperity required that the North free the national government from the grip of the slave power. "Slavery is monopoly," Leavitt declared, referring to the three-fifths clause of the Constitution: "It confers exclusive privileges." If the "bank monopoly" claimed representation in Congress, or if the North received extra representation on the basis of its capital investments in banks or "manufactories," the result would be the same. Political representation for property conferred special privilege and sustained monopoly. Monopoly, in turn, threatened to destroy republican government.[24]

Alvan Stewart, whose perfectionist arguments characterized the New York Liberty party's constitutional doctrine, pressed a similar economic argument in the East: "*Why is this country periodically in such deep Distress, without Famine, Pestilence, or War?*" The answer lay in the incapacity of the slave system to support itself. By Stewart's calculations, the South drained twenty million dollars each year from the free states. This debt "never has been, and never will be, paid." For an example of the process, Stewart turned to the shoe manufacturers of Lynn, Massachusetts. There, the distress of workers and farmers in hard times resulted not from the actions of manufacturers and merchants but from those of the slaveholders. Stewart used as an illustration a tanner who bought green hides from local farmers on credit. In turn, a leather merchant bought the tanned hides on credit and set twenty men to work to prepare the leather for the shoemakers of Lynn. The Lynn manufacturer "has one hundred men doing job-work . . . and this Lynn boss, from time to time, sends off his manufactured shoes and boots to the commission merchant in New York, who sells them, directly or indirectly, to Southern merchants, who fail." The downward spiral began: the New York merchant is unable to pay the Lynn manufacturer and the Lynn workers go unpaid; the leather merchant is ruined and his workers go unpaid; the tanner is ruined and the farmers who supplied the hides go unpaid. All "are left to contemplate the mode and manner of shoeing and booting an idle, vagabond, slaveholding population."[25]

Leavitt and Stewart were eager to put economic arguments to anti-slavery use, but their appeals involved more than simple opportunism. The notion that northern capital drained into the South where it was lost reinforced a faith in economic development at a critical point, when hard times directly challenged the optimistic projections of the proponents of progress. The Lynn shoe manufacturers whom Stewart cited faced angry workers when hard times threatened the livelihood of shoe workers. For the workers, whose artisan status as independent cordwainers declined with the centralized production of shoes, the cause of their current misery seemed close at hand and directly tied to exploitation by the proprietors of the central manufacturing shops. For the bosses of the central shops—men who had embraced temperance reform, enthusiastic religion, and (in several cases) abolitionism—the cause for their own periodic embarrassment, and the true cause of their workers' woes, lay in the unproductive and monopolistic nature of slavery.[26] The solution to this problem, Leavitt insisted, lay at the ballot box, where the political struggle against slavery could unite the interests of capital and labor.

Salmon P. Chase, the leader of the western Liberty party, found Leavitt's and Stewart's views appealing and employed them together with his own constitutional analysis to attract Democratic voters to antislavery principles. The *Philanthropist* (published in Cincinnati in the 1840s until its editor, Gamaliel Bailey, moved to Washington, D.C., to launch the *National Era*) provided a forum for such views.[27] William Elder, then a Liberty party organizer in Pittsburgh, informed Chase early in 1845 that the workingmen's movement of that city had endorsed the party's principles (drafted in the main by Chase). A physician and lawyer native to western Pennsylvania, Elder successively practiced both professions in Pittsburgh before resettling in Philadelphia in the late 1840s as a disciple of Henry C. Carey and a prolific writer on questions of political economy. Like many abolitionists,

Elder had first been stirred to reform by the anti-Masonic movement; in 1839 he had won election as recorder of deeds for Allegheny County on a Whig–Anti-Mason fusion ticket. At the same time, he befriended the pioneering black nationalistic Martin R. Delany, whose advocacy of emigration countered the anticolonization efforts of eastern abolitionists. Elder sponsored Delany's medical education and was credited by Delany with playing a critical role in his appointment as major of U.S. colored troops, detailed to recruit blacks into the Union army during the Civil War.[28] With the organization of the Liberty party, Elder took a leading role in the establishment of the Pittsburgh organization and began to discern a relationship between the antislavery struggle and broader currents of discontent among workingmen.

From the outset, Elder's conception of antislavery politics followed those of Chase's western Liberty movement and contradicted many of the views of Gerrit Smith and the party's standard-bearer, James G. Birney. Indeed, Elder had grown impatient with the "old abolitionists." "Some of them are such bigots," he wrote to Chase, "that native americanism seems to them the perfection of religious benevolence." If they were forced to choose between their antislavery sentiments and their anti-Irish prejudices, Elder thought they "would sooner send the niggers to Hell than go to Heaven with catholics." The new political focus which Chase and Bailey brought to the Liberty party "operated like an emetic upon old abolitionism," which "has thrown up all its undigested truck." A serious political assault against the slave power required reformers to make new and more effective abolitionists "out of the green stuff," the workingmen, ignored or spurned by the old abolitionists.[29]

In the remnants of the workingmen's movement in Pittsburgh, Elder found some of the "green stuff" he was looking for. Early in January 1845, he reported to Chase that resolutions passed by the Pittsburgh Liberty convention and published in the party's local paper had been endorsed by the "old trades union locofocos." Support from this quarter was as welcome from Elder's point of view as it was unexpected. He could not suppress his delight that "hard fisted . . . antibankers," men "whose motto is equal change and damn the aristocracy of wealth, hurrah for the flag and let the bible take care of itself," had approved Liberty principles in "one of their radical blood and thunder conventions." A good deal of social distance separated these radicals and the Liberty men, but Elder believed it could be bridged.

"A'nt we democrats," he exclaimed with self-conscious enthusiasm, "and won't loco focoism take notice?"[30]

Like Chase, Elder had become increasingly concerned with the ways in which antislavery principles "branch into practice." After the Pittsburgh fire of 1845, Elder moved to Philadelphia, where he edited the *Liberty Herald* and played a locally prominent role in the Free Soil campaign of 1848. In the same year, Elder attended the Industrial Congress in Philadelphia as a representative of the Philadelphia Union of Associationists. As the political opponents of slavery prepared for the 1852 elections, Elder hoped that they could divest themselves of the moral focus of the old abolitionists. The movement's success now required that those who would end slavery by political means understand and accept "that slavery, considered as a sin . . . offers no complete basis for political party, and no nucleus for a political organization." When the *National Era* urged its readers to take "the Democratic principle as its central idea" and to apply it "to the solution of all the political questions now pressing upon the public mind," Elder endorsed the call, adding that if the friends of freedom would take the time to analyze "the classes of voters in the North," they would quickly become satisfied that such a political focus was both necessary and wise.[31]

It seemed clear that antislavery reformers might as well surrender to the enemy "all the prosperous, prudent classes, who prefer their prosperity and their ease to the odiousness and onerousness of reform and agitation." It was useless to agitate among the prominent and securely established "mercantile and manufacturing men," or to seek support among "aspiring politicians," "leading churchmen," or the "aristocratic capitalists and idlers." On the antislavery side of the scale, Elder placed the original Liberty party supporters—"the men of the martyr spirit, and the conscious class." Liberty ranks had swelled from seven thousand in 1840 to sixty-two thousand in 1844, and though it was unreasonable to expect Liberty men to carry antislavery principles into political practice by the weight of their number alone, they provided a reliable and consistent basis of support. The 1848 campaign had brought a "large auxiliary force" of Conscience Whigs and Barnburner Democrats into the antislavery camp, and victory was within reach if the original Liberty men could appeal to "the class of voters who are not committed by interest or affection to the present ruling parties."[32]

Elder urged antislavery reformers to consider the interests of "the multitude of working men employed at wages by capitalists." With support from workingmen, antislavery reforms could be realized; without that support, Elder feared reformers would remain a dedicated but politically insignificant faction. Elder believed that workingmen could be won to the antislavery cause because their "civil freedom" inspired them with ambitions and aspirations that made them restless and resentful of "their own social and pecuniary privations" and encouraged them to seek "the more equal distribution of wealth in their own world." At the moment, Elder admitted that these concerns kept workingmen from extending any "effective sympathy to the slave of the South." Because workers were not "at ease in their own condition," they did not feel the "impulses of disinterested philanthropy" that fired the hearts of abolitionists. Because workers' experiences and concerns did not "easily apply to the slave's condition," abolitionist depictions of the horrors of slavery and the inhumanity of human bondage did "not come easily home to their sympathies." The workingmen of England and Ireland had "tacitly" assented to emancipation doctrines at home, but "not an immigrant in a hundred" would embrace abolitionism in America. The same could be said of most of the "native laborers" as well. As matters stood, workers remained "indifferent to the demands of Abolitionism."[33]

The central concern of workingmen—legitimately in Elder's view—was labor's relationship to capital, "or the *system of property*." Workingmen in America had never feared bondage, but they had found that their freedom was not always a "positive and productive blessing": "Indeed, there are some pinching places in the toiler's experiences where the Declaration of Independence does feel like 'a rhetorical flourish,' and that 'inalienable liberty' a mockery, which, while it forbids the sale of the man's bones and muscles upon the auction-block, nevertheless allows the sale of all there is in them every day at the counter of the employer, without hope of an alternative for free choice."[34] It was not that workers were necessarily opposed to the liberation of the slaves. Rather, Elder insisted, the way abolitionists proclaimed the blessings of freedom left workers cold and resentful. Garrison's celebration of freedom ("to go and come, rise up or lie down, labor or rest, just as the free spirit shall elect") expressed the romantic urge to be free of coercion and restraint, but these sentiments did not encourage those who toiled long hours for small wages to identify their interests with the plight of the slave.[35]

An antislavery movement that would make the "Democratic principle" its central idea would appeal to workingmen. Wage earners voted with the Democracy, Elder believed, because the party of Jackson appeared to offer them some means of resisting the "forms of oppression" that affected them. An antislavery party could do no less. It would have to bring to the workingmen "a system of rights and remedies . . . or give them a method of exerting their political power hopefully" if it were to succeed. Fundamentally, workers were "not hostile" to antislavery goals, "but they are not concerned." On occasion, workingmen reacted with "violent injustice" to antislavery agitation, but Elder insisted that they did so "not from any sentimental antagonism" to abolition but from a profound frustration with "its annoyance," as a reminder of their own unfulfilled ambitions. If an antislavery party appealed directly to the interests of workers, Elder believed "they will allow you to add whatever philanthropy to remote objects you please." [36]

Because men were moved to act by "interests," not by moral principle, the "one idea" of the original Liberty party seemed pointless to Elder, who doubted as well the effectiveness of an "omnibus reform party" such as the Free Soil coalition of 1848. He remained convinced that third parties, organized around one or more reform principles, could not accomplish antislavery goals. Despite the efforts of the Liberty and Free Soil parties, traditional party identities endured because they appealed directly to people's interests. In certain specific ways, the existing parties met the needs of their constituent elements. The Whigs and Democrats held out promises and possibilities that permitted voters, in pursuit of their own interests, to submerge individual "objections" to certain party programs and overlook the party's collective "inconsistencies." Party activity involved a wide range of practical concerns, and it was naive of reformers to expect the expedient character of the political system to wither before an advancing moral hostility toward slavery. Those who stood with Henry C. Carey in insisting that a protective tariff represented the best interests of "the industrial classes" were not likely to ignore their interests and join with advocates of free trade simply to oppose slavery. Similarly, one could not expect to unite on the single issue of antislavery the "Radical Democrats" with their "cry of anti-bank, no monopoly, and no class legislation" with those who would grant equality before the law while holding "firm for order, and for all the defences of individualism, and all the distinctions of wealth, education and rank, that free competition can produce." Antislavery reform, in short, would have to advance in the context of real and continuing economic and political differences; moral sentiment would never overcome them. "A political party and policy cannot be built upon a sentiment," Elder declared. Moreover, the "legitimate business" of government was not to pursue moral reform: "The 'Higher Law' is not of the rule of representative legislation." Rather, political policy and party action "must grow out of interests—*all* the interests which government is concerned about."[37]

The task of reformers was to impress upon the varied and competing interests of the North "that Southern slavery . . . touches every concern of our lives, mingles in every speculation, and mixes with every form of business." "Capital and labor" were the true parties in the struggle against slavery, and once "all the parties of progress" perceived this harmony of interests—"but not till then"—slavery would die. "Reform, to get recognized and legislated into force, must first get itself infused into the life and manners of the people, and thence reflected in the political administration." The difficulty was that southern slavery was not yet "*the* question with the uprising mass of society." At the moment, workingmen's freedom consisted of the right to wage "a hard fight for the means of life" and little more. In Elder's view, workingmen correctly insisted "that the laborer ought to be the partner and not the machinery of capital." They would support abolition when they thought it would advance the harmony of class interests. "God will yet make a beautiful world," Elder concluded. Important distinctions remained between "the mob and the millionaires: the mass and the upper ten," but all were alike in their humanity, and the laws of political economy worked toward the ultimate harmony of their interests.[38]

Elder's sensitivity to the pinched circumstances of northern wage earners never dampened his faith in the progressive character of the advancing industrial age. Elder denounced the "mischiefs" of "insane individualism" and rejected laissez-faire doctrines because they projected "the everlasting riot of a divinely authorized cut-throat strife between capital and labor." "Political economy is not a theory of market values," Elder insisted. "It is, or ought to be, a system or theory of the productive power of a people."[39] Cooperation between labor and capital represented the central goal of utilitarian reform. In its pursuit, reformers understood the discontents and to a degree championed the cause of workingmen. Thus Daniel R. Goodloe, editor of the *National Era* and himself a writer on matters of political economy, supported the shoemakers' strike of 1860. "We sincerely wish success to the journeymen," Goodloe wrote in the *Era*. "The great defect of the social system," he continued, "is the necessity which constrains the laboring class to work at such prices as capitalists choose to accord them and the great desideratum is the discovery of some remedy for the evil." The solution, of course, was less clear to Goodloe than the problem, but he believed that cooperation was the key. In the pursuit of cooperation, the state assumed a new role. "Political government," Elder concluded in the 1880s, existed to control the excesses of individualism and competition and to interpose in the affairs of men "a rule which respects liberty, while it provides for and defends its exercise." "Control and protection" were the proper functions of the state, and "if democracy be not political atheism," Elder insisted that "it must accept this union of supervision and sustentation."[40]

As antislavery reformers shifted the focus of their concerns from individual moral action to what Elder later referred to as the supervising and sustaining role of the state, they confronted, as Elder did, the legacy of "disinterested philanthropy" maintained by the established Protestant clergy. The logic of utilitarian reform transformed slavery from a private moral concern into a proper concern of the state. By the same logic, organized Protestant benevolence seemed to be a misguided approach to unwholesome poverty and its related ills. Organized benevolence stood as a final barrier in the North to the public triumph of a utilitarian analysis of the causes and cures of pauperism, vice, and ignorance.

The doctrine of disinterested benevolence derived from the theological shifts of the Great Awakening and particularly from the writings and abolitionist reform efforts of Samuel Hopkins. In its most extreme expression, the traditional Calvinist insistence on irresistible grace denied the spiritual relevance of individual will and correspondingly negated the moral benefits of benevolence and good works. The traditional disjunction in Calvinist thought between the spiritual irrelevance of good works and the social desirability of sustaining the moral stewardship of the church had been highlighted by Jonathan Edwards during the Great Awakening. Thereafter, in the era of the Revolution, it fell to Hopkins, as Edwards's chief disciple, to accommodate the Calvinist concept of grace with the civic values of the new republic.[41]

Among "new light" Congregationalists and Presbyterians of the revolutionary and early national eras, Hopkins softened the effects of irresistible grace and created a broader field for Christian benevolence. Hopkins was a pioneering abolitionist among the New England clergy. His doctrine of disinterested benevolence built upon Edwards's emphasis on the absolute Providence of God to argue that a joyous acceptance of divine will (a willingness to be damned) freed men of pride in the commission of good works. By the early nineteenth century, "Hopkinsianism" underlay the organized benevolence and moral stewardship of Presbyterians and Congregationalists in New England, New York, and the developing Northwest. Under the 1801 "Plan of Union," Presbyterians and Congregationalists combined to carry their faith into the New England–settled West. Moral stewardship soon took institutional form in benevolent societies such as the American Bible Society, founded in 1816. The early benevolent societies, in turn, provided an organizational model for the moral reform energies associated with the Second Great Awakening of the late 1820s and early 1830s. These new societies—most notably the American Temperance Union (founded in 1826) and the American Anti-Slavery Society (founded in 1833)—combined postmillennialist perfectionist doctrines with middle-class desires to assert social control and soon pitted the "ultraist" middle-class reformers against the organized benevolence of the established clergy and their constituency.[42]

Nineteenth-century reformers wished to reach beyond the revolutionary legacy of disinterested benevolence as they identified a new role for the individual in society and reshaped traditional notions of moral responsibility. Early in the 1840s, William Lloyd Garrison led a radical abolitionist assault on organized benevolence, denouncing the "corruptions of the Church" as "more deep and incurable than those of the state." Although a number of abolitionists (most notably Lewis Tappan) initially defended organized benevolence as a potential instrument for antislavery reform, they soon found their position eroded by what one contemporary described as an increasingly "*proslavery* Christianity and *anti-Christian* abolitionism."[43]

Abolitionists, of course, were not anti-Christian, but they were increasingly hostile to the sentimental appeal for charity which the Protestant clergy sustained through a multitude of benevolent societies. Stephen Colwell, a Pennsylvania ironmaster and railroad builder, added to the Garrisonian denunciation of the clergy his own endorsement of state action to suppress pauperism and to promote Protestant virtues. A native of western Virginia, Colwell entered the iron manufacturing business in the outskirts of Philadelphia in 1836 after a brief career as a lawyer in southern Ohio and Pittsburgh. Associated with William Elder as an acolyte of Henry C. Carey, Colwell remained moderate on the slavery issue until the mid-1850s, when it became clear to him that "the fanaticism of the South has outdone that of the North." When, in his view, the South adopted the doctrine that "upholds Slavery as a moral industrial institution," a struggle for immediate emancipation had become inevitable. "I shall look for an early and violent end of the institution in the United States," wrote Colwell in 1856, "and for the utter ruin and prostration of that proslavery society." As a director of the Pennsylvania Central, the Reading, and the Camden and Atlantic railroads, Colwell became a prominent member of the Republican party and of its wartime reform and relief organizations. He presided over the organizational meeting of the Union League, took an active role in the operations of the Sanitary and Christian commissions, and served actively on James Miller McKim's Port Royal Relief Committee, which launched a wartime free labor experiment among blacks of the South Carolina Sea Islands.[44]

To the distress of contemporary churchmen, Colwell published two volumes in the 1850s to demonstrate that Protestants were not sufficiently concerned with the material needs of the poor and that Christian benevolence could not be expressed properly or effectively through the organized activities of benevolent societies. Colwell argued that American Protestants could best ensure the supremacy of their cultural values through public education and the equal application of the law. Because Protestant values were "woven into the texture of our laws and political institutions," he reasoned that "our Revolutionary Fathers" had conceived the American state to be "a benevolent institution which they constructed and in which they offered to receive every human being who would enter and conform to its regulations." The task of instilling Protestant values could no longer be left to voluntary associations or even to the family. The inculcation of Protestant virtues became the proper function of the state, informed by the sensitivity of individual Christian citizens. A Christian education and "training for an active and useful life" represented "a public consideration" as well as a family responsibility. If the task of education were left entirely to parents, Colwell believed that half of the nation's youth would be abandoned "to practical heathenism." Although "the duty of the parent stands first," Colwell concluded, "if that is neglected, the State is in loco parentis."[45]

Both the practical heathenism which Colwell feared in the young and the "stubborn and wicked conservatism" which he denounced in the benevolent societies resulted, in his view, from a failure to distinguish between moral concerns and the "maxims and practices of business." The confusion between religion and business—between a private moral sphere and public concern with political economy—resulted from the explosion of economic energies and the rapid growth of entrepreneurial talents that marked the progress of economic and social development across the North. "In the midst of all this turmoil," Colwell observed, a "business morality" emerged, "exhibiting a punctuality, and adherence to contracts, and honesty in the execution of trusts, a faithfulness to promises—far exceeding what the world had ever known." Naturally, this business morality "borrowed some of its maxims from Christianity" and claimed for the pursuit of individual gain a higher moral purpose. "This vast movement had a tinge of Christian colouring thrown over it," Colwell continued. Appeals to Christian virtue gilded many of the "deformities" of the new ethic but could not sanctify them. Accordingly, organized benevolence created the illusion that the needs of the poor could be met through charity and disguised the fact that selfish materialism had become one of "the great barriers to the progress of Christianity." Colwell commended the socialists for exposing the "hideous skeleton of selfishness," which produced injustice. In response, he called for a practical demonstration that established Protestant values embraced "the equality and the brotherhood and mutual kindness" sought by socialists. In such a setting, the "amelioration" of the conditon of labor "implies neither revolution, bloodshed, nor robbery," concluded Colwell, but it did demand that reformers divorce the moral concerns of religion from the laws of political economy.[46]

The utilitarian focus on slavery as part of a larger middle-class concern with poverty answered many of the complaints labor reformers leveled at moral abolitionists in the 1830s. Without countering Garrison's dictum that "Poverty Is Not Slavery," the utilitarian antislavery appeal asserted that slavery produced and sustained pauperism. Reformers intended to close the gap that had once set abolitionists apart from the concerns of workingmen. The political realignments that took place in the 1850s suggest that antislavery reformers enjoyed some success in this regard. Although immigrant Catholic workingmen remained overwhelmingly in the antiemancipation ranks of the Democracy, native-born and immigrant Protestant workers appear to have embraced the liberal antislavery appeal in sufficient numbers to produce a Republican majority. With this goal accomplished, the stage had been set to confront what Colwell identified as the "real question" agitating North and South: "Where is the political power of the country to be lodged? Who is to wield its patronage? and, Where is its wealth to be concentrated?"[47]

Principle and Party

5

SECTIONAL politics in the antebellum decades centered on disputes over the proper uses of national power. On one side, slaveholders demanded and received federal intervention and jurisdiction in the capture and return of fugitive slaves. Slaveholders also demanded constitutional protection in the "reserved rights" of the states to isolate their peculiar domestic institutions from intrusions by the national government. On this issue, North and South steadily diverged. As John C. Calhoun explained in 1830, "the truth can no longer be disguised" that slavery and the South stood "in regard to taxation and appropriation in opposite relation to the majority of the Union."[1] The tyranny of the majority which Calhoun feared took specific form in the years that followed in the writings of northern political economists and in the agitation of antislavery reformers. On both fronts, northerners pursued a national state dedicated to freedom. At the same time, they associated the superintending and sustaining functions of the state with national progress. By the 1840s, the abolitionists' political demand that the national government divorce itself from slavery directly challenged existing federal protections of slaveholding interests and promised to exert the powers of the national state in a manner that promoted freedom.

This utilitarian perception of the proper application of state power prompted Wendell Phillips's observation in 1863 that in matters of public activity "the State has a right to ask 'In what do you invite [the public] to indulge? Is it in something that helps, or something that harms, the community?'" Phillips spoke on this occasion to defend a Massachusetts law prohibiting the sale of intoxicating liquor, but the principle he invoked applied as well to all interactions between the state and civil society. As Phillips explained, "moral suasion" exerted beneficial influences over "the individual in society," whereas state action served to improve and protect the entire community. When state action violated moral principle, as it had in the antebellum capture and return of fugitive slaves, Phillips called for individual acts of civil disobedience. But when legislation reflected the moral will of the people, "the era of *public opinion* is finished, that of *law* has commenced."[2]

In the more immediate situation of party politics in the Jacksonian era, the reformers' demand for state action to expand the sphere of freedom required a rejection of the southern ties of the Democratic and Whig parties. The willingness of prominent Whigs and Democrats to assert federal responsibility for the enforcement of the Constitution's fugitive clause became a matter of central concern. Reformers set aside the older political debate over state versus federal authority and denounced the Supreme Court's decision in the *Prigg* case in 1842 and the federal Fugitive Slave Law of 1850 as tyrannical intrusions of national power. In both cases, the national state required the subordination of free institutions to the extraterritorial claims of the slave power. The antislavery objective—to divorce the state from the corrupting influence of slavery—intended to reverse this process and leave slavery (if it could survive in isolation) wholly dependent on the municipal regulations of the slave states.

In retrospect, the two-party system obscured rather than resolved fundamental sectional disputes over the power of the state and in this sense functioned successfully. Democrats and Whigs consistently avoided the harshest aspects of the sectional conflict for a quarter of a century and repeatedly (until the collapse of the Whig party after the elections of 1852) survived the challenges of antislavery third parties and coalitions. Among antislavery reformers, party identities remained strong throughout the antebellum decades. The political significance of antislavery reform did not derive from its capacity to rearrange party loyalties or to overcome party prejudices. Rather, antislavery reform advanced liberal tendencies in both political groupings, which triumphed with the North's military victory over the slave power and dominated national politics for the rest of the century.

Although antislavery principles failed to take root in either the Whig or Democratic parties, antislavery reformers displayed a marked preference for Whig principles and policies and a corresponding distrust of the Democracy. The Whig party appealed successfully to the reformers' cultural values and seemed to most of the enemies of slavery to be the proper vehicle for the political advancement of antislavery reform. Reflecting their Whig bias, reformers dated the slave power's ascendance from Andrew Jackson's election as president in 1828. Although Whigs, too, came in for criticism (particularly when they descended to the level of the Democracy in unseemly scrambles for office and spoils), most reformers regarded themselves as the conscience of the Whig party and believed that they could influence the course of mass politics without succumbing to its potential corruption. Accordingly, most reformers regarded it as the purpose of independent political action not to destroy the Whig party but to overcome its tendency toward expedience in matters relating to slavery and to advance those principles which both parties (but particularly the Whigs) should hold dear. As the Whig-oriented Liberty and Free Soil party veteran Austin Willey of Maine recalled in 1860, the political struggle against the slave power required a battle against the North's "trained, prejudiced, blinding political partyism reduced to a 'machine' in the hands of office-seekers." A heroic struggle—"nearly an age of martyrdom"—had been required to recover the republican virtue enshrined in "the old Declaration."[3]

Reformist hostility to "partyism" reflected the anti-Jackson sentiments of Yankee reformers, but it also expressed their liberal ambivalence toward mass politics. Reformers agreed with Wendell Phillips that universal suffrage and wide political participation promoted social harmony by diffusing popular discontents. As Phillips argued with reference to the Chartist movement in England, the popularity of partisan politics in the United States contributed to a greater degree of social order in comparison with England and Europe. The frustrations of the Chartists' struggle for democracy demonstrated to Phillips's satisfaction that the workingmen of England were "bound hand and foot in the power of the rich." To vote as independent men, free from direction by their employers, English workingmen risked "losing home and work." "What a contrast to our own land," Phillips concluded, "where each man is proud of his party."[4] At the same time, however, reformers denounced the narrow spirit of "partyism" because it encouraged the pursuit of favor and advantage in the distribution of economic benefits. It was here that reformers saw with particular clarity the dangers of mass politics and the divisive and corrupting influence of the slave power. As long as northerners focused their political energies on party-centered struggles for patronage, the consolidated interests of the slave power prevailed at the national level regardless of which party controlled the government. Under such conditions, party politics assured the national ascendance of the slave power. By uniting the producing classes of the North in a principled struggle against the slave power, antislavery reformers intended to embrace political democracy and to elevate mass politics above the clash and din of competing classes and interests.[5]

Although antislavery reformers consistently criticized party strife, they were by no means free of its effects. Some reformers—notably William Elder, Amasa Walker, Henry Wilson, and Salmon Chase—attempted to press beyond the cultural limits of Yankee reform. But with few exceptions, antislavery reformers consistently regarded the Democracy as the agent of the slave power and saw in its appeal to northerners (particularly to foreign-born Catholics, who increasingly filled the ranks of the working poor) evidence of slave power aggression.[6]

Antislavery reformers consistently found it easier to resist the corrupting influence of the Democracy than to separate themselves socially or politically from the influence of their Yankee-Whig traditions. The tenacity of their anti-Democratic sentiments exerted a powerful influence on the direction of antislavery politics. To an extent, reformers recognized that the dangers of aristocracy and despotism lurked in the "money power" of the North as well as in the slave power of the South. As William Jay observed in 1850, "the truths we advocate are unpalatable to the two extremes of Society." Most reformers agreed with Jay's assessment that the "coarse & vulgar prejudices of the rabble" blinded the lower classes to the "disinterested benevolence" that filled the hearts of reformers. "At the same time," Jay noted, "we disturb the tranquil consciences of the rich, thwart the calculations of the politicians, and interrupt the harmony subsisting between our merchants and their Southern customers." Like all reformers, Jay deplored the expedient spirit of "partyism" and distinguished his pursuit of principle from party management. Yet like most of his reformist colleagues, he continued to associate political corruption most directly with the Democracy and with the "rabble" to which it appealed and only secondarily with the self-seeking "higher classes."[7]

When reformers distinguished themselves from the higher classes, they particularly had in mind the prominent New England textile manufacturers and merchants, men with well-developed commercial ties to the South. These Cotton Whigs, led by the New England industrialists Abbot Lawrence and Nathan Appleton and by the younger patrician-politician Henry C. Winthrop, forged what Charles Sumner and the Conscience Whigs denounced as an "unhallowed" alliance between the "lords of the lash and the lords of the loom." Indeed, Lawrence and Appleton conceived their mature industrial ventures—the great textile mills at Lowell, Lawrence, and Manchester—to be compatible with southern slavery in the existing states. Yet the Cotton Whigs were not defenders of slavery in any fundamental sense, and the distinction between "Cotton" and "Conscience" faded as the Republican party emerged. Cotton and Conscience Whigs closed ranks to oppose the annexation of Texas and the extension of slavery into the Southwest. By the time of his death in 1855, Lawrence had grown dissatisfied with the Whig party's failure to halt southern expansion. And Appleton argued in the manner of Henry C. Carey that slavery could not compete with free labor as an economic system and that the South must inevitably submit to the economic hegemony of the industrial North. Lawrence's son, Amos A. Lawrence, supported Eli Thayer's colonization scheme in Virginia as well as John Brown's early plans to liberate and arm slaves—and he did so without abandoning the conservative Whig principles of his father.[8]

The cultural bias of antislavery reform remained strong even as ties to the national Whig party weakened. Although a gradual alienation from the Whig party occurred as antislavery politics advanced, a persisting Yankee suspicion of the Democracy marked its limits. Antislavery reformers shed their Whig identities reluctantly, if at all. Those who left the Whig party for the Liberty and Free Soil organizations in the 1840s generally conceived themselves to be independent Whigs, and they labored zealously to keep their new political operation free of any Democratic taint. Despite the influence of antislavery Democrats in the Republican coalition of 1856 (and throughout the Civil War) Republicans successfully defined their party as the heir of Whig anti-Democratic sentiments.[9]

The identification of antislavery reform sentiment with Whig politics remained strong enough into the 1850s to sustain the belief among a number of prominent Whig politicians (including leading antislavery personalities William H. Seward and Thaddeus Stevens) that their party would champion northern free labor principles. Throughout the early 1830s they and antislavery reformers generally associated Jacksonian states rights arguments with a defense of slavery. Correspondingly, Whig assertions of positive federal powers seemed to provide an avenue for antislavery reform. Reformers initially looked to antislavery Whigs in Congress for the leadership necessary to carry antislavery principles into effect. Thus John Quincy Adams represented the principled soul of the Whig party. Associated with Adams were William Slade of Vermont, Joshua R. Giddings of Ohio, Seth Gates of New York, and the future apostate Caleb Cushing of Massachusetts, all Whigs with New England ties espousing antislavery views.

During the late 1830s and early 1840s, the national Whig party began to lose its overwhelming appeal for antislavery reformers. When, for example, antislavery Whigs in Congress stood with their party in December 1839 to elect a slaveholder Speaker of the House over a man whom Lewis Tappan believed to be an abolitionist despite his Democratic ties, the New York abolitionist expressed his displeasure with Whig party discipline. Principled men must not allow party interests to blind them to the claims of freedom, Tappan lectured Gates. To Giddings, he invoked the memory of William Leggett and insisted that the principles of the Democratic party did not preclude abolitionist views. Tappan did not expect Gates or Giddings to "neglect the great principles of the Whig party," but he believed that party concerns could not be equated with political morality. Party interests must be "postponed" when they competed with "the claims of the slave, and the perpetuity of our free institutions as connected with the cause of human rights." Professed abolitionists in Congress, Whig and Democrat, should subordinate "all our political and financial subjects" to the antislavery cause.[10]

The spectacle of the 1840 Whig "hard cider" campaign, combined with President Harrison's sudden death and the return to the presidency of a southern slaveholder, sparked further disillusionment with the Whig party as a reliable basis for antislavery reform. "I feel disgusted with party strife," Salmon P. Chase wrote an abolitionist friend regarding the 1840 Whig campaign, "and am greatly chagrined on seeing the means to which both parties resort to gain votes." "Fully satisfied" that the Democratic administration of Van Buren was corrupt, Chase believed that duty required him to oppose the Democracy and vote for the Ohioan, Harrison. Nevertheless, the nature of party politics disheartened him. Politicians should pursue principle and elevate the masses. Now, as the Whig opposition hungrily pressed for victory, Chase feared "the result of this excited contest upon the religious and moral character of the country."[11]

By the early 1840s, the fledgling Liberty party (still small in numbers and vague as to its political program) represented an important step away from the traditional distinction between moral reform and politics and an important challenge to the Whig ties of antislavery reformers. So, too, the widening of Garrisonian reform concerns and an emerging disunionist stance revealed frustrations with traditional reform tactics as well as with Whig politics. George Bancroft's earlier assertion, initially startling to the enemies of Jackson, that Whigs were narrow materialists and that the Democracy (the party of "morality and mind") represented progress in America, suddenly had the ring of truth for some of the politically restless reformers. Early in 1840, when the future Liberty party standard-bearer, James G. Birney, expressed his view to William Goodell (also an original Liberty party organizer) that "the Whigs would probably carry our Antislavery view," Goodell firmly disagreed. "He says," recorded the startled Birney, "the Whigs being the Aristocracy of the country, or, at least, so considered by the people, never can get the ascendancy enough to accomplish the work of Emancipation; that our hope must be in the Democracy whose principles will insure their ultimate triumph in the government,—and that their professed principles are more akin to ours than those of the Whigs." [12]

Although the political success of antislavery reform required an appeal broader than the area of Yankee influence, antislavery coalitions with Democrats invariably divided reformers and prompted high-minded Whiggish denunciations of ambition, expediency, and abandonment of principle. Those who urged such coalitions aroused suspicion and even anger among their Yankee-Whig brethren. No one attracted more criticism in this area than Salmon P. Chase, who labored incessantly in the West to build an antislavery-Democratic coalition and to prevent the Liberty and later the Free Soil party from becoming secure but politically isolated havens for antislavery Whigs.

Like a number of reformers, Chase moved from the Anti-Masonic to the Whig party. In contrast to most of his colleagues, however, his alienation from the Whig party came early. When he abandoned the Whig organization for the new Liberty party in 1841, he insisted that independent political action was needed to bring "the whole question of slavery before the people." Freed of the restraint of national party ties, "we shall be able to accomplish immense good for the country, by checking the ruinous measures of one party and aiding & carrying the beneficial propositions of another." By 1850, however, Chase had learned that the "baneful spirit of partyism," however lamentable, persisted and inevitably affected the course of reform. "The only path to harmony," he observed in 1850, when antislavery hostility to the Democracy was particularly strong, "sometimes is through division." Political independence continued to be necessary, but Chase insisted that neither the Liberty nor the Free Soil party could "be permanent, or long efficient." If a party intended to have any effect, it "must take ground on all questions so far as they are of practical importance as actually existing political issues." Moreover, "taking such ground" on all of the issues of the day, reformers "must be either Democratic or Whig in sympathy." "Perfect independence," by which Chase meant "equal indifference to both parties," was impossible and only cloaked the lingering Whig sympathies of Yankee reformers.[13]

Outside of the ranks of Gerrit Smith's Liberty abolitionists, antislavery reformers agreed with Chase that the purpose of independent political action was to encourage the established parties to pursue antislavery reform goals. But most reformers disagreed sharply with Chase over the capacity of the Democracy to advance reform principles. Chase repeatedly acknowledged that "the outside appearance of the Democracy is bad," but he consistently maintained that "the fire of regeneration is burning within." He did not advocate that reformers join "*in party action* with the Old Line Democracy" because conservative Democrats showed little interest in seeking the support of the "nonslaveholders and liberals of the country." Rather, Chase urged political cooperation among "antislavery Democrats" and "liberal whigs" under the banner of the "Independent," "Free," or "Radical Democracy." The Democracy, Chase insisted, "is sure to become antislavery—reliably antislavery I mean—long before the Whig Party will." Once converted to the antislavery cause, the Democracy would carry the freedom national doctrine into effect. "Our motto should be no more slave states—no slave territory—no nationalized slavery—retrenchment in expenditure—reform in administration—power to the people and restriction upon the executive."[14]

By 1842, Chase's disaffection from Whiggery was complete. "What good is to be gained by cleaving to the Whig party?" he asked Joshua Giddings, then completing his first term as a Whig congressman from Ohio's Western Reserve. "I never expected it would hang together a year after Gen. Harrison's election: and it is split up sooner & more irrevocably than I anticipated." The purpose of antislavery political action, Chase continued, was to inculcate the principle that "the nation is a non slaveholding nation—that slavery is a custom of state law—local—not to be extended or favored, but to be confined within the states which admit and sanction it." The Whigs as a party would never embrace this principle of denationalization because it ran counter to their insistence on the positive powers of the national government. "The most they will do is to *tolerate* liberty," Chase thought. "They will not do it at all unless attachment to liberty is made subservient to party ends & secondary to party obligations." [15]

Like Chase, all of the reformers who favored antislavery coalitions with Democrats overcame an initial hostility to Jackson and a related identification with Yankee-Whig values. John P. Hale of New Hampshire, an early advocate of antislavery fusion with Democrats, supported John Quincy Adams in 1828 and denounced Jackson as "unqualified" for the presidency. Amasa Walker of Massachusetts emerged as an antislavery Democrat in the mid-1830s after supporting Henry Clay and the Anti-Masonic party. And Henry Wilson, although nominally a Whig in the Massachusetts legislature, identified himself with "the poor men" of New England, "with whom I have been reared and with whom I now stand." The son of a day laborer, Wilson built a modest fortune as a shoe manufacturer before turning to politics and reform. In the legislature, he counted among his political allies two leading Democrats, George Boutwell and Nathaniel Banks, and frequently crossed party lines to support Democratic reforms: abolition of imprisonment for debt, enactment of mechanics' lien laws, and public control of Harvard College and other state-chartered corporations. As an antislavery politician, Wilson described the Free Soil party as the "Free Democracy," which stood in opposition to the slave power, to the "wealthy corporation influence," and to the "selfish, conservative and corrupt money power." [16]

For James G. Birney, Gerrit Smith, and other Liberty party members dedicated to preserving the moral purity of abolitionist political action, cooperation with the Democrats seemed dangerous if not immoral. Noting that Chase and his coworkers in the western Liberty party had organized ward meetings in Cincinnati in the spring of 1842, Birney feared that Chase did not share the original Liberty party identification of politics with "religious duty." Birney found Chase "sanguine—perhaps too much so—of speedy success." Listening to Chase's enthusiastic plans, Birney also noted that Chase's moral concern for the oppressed slaves seemed to be subsumed in principles of political economy. Chase "possesses no more sympathy with the free colored class than with any other class," Birney remarked. "*They* are to be admitted to the rights secured to all men by the Constitution and asserted in the Declaration of Independence. No sympathy is expected for the slaves. The government is to be made free from the influence of the slave power, & slavery to become (if it survive) strictly a *state* institution." [17]

Birney also had personal reasons to resent Chase's activities. Because Chase looked on the Liberty party not as an end in itself but as a means of drawing Yankee reformers away from their Whig ties, he opposed Birney's candidacy in 1844. William Jay, who would attract a larger number of Whig voters, seemed to Chase a more sensible choice. The Liberty party should continue to distinguish itself from "the Whigs and Democrats, *as parties*," Chase contended, but "there are many *men* in the Whig Party, whom Liberty Men should honor for their steadfast adherence to principle." Jay was high on that honor roll. More important, Jay's candidacy would encourage antislavery Whigs to act independent of their party. [18]

Chase's course alarmed Liberty abolitionists such as Birney, and those reformers who remained politically firm in their Whig faith regarded him as a threat to the anti-Democratic unity of their Yankee communities. Joshua Giddings in particular revealed the strength of these Whig sympathies and fears. A successful Western Reserve lawyer and Chase's rival as leader of western antislavery forces, Giddings embraced moral reform in 1837–38, when he joined the Ashtabula Temperance Society and won that county's Anti-Slavery Society's endorsement as Whig candidate for Congress. Giddings won the election in 1838—Western Reserve voters returned him to Congress regularly until 1860—and joined John Quincy Adams in the fight against the gag rule. During that fight, Giddings came to idolize Adams, whose sense of duty and defense of the "transcendant sovereignty" of the people against the corrupt Democratic doctrine of "state Sovereignty" seemed to the young Ohioan to be the essence of Whiggery and of antislavery reform. To Giddings, the Whig party provided a natural home for antislavery men. Antislavery Whigs, in turn, could be relied upon to transform the enemies of Jackson into a party of northern principles. [19]

Giddings gained considerable prestige in antislavery circles when he was censured in 1842 by the House of Representatives for his stern, nationalistic opposition to the Tyler administration's policy in the affair of the slave ship *Creole*. Giddings focused much of his wrath on Secretary of State Daniel Webster, who sought the extradition of rebellious slaves who had taken control of the *Creole* and forced its crew to sail to the British West Indies. Notwithstanding Webster's role in the affair and the joining of southern Whigs with Democrats in the censure vote, Giddings insisted that the Democracy—as the party of the slave power—engineered the censure. Giddings promptly resigned his seat, stood for reelection, and won an overwhelming vote of confidence on the Reserve. But the November 1842 elections brought a statewide Democratic victory in Ohio for which Giddings blamed Chase and the Liberty party. In the wake of the election, Giddings published a series of essays in the *Western Reserve Chronicle*, which insisted upon a Whig foundation for antislavery reform and damned the Democracy as the agent of the slave power. Giddings warned that the Democratic victory in Ohio would result in the election of a Democrat (and, in his mind, a defender of slavery) to the Senate. Had "the friends of northern rights" held firm in Whig ranks, Giddings concluded, Ohio would have been spared such a disgrace. As it was, "we must look for the election of a man who will lend his influence generally to the slaveholding interests." Because of the independent stance of the Liberty party, antislavery men—that is, Whigs—"were divided, and of course conquered." [20]

In Giddings's analysis, antislavery opposition to the slave power required a Whig defense of northern rights, particularly northern "pecuniary interests." Giddings regarded the defection of Liberty men as unnecessary in principle and self-defeating as a mode of antislavery political action. "Our Whigs," he insisted, "are willing to sustain *all* our rights, and our Liberty men have no further objects in view than the support of such rights." Giddings admitted that as a party the Whigs had been "lukewarm" in defense of northern rights but insisted that the Democracy had "violently *opposed* these rights." The alternative to Whig unity was Democratic victory. It followed that the independent course of the Liberty party "delivered over our interests to the disposal of those whose bitterness against the rights of man can scarcely find utterance in our language." [21]

At the core of Giddings's defense of a Whig basis for antislavery reform was the direct relationship he perceived between his party's economic policies and an antislavery defense of northern rights. As an example of this kinship between economic interest and reform, Giddings argued that the Nullification Crisis of 1832–33 prompted Democrats to lower a tariff that had encouraged New England manufacturing and benefited Ohio farming. The tariff reduction, forced by South Carolina's intransigence, violated "the rights of the free States." Similarly, if Ohio's legislature elected a Democratic senator, his service to the slave power would require opposition to harbor improvements and to the completion of the Cumberland road. The Democracy, controlled by slaveholding interests, opposed progressive economic measures because everything that was "highly desirable to a free people" tended to be "dangerous to the interests of slavery, which must ever depend upon the ignorance and stupidity of the slave population." [22]

Giddings believed that the "pecuniary" interests of the North went hand in hand with a "moral" hostility to slavery. He believed as well that the Whigs would unite northern interests against the usurpations and aggressions of the slave power. Why, he asked, did Liberty men— almost all of whom had been recruited from the Whig party—fail to see that Whig economic principles were essential to a defense of northern rights? If antislavery men abandoned the economic interests of "the friends of internal improvements, and of the tariff," they should not expect to receive any help from this group when they pressed for reforms "of far less pecuniary importance": "If one class of our northern men will tamely surrender our *pecuniary* interests, may we not expect that another portion will . . . yield up our *honor* to the demands of the southern States? . . . Can any man of reflection suppose that we can extricate ourselves from the *moral* influence of slavery while it continued to control our pecuniary interests?" [23]

Giddings remained adamant in his opposition to the Liberty party defectors through the 1844 elections. He actively supported Henry Clay, insisting that any Whig would protect northern rights equally with southern rights. At the same time, he denounced the Liberty party's candidate, Birney, charging that his sale of slaves in Alabama, where state law prohibited their manumission when Birney moved North, was an act "a hundred times worse" than Clay's ownership of slaves in Kentucky. Giddings was not alone among leading antislavery reformers in his advocacy of Whig unity. David Lee Child, a Garrisonian abolitionist who made no secret of his Whig sympathies, and Jacob M. Howard, an antislavery Whig from Detroit, shared in directing the anti-Birney campaign in reform circles. Child hoped that the Whig campaign would "drive these Bedlamities," as he branded the Liberty defectors, "from their last retreat." With such support, Clay made effective use among Yankee-Whig voters of the antislavery records of Giddings and the venerable John Quincy Adams.[24]

The unwillingness of the national Whig organization to adopt antislavery principles increasingly embarrassed Giddings and his fellow antislavery Whigs. At the same time, the relationship they perceived between the slave power, the Democracy, and irresponsible Locofoco appeals to gullible voters seemed clear and damning. Until the 1848 bolt of the Conscience Whigs, Giddings and his associates labored with some effect to isolate the Liberty movement and to establish antislavery politics on a Whig base. After the 1844 national Whig defeat, Giddings joined other Whig loyalists to charge that Liberty men were responsible for the victory of the expansionist James K. Polk. As northern hostility to annexation grew, the first successful antislavery coalitions emerged under Whig control and Giddings had good reason to believe that the Whigs would become the party of northern principle.

In this regard, Giddings looked with particular favor on developments in New Hampshire and Maine. In New Hampshire, John P. Hale led antislavery Democrats into a Whig-dominated coalition. Despite his early hostility to Jackson, Hale won election to Congress as a Democrat in 1843 and joined with leading antislavery Whigs—Adams, Giddings, and Slade—to vote down the gag rule. Although privately opposed to the annexation of Texas, Hale remained loyal to the national Democratic party through the 1844 election. In January 1845, however, he broke his silence, denounced annexation, and found himself promptly dropped from the New Hampshire Democratic ticket. With Liberty party support, Hale ran for reelection as an Independent Democrat. Although he did not win, he successfully deadlocked the congressional race and, with Whig support, won election to the state legislature. In the legislature, following complex maneuvering, Hale's Independents cooperated with the Whigs and, in June 1846, the coalition elected Hale to the United States Senate.[25]

With Hale safely in the Senate, the battle for the disputed congressional seat focused attention on Hale's lieutenant, Amos Tuck. Tuck served one term in the state legislature as a Democrat before joining Hale in his break with the party over annexation. Like Hale, Tuck felt strong bonds with liberal Whigs. When the Whigs agreed to support Tuck for Congress in the March 1847 elections, Tuck agreed to deliver Independent Democratic support for the Whig congressional candidate in the western district of the state. Tuck described the Whig candidate as a respectable man who had been kept out of office by "low lived hostility" among Democrats. Despite his earlier Democratic ties, in Congress Tuck was "decidedly favorable to the Whigs" and correspondingly suspicious of the prominent antislavery Democrats Preston King and David Wilmot, who he believed would never allow their opposition to slavery to inflict real injury upon the Democratic party.[26]

Giddings believed that the movement begun in New Hampshire would spread. In July 1846, he toured Maine, where he "consulted with Whigs and Liberty men very fully and with some democrats" on the issue of antislavery political unity on Whig principles. "*There will be such a Union in this state as there was in yours,*" Giddings predicted to Hale. Whigs would provide the format for antislavery union: "Even the Democrats approved my doctrine although my facts certainly bear hard upon the radicals [that is, Locofocos] of that party."[27] With some reason, Giddings hoped for similar developments in Ohio although Chase and the Democratic character he had already given the western Liberty movement stood squarely in opposition.

As early as 1843, Chase insisted to Giddings that the principles of the Democracy "are in exact harmony with the principles of the Liberty men." Rather than attribute these principles, as Giddings did, to "pretence & hypocritical profession" on the part of Democrats, Chase referred to the Democracy's "ignorance of the proper application of these principles to slavery as it exists in this country." The Liberty party offered a useful means of instructing the people in a proper antislavery course. In place of Giddings's view of the Whig party as the defender of "Northern Rights," Chase proclaimed the Democracy as the party of "Constitutional Rights, Liberty, Justice, Free Labor."[28] The struggle for control over the direction of antislavery politics took place on many fronts. Nowhere, however, did the contest between Whig and Democratic values assume greater importance or attract more sustained scrutiny than in the developing conflict between Giddings and Chase in Ohio.

Chase's victory over Giddings in the Ohio Senate race of 1849 came to symbolize the tension between principles and expediency in antislavery politics. It also illustrated the persisting fears of Democratic corruption and a corresponding drive to maintain Yankee-Whig unity under the Free Soil banner. The sentiment was widespread at the time, and it would persist into the late nineteenth century, that Chase won election at the expense of moral principle. In this case, Albert Gallatin Riddle, a Whig free soiler from the Reserve, acted as the conscience of antislavery reform. An ardent Whig of antislavery views, Riddle followed Giddings out of the national Whig party after the nomination of Zachary Taylor in 1848. During the 1848 Free Soil campaign, Riddle won election (with Whig support) as a Free Soil candidate to the Ohio legislature. As a member of the legislature, Riddle denounced Chase's coalition of Free Soilers and Democrats and nearly thirty years later resurrected the event for the readers of the *Republic* as a case study of personal political corruption—the pursuit of "expediency" at the expense of "morality."

In the late nineteenth century, as liberal reformers drew their principles around them as a barrier against the corrupting influence of mass politics, Chase's actions assumed the dimensions of a crime. "Its shadow," wrote Riddle, "always fell upon him and hovered near and darkened his pathway at the critical places in his political life."[29] In the same manner that liberal reformers in the Gilded Age identified the political meanderings of Benjamin F. Butler of Massachusetts with the horrors of democratic excess, Chase's victory over Giddings came to represent the corrupting influence of ambition. In 1897, Theodore Clarke Smith concluded in his pioneering historical study of the Liberty and Free Soil parties that Chase's "whole connection with the affair . . . and especially his action toward Giddings, leave an unpleasant impression." Giddings's son-in-law, the Indiana antislavery leader George Washington Julian, reviewed Smith's volume for the *American Historical Review* in 1899 and gave special praise to the author's abilities at "character-sketching," particularly "the admirable account of the famous coalition in the Ohio legislature in 1848, by which the Free Soilers secured a United States senator." In Julian's view, Smith had portrayed Chase "in his true attitude and real lineaments."[30]

Theodore Clarke Smith's sharp distinction between morality and expediency in public affairs adequately described the suspicion with which late nineteenth-century liberals regarded popular politics, but it distorted the mood and behavior of antebellum reformers by ignoring their universal eagerness to harness the democratic spirit of the age to their antislavery cause. Indeed, neither Chase's obvious personal ambitions nor his opportunistic political maneuverings distinguished him from his critics in the antislavery movement. Consequently, although Chase's reputation for political expediency is not undeserved, the means by which he won election to the Senate and the manner in which his election became an object lesson in political morality for the rest of the nineteenth century require examination for what they reveal about the political realignments of the 1850s and the relationship between antislavery reform and the course of mass politics in America.

Chase won election to the Senate by exploiting a bitter party rivalry in Ohio and forging from it a productive coalition of antislavery independents and regular Democrats. Before the 1848 elections, Ohio's Whig-controlled legislature created an intense party dispute by dividing Hamilton County (which included the city of Cincinnati) in such a way that the Democrats could be expected to lose a legislative seat traditionally under their control. The Democrats refused to accept the redistricting scheme and elected Democratic candidates under the old plan. The new legislature, which met in December 1848, found itself confronted by the rival claims of Whig and Democratic representatives from Hamilton County. Moreover, in the wake of the 1848 national Free Soil campaign, antislavery forces in the state agreed that the new legislature offered an excellent opportunity to elect an antislavery senator and to repeal Ohio's black code. Because neither Whigs nor Democrats controlled the legislature, and reform-minded forces, if they acted independently of party ties, could control the balance of power, the Hamilton County issue provided Chase with an excellent opportunity to engage in the independent political action he had long advocated. Not surprisingly, he moved quickly to put himself in the Senate race. He would be "highly gratified," he announced, to receive antislavery support for the Senate seat. "I do believe," he added in support of his candidacy, "that I understand the history, principles & practical workings of the Free Soil movement as thoroughly as most men, & nobody, I presume, will question my fidelity to it."[31]

Questions of ambition aside, Chase believed that he deserved public praise and political support from antislavery forces for his tireless labors and consistency of principle. "The only comfort I have in my position," he wrote to his wife in the midst of the battle, "is that . . . I am generally believed to be better qualified than either of the candidates who may be elected."[32] There is no doubt that Chase lobbied long and hard for his election and that his assertions of the righteousness of his cause goaded his critics (principally antislavery Whigs on the Reserve) who felt that they had been wronged. But there was a political dimension to Chase's candidacy—and to the opposition it attracted—that underlay the questions of personal ambition and integrity. At stake was the relative Democratic or Whig character of northern antislavery politics.

Although Giddings and his supporters on the Reserve insisted on Free Soil party independence after the 1848 elections, Chase considered their antislavery views to be characterized by "Whig ideas and Whig connexions," and he worked skillfully for a coalition with the Democracy. "If the Free Soilers and democrats are brought to act together," Chase observed to his wife, "it is quite possible that I may be ultimately elected to the Senate."[33] The efforts of antislavery forces from the Reserve to maintain Free Soil independence in the Ohio legislature and to oppose a coalition with Democrats found an able and persistent advocate in Albert G. Riddle. Chase spoke well of Riddle and continued to cultivate his favor long after Riddle had made his opposition to a Democratic coalition clear. Nevertheless, Chase's success in establishing an antislavery coalition with the Democracy deeply and permanently alienated Riddle, who acknowledged that Chase "was never a partisan, was never a party man." Yet Chase's political independence seemed to Riddle to have been manipulative, opportunistic, and devoid of principle. "Parties were his implements," Riddle recalled, "to be taken up or laid down with comparative facility and indifference." It seemed to Riddle that Chase had "sold out to the democrats" so he could win election to the Senate. In the process, former Whigs who had joined the Free Soil party had been betrayed to "Locofocoism." Riddle had hoped for a different result and had worked hard to achieve it. Realizing that most of the Free Soilers in the state house were "bolting Whigs . . . elected by the conjoint action of the Free-soilers and the remnant of Whigs," Riddle had hoped that a caucus of free-soil Whigs could wield the balance of power in the legislature, elect an antislavery senator—preferably Joshua Giddings—and abolish the black code.[34]

As events unfolded, it became abundantly clear that honor and the pursuit of antislavery goals were closely tied in Riddle's view to Whig political identity. As Riddle's plan developed, Dr. Norton S. Townshend, a legislator from the Reserve who had entered the Free Soil party via the Liberty party, was put forward as the Free Soil candidate for Speaker of the House. By holding fast to Townshend's candidacy, the Free Soil bloc—composed of bolting Whigs from the Reserve—hoped to prevent the House from organizing until demands for an antislavery senator and the repeal of the black code were met. In this manner, Free Soil independence would permit antislavery Whigs to influence the course of the regular Whig organization without compromising with the Democracy.

Chase's counterstrategy relied first on his personal friendship with Townshend, an old Liberty party colleague. Although Townshend had been elected as a Free Soil candidate from Lorain County, an area of traditional Whig strength, and notwithstanding Riddle's reliance on Townshend's independent candidacy as Speaker, Townshend appears to have been predisposed from the outset to follow Chase's leadership. More problematic from Chase's point of view was the support of John F. Morse, an antislavery Whig from the Reserve who had been elected as a Free Soil candidate by the traditionally Whig electorate in Lake County. Alone among the Free Soilers in the legislature, Townshend and Morse had won election over Democratic and Whig opponents. In the end, Townshend and Morse broke ranks with Riddle and with the Whig free soilers to provide the essential votes for the antislavery Democratic coalition that sent Chase to the Senate.[35]

Chase regarded Riddle's efforts to maintain the independence of the Free Soil caucus as a plan designed to create the basis for an antislavery coalition with Whigs. "The object seems to me plain enough," he wrote privately in mid-January. If the Whigs "can cut Townshend & myself down, & terrify Morse into unquestioned acquiescence into the decisions of the Whig Freesoil Caucus, the course will be left clear . . . for the unchecked sway of Free Soilism of the Whig stamp." In the meantime, Chase courted leading Democrats whom he found agreeable to the proposition "that it was very important that the reliable Freesoil members & the Democrats should cooperate together." The Democratic leadership made the terms of that cooperation explicit. The Hamilton County issue should be decided in favor of the Democrats in exchange for Democratic support for the repeal of the black code. Democrats would support Chase for the Senate "provided . . . the Democrats shall have the two Supreme Court Judges." The Democrats wanted "a distinct understanding" of such a bargain with Morse and Townshend. Chase thought an understanding could be reached if Morse and Townshend were presented with "a private note" from half a dozen prominent Democrats "distinctly stating that the signers will steadily vote for a Free Soiler" for senator. Chase thought Morse needed and deserved such a specific commitment. It must be remembered, he noted, that Morse's Western Reserve district was heavily Whig and that his willingness to cooperate with Democrats could be turned against him by those who viewed all Democrats as "desperate haters of all good, enemies of black law repeal etc. etc."[36]

Within a few days, Chase's supporters had secured the desired pledge from the Democrats. The test of Democratic sincerity would be support for Morse's bill to provide schools for blacks, the first step toward a repeal of the black code. Stanley Matthews, Chase's political manager in the legislature, reported that it had been agreed to get the school measure through the Senate first, "before the suspicions of the Whigs are aroused." Then, in the House, Morse was to support the Democrats on the Hamilton County issue and the Democrats would ensure the passage of Morse's school bill. The success of the agreement relied heavily on Democratic party loyalty. "It has been exceedingly difficult," wrote Matthews, to get many of the Democrats "who had been deeply committed on the other side of the question" to agree to support schools for blacks. "Nothing could have effected it but the most determined & rigid application of party discipline." Nevertheless, as long as the Whigs did not decide to oppose Morse's bill simply to break up the antislavery-Democratic coalition, Matthews was confident that the repeal of the most obnoxious black laws was safe.[37]

Much to Riddle's annoyance, events unfolded as Chase had planned. Townshend, whom Riddle supported for Speaker, joined with Morse and Isaac Van Doren (a Free Soil legislator elected with Democratic support) to elect a Democrat Speaker of the House. The Democrats then promptly elected Chase's manager, Stanley Matthews, clerk. Alarmed by the defection of Townshend and Morse, Riddle managed to secure an adjournment and the following day delivered seven of the Reserve Free Soil votes to the Whigs to elect their candidate as sergeant-at-arms. On the major issues, however, Chase's coalition held firm. When Townshend, as chairman of the committee to settle the Hamilton County dispute, presented the majority report declaring the division unconstitutional, the measure carried the House by a majority of one, with Townshend, Morse, and Van Doren all voting with the Democrats to form a majority. The antislavery-Democratic coalition then moved to pass Morse's school bill and, shortly, to elect Chase to the Senate.

Despite its success in passing antislavery measures, the coalition Chase manufactured proved to be a bitter pill for Free Soil Whigs on the Reserve to swallow. "Chase is an able man, and will prove an able Senator," Giddings observed grudgingly several weeks after the election. But Giddings added that Chase lacked "a knowledge of popular feeling and of popular sentiment, and is not qualified to lead a party." "His policy last winter came near ruining us in this State," Giddings charged. The Free Soil party, from Giddings's point of view, had been discredited by Chase and the Democratic coalition. The defection of Morse and Townshend prevented Free Soilers of Whig sympathies from using Giddings's candidacy for the Senate as a means of forging antislavery unity on Whig terms. Yet the Whigs had little hope for success. Recalling the events that had led to Chase's election, Riddle himself acknowledged that Chase had instructed his supporters to vote for Giddings if the Whigs could be won to the congressman's support. There was, as Riddle admitted, "never at any time a reasonable hope" that Giddings could be elected. It was Riddle's plan that the Free Soilers "would unanimously vote for Giddings until the hopelessness of his election was practically shown." At that point, Riddle proposed to support Chase. Exercised in this fashion, Free Soil independence would permit men of Whig principles to control antislavery political action. Chase's efforts prevented such a development, and Riddle noted with scorn that, with his victory secured, "Mr. Chase gave the usual party banquet to the Democrats, and was claimed and assumed to be a Democratic Senator until the repeal of the Missouri Compromise."[38]

Chase's election to the Senate illustrated to Yankee-Whig reformers the subtle dangers awaiting well-meaning men who strayed too far into the practice of mass politics. As the northern proponents of progress embraced mass politics to divorce the national state from the slave power, the reformers' distinction between Whig propriety and Democratic expediency assumed increasing importance in antislavery politics. The boundary between political principle and expediency assumed an increasingly moral significance as well, as antislavery reformers endeavored to master and direct mass politics. The theme of political morality defined the limits of acceptable behavior; it also provided an instrument to discipline errant reformers who wandered from the standards of propriety toward which the masses must be raised or by which their excesses must be checked.

Whigs and Democrats

6

T H E political success of antislavery reform required a liberal transformation of the American party system. As doctrines of antislavery reform took hold and developed among northern Whigs and (to a more limited extent) among Democrats, the character of the two-party system changed. In the rhetoric of reform, this change marked the triumph of antislavery principles over the partisan character of antebellum politics. In the emerging Republican party, most reformers saw a coalescence of liberal sentiments that signaled the victory of freedom over slavery. As long as the divisions of the two-party system muted northern antislavery sentiment in pursuit of national party unity, reformers tended to look on party politics as the means by which the slave power maintained its influence over the national government. This view, that the Republican party as the party of liberalism and progress in America reshaped and redirected national politics, appealed widely to reformers. It appealed as well to historians of reform, who have seen in the Republicans' rise to power not simply the triumph of virtue over evil but a radical fusion of progressive forces capable of fundamentally altering the American political and social landscape.[1]

Historians concerned with the radical impact of antislavery reform have perceived—as did the most sophisticated of the reformers themselves—that growing sectional divisions and the political transformation they produced reflected a fundamental conflict in American society over issues involving the intrusion of the state in matters affecting labor and capital. Neglected in this concentration on fundamentals, however, is the manner in which the American party system advanced the liberal doctrines that antislavery reformers espoused. Although the national Whig and Democratic parties attempted to mute sectional divisions and to avoid agitation of the slavery issue, liberal doctrines took root in both parties and gave rise to distinctive but parallel views of the ideal liberal state.

In the Whiggish view embraced by the majority of reformers, the liberal goals of antislavery reform required a state active in the pursuit of moral and material progress. Detached from the individual scramble for material gain, the liberal state, in this view, assumed the attributes of divine stewardship. The government of man approached the government of God. When the New York Whig Senator William H. Seward expressed this sentiment in his "higher law" speech opposing the Compromise of 1850, the pronouncement secured his reputation among antislavery Whigs as a reformist statesman. "When God had created the earth," said Seward, "He gave dominion over it to men." The American state existed as God's agent in the advancement of man's moral and material progress. When Seward reached beyond the Constitution to appeal to "a higher law . . . which regulates our authority," he did so not to lay aside constitutional proscriptions (in the anarchistic manner of Lysander Spooner) but to reinforce the Whig notion of an active state. God's higher law devoted the earth to "the same noble purposes" to which the Constitution obligated Congress in its policies toward the territories. The "higher law" and the Whig notion of an active state pointed in the same direction. Seward envisioned a national government directing the judicious development of western lands, the financing of internal improvements, and the discouragement of slavery through a policy of nonextension and compensated emancipation. "We cannot establish slavery," Seward concluded, "because there are certain elements of the security, welfare, and greatness of nations, which we all admit." In the name of "union," "justice," "welfare," and "liberty," slavery could not be extended into the territories, and the national state stood divorced from the slave power.[2]

For most reformers, these Whig sympathies, which appealed strongly to the reformers' Yankee Calvinist values, were difficult or impossible to abandon.[3] As Wendell Phillips acknowledged in 1863, there was much that was "good," "virtuous," and "correct" in the Whig doctrines. But the Whigs had "one great defect" in Phillips's view: they "had no confidence in the people, no trust in the masses." For most reformers, sharing these Whig views, the antislavery principles they espoused required hostility to the Democracy as the party of Locofoco radicalism, the party of the slave power and, by the 1850s, the party of the immigrant masses as well. In Phillips's characterization, Whigs looked at the world as if in a probate court "in which the educated and wealthy were the guardians."[4] Herein lay the importance of the antislavery Democrats who denounced Whig ties to established wealth and who enlisted mass politics in a parallel pursuit of a liberal state. Whereas antislavery Whigs emphasized the proper uses of state powers, antislavery Democrats championed doctrines of laissez-faire and equal rights as the means by which the state rose above the competing forces of society. Proposing to divorce the national government from the corrupting influence of the slave power, antislavery coalitionists such as Chase, Henry Wilson, and Amasa Walker, as well as the Barnburner Democrats, worked to build popular antislavery support on a liberal Democratic base.

As antislavery reformers aroused liberal tendencies among Whigs and Democrats, they rejected the two-party system's accommodation of slaveholding interests. In the sectional confrontation that ensued, antislavery Democrats coalesced with antislavery Whigs in sufficient numbers to carry the new Republican party to victory in 1860. That victory and the unionist resolve of the War Democrats ensured a northern triumph over secession and slavery in the Civil War. Although the patriotic sentiments that the war aroused across the North facilitated the Whig-Republican characterization of the Democracy as the party of the slave power and treason, the North's triumph rested on a broader political base than the Republican party itself. In time, the maintenance of Democratic ties by some men of liberal sentiments—notably Samuel J. Tilden and George Bancroft—no longer shocked or surprised the once fervent Whig-Republicans. By 1885 (following Grover Cleveland's narrow victory over James G. Blaine), the old abolitionist Samuel May understood why Bancroft "& many another" stayed with the Democracy: "Viz. that *democracy,* as a principle, as a doctrine, as a political foundation, is right, however little honored or greatly dishonored, by its followers." In the postwar setting, parallel liberal views of the sustaining and superintending functions of the state resumed a political competition begun in the late 1840s. May had once thought that the Republican party elevated politics above such competition. In 1884, however, he had been unable to vote for either candidate, and his discomfiture underscored the nature and effect of the party system. With the slavery issue resolved, the parties arrayed their distinctive constituencies in a continuing contest for political office and patronage. It was a contest that muted growing divisions of class as well as ethnic and religious divisions characteristic of industrial America. It was also a contest in which disgruntled liberals moved uncomfortably from one party to the other.[5]

For some time, however, the anti-Democratic focus of the old Whig party remained strong in the Republican organization and kept the relatively small but influential group of Democratic Republicans suspicious of the new party's Whig tendencies and conscious of the limits of what they conceived to be a temporary coalition. For the Whig-oriented majority, Republicanism represented an antislavery fusion on a reliably anti-Democratic base. Issues that had once divided northerners and diverted attention from the fundamental issue of slavery seemed to be finally and properly contained in a common struggle against the slave power. Under the circumstances, Democratic Republicans regarded Republican successes with more caution. As Chase confided to Benjamin F. Butler of Massachusetts in December 1862, circumstances required him to devote his energies "to the Salvation of our country," although he had not abandoned his identity as a Democrat. In the turmoil of the Civil War, one stood either on the side of freedom or of slavery. For that reason, Chase insisted, "the party which now opposes the national Government is not in any just sense the Democratic Party and ought not to be so called." Instead, Chase looked forward to the restoration of a liberal Democracy, to "a new party really democratic and really republican."[6]

In the partisan rivalries that shaped the course of antislavery reform, the predominance of Whig sentiment in antislavery ranks gave the entire movement an anti-Democratic tone. Wherever the antislavery banner heralded Democratic successes, antislavery Whigs warned of the dangers of political expediency and denounced the deviousness of Democratic politicians. In Ohio, where Chase successfully engineered an antislavery coalition with Democrats, Whig Free Soilers on the Western Reserve remained hostile to Chase as the state's new antislavery senator and continued to be suspicious of his Democratic ties. The old-line Democracy in Ohio seemed to be unmoved by Chase's antislavery successes, and Whiggish observers insisted that the venture must soon fail. Viewing the scene from Massachusetts, Charles Sumner pronounced the course of the Ohio Democracy "disheartening." "I trust even you must despair of them" he chided Chase. Closer to home, the Cleveland editor John C. Vaughan led a Whig antislavery attack. A native of South Carolina, Vaughan joined the Kentucky abolitionist Cassius M. Clay as editor of the *Louisville Emancipator* before moving north in the 1840s to edit the *Cincinnati Gazette* (a cautiously antislavery Whig paper), the *Cleveland Free Democrat* (which bore the name of Chase's successful coalition without sharing its Democratic views), and later (with Joseph Medill) the liberal *Chicago Tribune*. Although Vaughan lent his support to Chase's efforts during the 1848 Free Soil campaign, he now vigorously attacked Chase's Democratic ties. "I still think well of Vaughan personally," Chase wrote to a political ally in Ohio as the attacks continued, "but he is not worth having as a *friend* politically."[7]

Chase held to his Democratic course despite the criticism. "I have not embraced democratic ideas for profit," he protested. "I believe in them with a very earnest faith; and I cannot be persuaded into any Whig alliance, real or apparent." It was his "great object," he said, to raise the Democratic party to antislavery ground. "This we can do if things can be so shaped as to preserve local harmony with the Democracy." Vaughan and the Ohio Whig Free Soilers pursued what Chase deemed to be a "foolish" course designed "to lead our friends in a direction counter to that indicated by the whole spirit of the movement."[8] Nevertheless, with the antislavery members of the Ohio legislature increasingly unwilling to "act in concert with the Democrats," there was little that Chase could do to maintain his coalition with the "old line Democrats of the Progressive school." Chase acknowledged that "it is now more necessary to preserve union among ourselves," although he hoped that the antislavery movement would not retreat "a hairsbreadth" from its earlier opposition to "every form of monopoly and unequal taxation—especially to corporate banking and to special privileges for bankers."[9]

To Chase's disappointment, Ohio Free Soilers (who nominated the Liberty party abolitionist and educational reformer Samuel Lewis for governor) largely abandoned the Democratic principles of the earlier coalition. The Free Soil convention that met in Cleveland struck Chase as a "Whig Freesoil Convention." Not only did the delegates reject Democratic principles, they included in their antislavery pronouncements the assertion that Congress possessed the constitutional power to abolish slavery in the states. Chase viewed this act as a direct "contradiction" of the 1848 Free Soil platform, which insisted upon the divorce of the federal government from the institution of slavery. (To some extent, of course, this resolution also illustrated the influence among Free Soilers on the Reserve of the higher law arguments of Lysander Spooner and the Liberty League.) To Chase's mind, the resolution reflected Whig views of federal power, views soon to be exalted by Seward in his "higher law" speech. At the very least, the resolution stood in direct opposition to Chase's definition of slavery as a function of municipal law, constitutionally divorced from the federal government. Determined to distinguish his Democratic analysis of free-soil doctrine from the Whig principles adopted on the Reserve, Chase spoke of the Free Democracy rather than the Free Soil party. In Chase's definition, the Free Democracy held that "personal relations between individuals" within the several states were the exclusive concern of the states themselves. It was the responsibility of the national government "to take care that, everywhere within its jurisdiction and not within a state, every person be protected in the enjoyment of his natural rights." By this logic, the northern states were as free to protect individuals within their borders from assaults by slavecatchers as the southern states were to enforce municipal slave laws.[10]

The legislative session of 1850–51 presented antislavery forces in Ohio with a second opportunity to elect an antislavery senator. Antislavery Whigs took particular interest in the post in part because Whigs traditionally controlled one of the state's senators, but more directly because the open seat had been filled by Thomas Corwin, a prominent Whig of antislavery sentiments. Corwin's strong opposition to slavery expansion during the Mexican War won praise in Whig reform circles, particularly from Joshua Giddings and Charles Sumner, both of whom hoped he would join the Conscience Whig bolt in 1848. To their disappointment, Corwin remained loyal to the national Whig organization and gave his support (albeit halfheartedly) to Zachary Taylor in 1848. When Corwin entered Millard Fillmore's reorganized cabinet as secretary of the treasury in 1850, the conservative Whig Thomas Ewing finished the last year of Corwin's term and Ohio's antislavery Whigs made it their chief item of business in the new session to redeem Corwin's Senate seat and replace Ewing with an antislavery senator of Whig views.[11]

As in the 1848–49 legislature Free Soilers (mostly of Whig sympathies) held the balance of power. With Ewing unacceptable to antislavery forces, attention quickly turned to Giddings and to John C. Vaughan. Chase warmly supported Giddings, in part because Giddings opposed Vaughan's bitter attacks against Chase and the Democracy. Chase now described Giddings as "thoroughly weaned from the Whigs" and urged Democrats to support his former rival as an efficient means of destroying "the last vestige of whig ascendance on the Reserve."[12]

At the outset of the new Senate contest, Chase had reason to believe that an antislavery-Democratic coalition might once more control the legislature. Norton Townshend, one of Chase's principal collaborators in the legislature during the winter of 1848–49, had won election to Congress in the fall of 1850 as a Free Democrat. Now, as the new legislature organized, John F. Morse (who, together with Townshend, had ensured the success of Chase's coalition two years earlier) won election as Speaker in the Ohio House. Chase was jubilant. "I rejoice in it on my own account," he wrote Morse, "as it proves that the advocacy of the repeal of the Black Laws and the election of S. P. Chase has not been *very fatal* to any who took the bold ground of right." [13]

But Chase's optimism shortly faded as it became clear that Whig Free Soilers would not break with their party's regulars and that the regular Democrats had no intention of cooperating with Chase's Free Democracy. Chase did not blame Whig Free Soilers for cooperating with the regular Whigs, but he did criticize them for refusing openly to "avow their Whig sympathies" and for the "sneaking way" they covered their cooperation "under the cloak of independence." In any case, the result was a deadlocked election: neither Giddings nor Vaughan could attract sufficient support from the regular Whigs, and regular Democrats refused to cooperate with the antislavery independents. In February, with the Senate election still undecided, the legislature adjourned for several weeks. During the recess, another antislavery Whig from the Reserve, Benjamin F. Wade, emerged as a compromise candidate. Although Wade had been careful to maintain his regular party ties (he had supported Taylor in 1848 and would remain a Whig until the organization of the Republican party), he possessed respectable antislavery credentials. As a state legislator in the 1830s and 1840s, Wade spoke out against slavery expansion, denounced the black codes, and opposed the capture of fugitive slaves. Appointed presiding judge of Ohio's third judicial circuit in 1847, Wade sharply attacked the Fugitive Slave Law of 1850, together with Daniel Webster's "Seventh of March" speech and its condemnation of antislavery reform. When the legislature reconvened in March 1851 and the balloting for senator continued to be deadlocked, Wade moved to the forefront and, on the twenty-eighth ballot, with a three-vote majority, Wade joined Chase in the Senate. [14]

Giddings, who had known Wade as a former law partner, could not conceal his personal disappointment and his distaste for the new senator. "He was ambitious," Giddings wrote to Sumner. "I stood in his way in 1848 [and] he went for Taylor and opposed freesoilers." "My objection to him is solely on account of his want of straightforward determination of purpose," Giddings added. "That leads me to fear he may leave us at some future date." For Chase, Wade's election added to antislavery strength of the Whig variety. "I *think* he will generally go with Seward," Chase told Sumner, adding that as "one of the original abolitionists," he did not think that Wade would be "derelict to the antislavery faith." [15]

Angered and alienated by Wade's victory, Giddings turned to the Free Soil party as a permanent alternative to Whig opportunism and a haven from the Democracy. Chase, who viewed independent political action as a means of advancing the position of the national parties, warned against efforts to protect the purity of the Free Soil organization. As long as the national parties silenced antislavery advocates in their ranks, independence was justified. But that time had passed, Chase argued, when "antislavery sentiment became so powerful as to carry its distinctive representatives into Legislative Assemblies State & National." At that point, "except for an occasional effort" during a presidential contest, or in a state where antislavery sentiment remained weak, independent third parties had "become impossible." A "mere freesoil organization" no longer served any purpose. "Composed of men of opposite political views on questions which divide conservatives from progressives and held together only by a common sentiment of hostility to slavery," such a party could have no political effect. [16]

In this spirit, Chase continued his labors in the Democratic fold. If the Democracy was to survive, Chase believed that its leaders "must yield to the pressure of antislavery sentiment." And when it became clear that the national Democratic party intended at its Baltimore convention to embrace the Compromise of 1850, Chase returned, reluctantly, to an independent position. Not all antislavery Democrats followed, however. New York Barnburners held fast to the Democratic organization. Chase had no enthusiasm for an energetic independent presidential campaign, but he wanted the Free Soilers at their Pittsburgh convention to keep on "the right ground" with "the right name." Chase preferred the name "Independent Democracy," which, in his recent correspondence with the New York Barnburner leader Benjamin F. Butler, he distinguished from the "Compromise Democracy."

The independents should nominate John P. Hale, Chase argued, and adopt the Buffalo platform of 1848, "modified by the introduction of judicious Land Reform and European Freedom Resolutions." On such ground, antislavery forces could weather the storm on a Democratic foundation and resume their efforts to control the political organizations of the free states once the "presidential crisis" had passed. Together with Lewis Tappan, Samuel Lewis, and others, Giddings attempted to maintain the Free Soil party on "high principles" in opposition to "the *extension* [and] the *existence* of slavery" and free of Democratic ties. Reluctantly, they accepted the name "Independent Democracy." As with the Barnburners, most antislavery Whigs stayed with their national party to press for Whig victory in the 1852 presidential race. Giddings, who hoped to make the Free Soil party the refuge of honest Whigs, lamented to his son-in-law George Washington Julian that "the antislavery feeling which John Quincy Adams myself and others have labored so long to create had been taken possession of by Seward and he is trying to use it for Scott's election." Giddings had no choice but to stand with Chase and the rather forlorn Independent Democrats.[17]

The course of the New York Barnburners, the largest single group of antislavery Democratic voters, assumed special importance in the internal antislavery political debate of the 1850s. Much to the chagrin of antislavery Whigs, particularly those in Ohio and Massachusetts, the Barnburners wasted little time after the 1848 Free Soil campaign to demonstrate their desire to restore Democratic party unity. Led by Preston King, Samuel J. Tilden, David Dudley Field, John Van Buren, and Benjamin F. Butler of New York, the Barnburners looked hopefully for signs that reunion was possible. There were compelling reasons for them to do so. Both Seward in upstate New York and Horace Greeley in New York City maintained strong antislavery records, yet both remained loyal to the national Whig party. Until the organization of the Republican party, Seward held fast to the conviction that the northern Whigs offered the best organizational base for antislavery political action. As governor of New York, Seward had been criticized by Lewis Tappan for appointing "a notorious slave catcher" commissioner of deeds in New York City. In general, however, Seward maintained sound credentials as an opponent of slavery and a friend of the oppressed blacks. If nothing else, Seward understood the importance of slavery as an issue that maintained Yankee reform loyalty to the Whig party. He served prominently as defense counsel in the celebrated murder trial of William Freeman, a black man charged by the state for the murder of a white family in Auburn, New York. It did Seward no harm politically to face as prosecuting attorney in the case the Barnburner leader John Van Buren, then New York's attorney general. Seward similarly joined with Chase to argue the case of John Van Zandt (who aided escaping slaves in Ohio) before the United States Supreme Court and to defend two men arrested in Washington, D.C., for assisting escaping slaves. Seward was sent to the United States Senate as a Whig in 1848, and his "higher law" speech in 1850 appealed strongly to Yankee reform sentiment across the North.[18]

Unlike the Conscience Whigs, Seward did not feel that his antislavery principles required him to bolt the party. He justified his loyalty by arguing that the Whig organization in New York endorsed emancipation. He insisted as well that there was nothing practical to be gained by separating the state organization from the national party. "The error is almost universal," he wrote Chase in the spring of 1848, "that national issues can be made in our general elections upon questions which are only locally discussed." Although Seward wanted to see an antislavery national government and judiciary, he regarded it as folly to expect such a development "until more than half of the People shall be impressed with the safety beneficence and justice of Emancipation." Regarding slavery, as other issues, politicians could advance only as fast as "the progress of the principle of Emancipation." In Chase's characterization, Seward intended to "maintain his own position as an antislavery man" and "to maintain it in the Whig Party and only in the Whig Party." As Seward himself put it, "no new party will arise nor will any old one fall." He joined the Republican party in the conviction that it was dominated by Whig leaders and Whig principles. The "Loco Foco party," as Seward described the Democracy, was the party of the slave power; the Whigs and their Republican successors were the party of northern principle. Nothing in the development of antebellum politics changed that view.[19]

As long as the New York Democracy remained divided between its Hunker and Barnburner factions, the united Whigs in New York could easily control the state. For such Radical Democrats as John Van Buren and Benjamin F. Butler of New York, the prospect of continued Whig ascendancy became too much to bear. The reunion of the New

York Democracy—which seemed inevitable under the circumstances—took place in two stages. The first came in September 1849, when both factions agreed to support a common slate of candidates for state offices without making slavery a test. The second came in 1850, when, with a gubernatorial election at stake, Barnburners laid their anti-slavery interests aside, joined with the Hunkers to nominate Horatio Seymour for governor, and accepted the national party's endorsement of the Compromise of 1850 with its harsh new Fugitive Slave Law and the popular sovereignty "solution" to the territorial issue.[20]

The course followed by the New York Barnburners became critically important to Chase, whose efforts in Ohio and in the Free Soil party looked to the Democracy as a basis for antislavery organization. "The Free Democracy of Ohio," Chase wrote Benjamin F. Butler in July 1849, "naturally regard with a good deal of solicitude" the efforts of Barnburners to reunite with the Hunker wing of the party. Chase considered the unity of the Democracy to be highly desirable, "but it must be reunion upon principle." With the exception of a resolution regarding the tariff (a resolution Chase had opposed), Chase described the Free Soil platform of 1848 as a proclamation of "Democratic Doctrine & Measures." "I have never met a Democrat in the Free States," said Chase, "who did not admit that every resolution adopted by the [1848] convention embodied sound democratic opinion." The great danger, he thought, was "the surrender or modification of antislavery principle for the sake of Hunker application and support." Such a development "would provoke and justify the contemptuous sarcasms of the entire Whig Press." In the future, the Democracy would lose the "moral power" of antislavery principle, and the antislavery "tide of opinion" would favor the Whigs throughout the free states.[21]

Chase urged patience and caution. The Free Soil organization had united "the old liberty men and nearly all the Progressive Whigs" on Democratic antislavery principles. Whigs such as Giddings who remained in the Free Soil party (now called the Free Democracy) seemed to Chase to be "so little whiggish, in the conservative sense of that term, that we may fairly assert them to be . . . Democratic." An unprincipled reunion of Barnburners and Hunkers would greatly damage the development of a Free Democracy and retard "the cause of human freedom & Progress in general." Chase advised the Barnburners to maintain their independence: "The old hunkers cannot go into the battle of '52 without uniting with us on our own platform, except to meet inevitable and disastrous defeat." The Hunkers did not covet political martyrdom, and Chase predicted that Democratic unity could be effected on antislavery principles.[22]

Chase's advice largely went unheeded by the New York Barnburners. Furthermore, as Chase predicted, the Whigs heaped ridicule on the Democratic reunion. Understandably, the reunion drew particularly sharp fire from the Conscience Whigs, who suppressed their anti-Democratic bias sufficiently to vote for the Barnburner leader Martin Van Buren in 1848. Denouncing the reunification of the New York Democracy as an outrageous betrayal of principle, Conscience Whig journals—particularly the *Boston Republican* and the *Cleveland True Democrat*—again equated the national Democracy with the slave power.[23] Among Conscience Whig leaders, Charles Sumner offered a model of Christian charity when he reported to Chase in the wake of the September 1849 reunion that "we are all much disquieted by the occurrences in New York." Sumner did not want to "judge our friends hastily," but he had the distinct impression that "our cause has been sacrificed in a vain desire for harmony of that ancient omnibus the Democratic party." Massachusetts Conscience Whigs, Sumner vowed, "shall keep to our ancient Anti-Slavery ways" and work to strengthen the independent Free Soil party. Sumner himself soon benefited from a Free Soil–Democratic coalition such as had recently elevated Chase to the Senate. For the time being, however, he shared the prevailing Conscience Whig hostility toward the Democracy.[24]

Chase and others who looked hopefully to the Democracy for future antislavery political success remained generous toward the apostate Barnburners. Even so, Chase expressed "doubt" about their course. That John Van Buren (whose antislavery principles Chase trusted) supported the reunion gave Chase cause to hope that Van Buren and his friends meant to bring the Democracy of New York "unreservedly" to the Free Soil platform of 1848. But Chase knew that the entire Democracy would not easily be won to antislavery principles and that the Barnburners' willingness to drop the slave issue as a test for political support created conditions that permitted candidates to "creep into office and into Congress who will betray the people of the Free States." Chase tied sympathy to caution: "It behooves all friends of Freedom to heed well what they are doing, and take care that they do not become so entangled in party mesh that they cannot withdraw themselves."[25]

With Chase, Gamaliel Bailey—who early in 1847 left the *Cincinnati Philanthropist* in the hands of Chase's supporter Stanley Matthews and moved to Washington, D.C., to launch the *National Era*—remained confident of the "honesty of the Radical Democrats" however much he questioned the incautious character of their course. To Sumner, Bailey urged that the friends of freedom "avoid denunciation." It was important not to question the Barnburners' "purity of intention." The abuse John C. Vaughan's *Cleveland True Democrat* heaped on the Barnburners (as it had earlier attacked Chase's Democratic coalition in Ohio) particularly upset Bailey. "This certainly is *not* the way to influence them for good," he warned Giddings, whom he urged to "give a hint" to Vaughan to temper his language.[26]

The reunion of the New York Democracy offered antislavery Whigs across the North an appealing opportunity to deliver a lecture on political morality. Henry B. Stanton provided them with a convenient focus. One of the original abolitionist rebels at Lane Seminary in Cincinnati in 1834 and later a member of the executive committee of the American Anti-Slavery Society, Stanton moved from Boston to Seneca Falls, New York, in 1847. (In 1848, his wife, Elizabeth Cady Stanton, joined with advocates of women's rights at the Seneca Falls convention to demand political equality for women.) In New York, Stanton identified politically with the Barnburners. As an abolitionist who now embraced political coalition with the Democrats, Stanton became a target for the critics of the Democratic reunion. As Stanton understood matters, however, the source of the criticism was simply Whig hostility to the Democracy. "The truth is," he wrote Chase, "they are free soil *Whigs* & still believe that something can be got out of the Whig party." When the political conditions were reversed—that is, when (as in Michigan) Conscience Whigs reunited with the national Whig party— neither the *Boston Republican* nor the *Cleveland True Democrat* discerned any "abandonment of principle."[27]

Antislavery Whig hostility to the Democracy remained strong despite a widening sphere of antislavery political activity and the success of Free Soil–Democratic coalitions in Ohio and Massachusetts. In both states, the excitement over the annexation of Texas provided the impetus for independent antislavery political action. Massachusetts Conscience Whigs held their first major rally in January 1845 in Boston's Fanueil Hall to announce their hostility to annexation. Observing the affair as a Liberty abolitionist, Elizur Wright estimated that one thousand delegates attended the meeting, "including our Beacon St. aristocracy." Wright reported to Chase that the rally "converted itself into one of the best antislavery congregations we have ever had," and he hoped that it would "go further than the Whig movers intended."[28]

Before the Conscience Whigs adjourned their gathering, they formed a "committee of correspondence" composed of Stephen C. Phillips, Charles Allen, and Charles Francis Adams to launch (in the manner of the revolutionary fathers) a "general consultation" with antislavery leaders in case of an "emergency." The joint resolution by the United States Congress sanctioning annexation constituted such an emergency, and the committee of correspondence sought the "advice and co-operation" of Chase, whose Southern and Western Liberty Convention in Cincinnati later in 1845 conspicuously called for independent antislavery action across party lines. Desires for cooperation were genuine, but the Conscience Whigs of Massachusetts were as strongly inclined as their Ohio brethren on the Reserve to see a Whig antislavery organization as the nucleus for the development of a party of northern principles.[29]

Sumner hoped that the Conscience Whig spirit of cooperation would produce "a new crystallization of parties, in which shall be one grand Northern party of Freedom." The antislavery principles of the Conscience Whigs seemed to Sumner to be beyond reproach, and he thought that their candidates should be supported by all men of antislavery views. Sumner could not understand why Liberty men in Ohio would oppose Joshua R. Giddings or why in Massachusetts they would oppose John Quincy Adams and John Gorham Palfrey. He assured Chase that Masschusetts Conscience Whigs were eager to eschew partisan politics "for the platform of Liberty, on which we can all stand together." The struggle against the slave power provided a secure foundation for the organization of northern interests in opposition to the slaveholding Democracy. Therefore, antislavery Democrats should rally to the Conscience Whig cause. Writing to Chase late in 1846, Sumner insisted that the old anti-Whig prejudices of northern Democrats had lost all significance: "John Quincy Adams said to me a week ago, as he lay on his sick-bed, 'the Tariff is an obsolete idea.' What other question could *seem* to separate us? I know nothing of the currency, or Sub Treasury. Opposition to Slavery is the idea which I wish to carry practically into politics, regarding it as paramount to all others, & I believe that I have your sympathy in this."[30]

Despite Sumner's eagerness to submerge conventional party issues in a Conscience Whig assault on the slave power, the rivalries characteristic of the two-party system shaped antislavery politics in Massachusetts as they did elsewhere across the North. In 1846—following a dramatic break with his conservative Whig mentors in his "True Grandeur of Nations" address in July 1845—Sumner toyed with the idea of accepting a Liberty party nomination to run for Congress against the conservative Whig leader Robert C. Winthrop. But the time did not yet seem right for an open break with the Whig party. Later in 1846, a group of younger Conscience Whigs, led by the future wartime governor of Massachusetts, John A. Andrew, bolted the state party and offered Sumner an independent nomination for Congress. Once again Sumner chose not to break with the Whig organization. Finally, in 1848, when Sumner proclaimed himself to be heartily "tired of the anomalous position forced upon dissenting Whigs here in Massachusetts," he accepted the Free Soil nomination for Congress. Political independence did not immediately bring political success, however, as Sumner lost his congressional race to the incumbent Cotton Whig, Winthrop. Later, when Winthrop resigned his seat to replace Daniel Webster in the Senate, Sumner once more ran unsuccessfully as the Free Soil nominee. Success for Sumner came through the coalition activities of Henry Wilson, who shared Chase's desire to fuse antislavery principles with Democratic programs.[31]

Although Wilson led Sumner toward coalition with the Democrats, most antislavery Whigs followed the path to reunion blazed by Horace Mann following the national Whig victory of 1848. Elected to Congress in 1848 to replace the late John Quincy Adams, Mann broke with the independent Conscience Whigs when he voted for Winthrop for Speaker of the House. Sumner urged Mann toward political independence, but the idea that the Free Soilers could defeat conservative Whigs and the slave power seemed as ludicrous to Mann as it did to Seward, Greeley, and other leading antislavery Whigs: "This is setting a mouse-trap to catch an elephant," wrote Mann. "The truth is," he continued, echoing Seward, "the pro-slavery feeling has increased at the South, even more than the anti-slavery feeling at the north." Mann admitted Winthrop's shortcomings on the slave issue, but as a Whig he was greatly to be preferred to a Democratic Speaker. If Whigs in Congress remained unified and loyal to the administration, Mann thought that it was possible to "get an anti-slavery territorial or Dist[rict] of Col[umbia] bill before the President," whom he believed would support such a measure. Had Winthrop won election as Speaker, the prospects for success would have been bright. With Winthrop's defeat, success seemed "doubtful." The alternative to supporting the Cotton Whig leader, as Amos Tuck of New Hampshire noted in justification of his own vote for Winthrop, was to follow the leadership of Preston King and David Wilmot, Democrats who were laboring to identify the free-soil movement with the party of the slave power.[32]

Henry Clay's compromise resolutions, introduced in the United States Senate late in January 1850, together with Daniel Webster's "Seventh of March" speech attacking antislavery agitation, made it clear that Mann's hope for an antislavery victory achieved by the existing Whig leadership was illusory as far as Massachusetts was concerned. Nevertheless, it was one thing to understand that party loyalty was useless as a reform tactic and quite another to abandon willingly the Whig organization as a basis for antislavery political action. That Conscience Whigs could defeat the conservative leadership of their party only by forming coalitions with Democrats did not make a union with the Democracy easy or signal the decline of party identities.

Charles Sumner's election to the Senate in the winter of 1850–51, like Chase's election two years earlier, marked the progress of antislavery coalition in the North at the same time that it revealed the prevailing influence of party loyalties. Henry Wilson, whose political success as an antislavery Whig had always been closely related to his ability to identify himself with Democratic economic reforms, emerged in the late 1840s and early 1850s as the principal manager of antislavery coalition in Massachusetts. The rise of Wilson, the son of a Farmington, New Hampshire, day laborer from the ranks of indentured labor exemplified the progress he and fellow reformers associated with the antislavery cause. On his twenty-first birthday in 1833, Wilson completed his indenture, abandoned his given name (Jeremiah Jones Colbath) and walked one hundred miles to Natick, Massachusetts, where he took up the tools of the cobbler's trade. At the same time he studied law and in the 1840s emerged from obscurity to a position of prominence as an antislavery politician and a manufacturer of shoes employing more than one hundred workers. With Charles Allen, Wilson led the 1848 Conscience Whig bolt from the national party convention in Philadelphia following the nomination of Zachary Taylor and joined in the call for a national Free Soil convention to unite antislavery factions of both parties. Antislavery reformers in Massachusetts looked upon Wilson's remarkable success with a mixture of enthusiasm and suspicion. On the one hand, the emergence of the "Natick Cobbler" as an antislavery political leader appeared to express the common man's opposition to slavery and the slave power. On the other hand, Wilson's plebian origins, his radical break with his past, and his aggressive behavior as a successful entrepreneur and politician inevitably raised fears among those who, like Charles Francis Adams, Stephen C. Phillips, and John Gorham Palfrey, associated reform principles with the decorum, intellect, and breeding they thought to be synonymous with Whiggery. Accordingly, Theodore Parker took it upon himself to instruct Wilson after his election to the Senate in 1855 (with Know Nothing help) to be *"a champion of Justice to all men."* And Parker urged humility in the pursuit of justice lest Wilson become too proud of his rapid rise to power and influence.[33]

As a state legislator, Wilson gained support for his antislavery coalition efforts from Amasa Walker and John B. Alley, men who like himself had risen to wealth and prominence with the expansion of the New England shoe industry. Among his allies, Wilson also counted two regular Democrats of considerable influence, George Boutwell and Nathaniel Banks. Although Walker, Alley, and Wilson were less socially prominent than the Conscience Whigs, who looked to Charles Francis Adams, Stephen C. Phillips, and John G. Palfrey for leadership, they proved to be considerably more effective in matters of practical politics. It was Wilson, primarily, who managed Sumner's election to the Senate by delivering the votes of bolted Whig Free Soilers to elect Democratic office seekers and by holding Democratic votes steady for Sumner's Senate election.[34]

Stephen Phillips led the Conscience Whig opposition to this political bargaining. A prominent Salem businesman and Whig politician, Phillips won election to three congressional terms in the 1830s and, with Charles Allen and Charles Francis Adams, led the Conscience Whig opposition to the annexation of Texas. In 1848, Phillips joined the Conscience Whig bolt to the Free Soil party. With Adams and company, he opposed the political maneuverings—particularly the Democratic leanings—of Henry Wilson. In the fall elections of 1850, Phillips stood as the Free Soil candidate for governor and, by attracting enough votes to prevent any candidate from receiving a majority, threw the election into the state legislature. The ensuing political fray ultimately sent Sumner to the United States Senate and left Phillips and the Conscience Whigs outmaneuvered and isolated by Wilson and his Free Soil–Democratic coalition. After gaining enough Democratic votes in the legislature to secure Sumner's election to the Senate—by a bare majority—Wilson delivered enough Free Soil votes to give the Democratic candidate, George Boutwell, the governorship. Stephen Phillips was stunned. "I learned with surprise & regret," he wrote Sumner early in January 1851, "that I am to be sent up to the Senate with Mr. Boutwell, to receive Whig votes or none." Phillips felt himself to have been "*publicly abandoned*" by the Free Soilers. What Charles Francis Adams referred to as an "unholy" and "immoral" association with Democrats, Phillips similarly denounced as "unprincipled and corrupt." Sumner's election involved "the overthrow of the Free Soil party, and, to a great extent, the abandonment of its cause." [35]

Although Phillips would shortly be reconciled with Sumner personally, he had been, as Samuel Gridley Howe put it, "much *miffed*" by the course of antislavery politics in Massachusetts and, with Charles Francis Adams, disassociated himself from Free Soil party politics thereafter. Whig Free Soilers of the "better class," as Adams described them, would continue to insist upon the incompatibility of antislavery principles and Democratic politics.[36]

Had the Free Soil coalition with the Democracy in Massachusetts been simply a tactical maneuver to secure the election of an antislavery senator, the disaffection of Phillips, Adams, and Palfrey, among others, might have amounted to nothing more than a transitory difference of opinion. After all, Charles Sumner was eminently acceptable to the "better class" of Free Soilers. Thus though Samuel Gridley Howe agreed with Horace Mann and Palfrey that honorable men "must look to the good" of the Free Soil party, he eagerly anticipated Sumner's election to the Senate. "You know I have never advocated or consented to the Coalition with the Democrats," Howe wrote to Mann. Cooperation with the Democracy seemed "unwise & useless" to Howe, who believed that "the free soil party might have carried the day in five years without coalescing with any body." But Sumner was the right man for the Senate. No one likely to be elected could "so well represent the antislavery sentiment of the North." Howe's distaste for the Democracy notwithstanding, he confessed that he had "come to wish & pray" for his friend Sumner's election.[37]

As it happened, however, the disaffection of the Conscience Whigs did not dissipate in the wake of Sumner's victory. Increasingly, antislavery reform became integrated with practical political concerns that continued to divide the friends of freedom. The relationship between antislavery reform and a wide range of state reforms—culminating in the Massachusetts constitutional convention of 1853—illustrates the array of interests that reinforced the anti-Democratic sentiment of antislavery Whigs and contributed to their growing hostility toward mass politics.

By the early 1850s—partly as a result of the third-party actions of the Free Soilers themselves—a number of long-standing disputes over the electoral process and the nature of representation emerged as major political issues in the state. At the heart of the conflict was the rapid pace of industrialization in Massachusetts and the heavy Irish immigration into the state during the 1840s. The new wave of immigration swelled the population of the cities—particularly Lowell, Lynn, and Boston—and raised demands for more equitable political representation. At the same time, Massachusetts's rural towns, weakened by declining population and dislocated by the collapse of household industries, regarded the growing cities with hostility and fear and understandably clung to the state's constitutional provision guaranteeing representation to towns.[38]

The existing electoral system served the Whigs well, and its inequities helped to create the conditions for Wilson's coalition with the Democrats. Guaranteed representation of towns sustained the Whigs in the countryside, and the practice in the cities of voting a general ballot (without ward divisions) effectively denied representation to Democrats and to antislavery independents. Thus, although Democrats and Free Soilers together repeatedly polled between 30 and 40 percent of the vote in Boston, the city's forty-four representatives remained in Whig control. Understandably, Democrats and Free Soilers of Wilson's temperament demanded representation by wards. In a closely related reform, Democrats urged the institution of a secret ballot in the cities to protect factory workers from political intimidation by employers. Although the state legislature provided for a secret ballot in 1851, a Whig-controlled legislature in 1853 emasculated the act by making the secret ballot optional for voters. In addition to these electoral changes, Democrats continued to agitate for a host of economic reforms that became part of the constitutional debate of 1853. The Democracy sought the passage of general incorporation laws, the abolition of property qualifications for officeholders, the repeal of the poll tax, the abolition of imprisonment for debt, and public control of Harvard College.

Amendments to the Massachusetts constitution initiated by the legislature required a two-thirds vote by two consecutive legislatures, so Free Soil and Democratic reformers looked to a state constitutional convention as the most effective means of securing the changes they desired. In the state elections of 1852, the Free Soil–Democratic proposal for a constitutional convention passed by a narrow margin (at the same time, however, voters defeated the Free Soil–Democratic coalition and returned the Whigs to power). At the constitutional convention that convened during the summer of 1853, rural delegates fearful of the Whig-controlled cities formed a shaky alliance with urban delegates angered by Whig opposition to the secret ballot and the ten-hour day. By a rule that permitted towns to send anyone from Massachusetts to the convention, Henry Wilson and Charles Sumner (both of whom supported the Democratic reforms) attended the convention as representatives of rural areas. Charles Francis Adams and John G. Palfrey—both opposed to the Democratic reforms—stood for election in their home districts and lost. Adams, who had been beaten by the Irish vote in Quincy, blamed his defeat on the "rotten . . . treachery" of Wilson, upon whom Adams relied to deliver the immigrant vote. After lengthy debates, the convention finally produced a document and submitted it to the electorate in the fall elections of 1853. The proposed constitution was a patchwork affair, but it contained two provisions of significance to antislavery forces and their Democratic allies. First, the proposed constitution provided for the abolition of the general ticket system in Boston and other large cities; second, the document reintroduced the secret ballot in the large cities. Henry Wilson, who ran as the Free Soil party's candidate for governor in 1853, strongly supported the new constitution. But the basis for coalition with the Democracy was badly damaged by Caleb Cushing (a Whig turned Democrat, then serving as President Franklin Pierce's attorney general), who announced his opposition to the proposed constitution and urged Massachusetts Democrats to end their coalition with the Free Soilers. Wilson's gubernatorial prospects were further damaged by the vigorous opposition of Adams, Palfrey, and other Conscience Whigs who consistently opposed the new constitution and the coalition with the Democrats. With deep divisions in antislavery ranks and the coalition weakened by Democratic defections, Wilson lost badly in the election, and the proposed constitution went down to a narrow defeat.[39]

For those struggling to organize antislavery politics on Democratic principles, it was becoming increasingly difficult to sustain the momentum that had been created by the Texas and Wilmot Proviso issues. In vain, Chase urged the New York Barnburners to maintain their independence until the 1852 presidential campaign was under way in earnest. He was more successful in keeping his supporters in Ohio independent minded. "I am thoroughly convinced," he wrote Edward Hamlin in April 1851, "that a radical democratic organization would bring the Old Line Democracy to our Platform." The task for antislavery Democrats throughout the North was to convince the conservative Democrats that they could not hope for success without the support of the antislavery wing. Once it became clear that "they must choose between us and the Slavepower," Chase reasoned, "they will not hesitate a great while. The free states have more votes than the slave states."[40] With the ranks of the Independent Democrats drastically thinned by the Barnburner defection, however, Conscience Whigs looked to their old party with new hope that it might become the party of northern principles. In large numbers and with notable enthusiasm, antislavery Whigs experienced a fresh sense of party loyalty in 1852 and, with the nomination of the cautiously antislavery war hero Winfield Scott, antislavery reformers once more identified principle with Whig victory.[41]

In Massachusetts, the resurgence of Whig loyalty contributed directly to the collapse of the antislavery-Democratic coalition and added to the difficulties Henry Wilson, John B. Alley, and others faced trying to fuse antislavery principles with popular discontents. Wilson and Sumner, still eager to maintain the coalition, put the best face possible on the altered political reality. "We were never so strong as at this time," Wilson wrote optimistically in February, adding that "we must keep clear of all parties until after the two conventions." Sumner favored "fraternizing fully with the Democracy" in Massachusetts, and even after Scott's nomination, he urged that state's antislavery forces to remain "absolutely uncommitted." Neither Wilson nor Sumner would openly support Scott, but they were fully aware of the strong pro-Scott sentiment among Conscience Whigs. Anxious to assist the Scott supporters and equally concerned with maintaining a working relationship with antislavery Democrats, Wilson, Sumner, and the supporters of the coalition insisted on the necessity of an independent presidential nomination. "Our friends generally hope Scott will be elected but they go for a coalition with the Democrats on State affairs," observed Wilson. Both interests would be well served by the independent nomination of an antislavery candidate such as Chase or Hale, who would provide a foundation for future coalitions and, by drawing mainly Democratic votes, help elect Scott. "I want to nominate Chase," Wilson told Sumner. With an independent antislavery coalition on Democratic principles, "we can whip Frank Pierce[,] let Scott go in and disorganize both parties." Wilson preferred Scott to Pierce, but he considered it to be his "first duty," and the duty of antislavery men generally, "to crush the Whig power in this state." Equally interested in defeating Pierce, Amos Tuck and George G. Fogg (John P. Hale's political managers in New Hampshire) warned that Hale's independent nomination would draw votes from Scott. The New Hampshire Democracy had recently defeated the antislavery-Whig coalition and had replaced Hale in the Senate. With the state Democratic party solidly in Pierce's camp, Tuck and Fogg preferred Chase to Hale as an independent candidate. "Go *immediately* to Washington," Fogg instructed Hale. "See Chase, and then determine carefully what you ought to do."[42]

Chase shared the Conscience Whig conviction that Scott's election was greatly to be preferred over Pierce's, and he might also have been willing to see the Free Democracy—as the Free Soil party styled itself for the 1852 campaign—serve Scott's ends. But Chase was equally concerned that the independent Free Democrats proclaim their hostility toward slavery and the slave power on decidedly Democratic principles. In a public letter to New York Barnburner leader Benjamin F. Butler, Chase predicted that Radical Democrats must ultimately decide to join the antislavery Democracy "openly and avowedly on the side of liberty and progress," or accept the domination of the "Compromise" Democracy, "intolerant alike of the claims and the friends of freedom." Reminding the New Yorkers of their antislavery vows of 1848 and pointing to the success of Democratic reunions on antislavery principles in Wisconsin and Vermont (as well as to the once successful antislavery-Democratic coalitions in Ohio and Massachusetts), Chase insisted that antislavery principles and Democratic principles were synonymous. Moreover, when Democrats acted forthrightly on these principles, they gained the support of those "whose attachment to Whig measures had been overcome by their devotion to freedom." The Barnburners remained in Pierce's camp, but Chase's goading had elicited their condemnation of the proslavery sections of their party's Baltimore platform. Despite his admitted "anti democratic prejudices," Richard H. Dana of New York City considered Chase's letter and the Barnburners' response "one of the best things of this generation." Although there were sound, practical resons for the Barnburners to maintain party unity, it seemed to Dana that "the concurrent [antislavery] testimony of men differing as they do . . . must carry weight." And Chase, despite his fears of Pierce, believed that if the Barnburners were true to their professions, "not much need be apprehended even from Pierce."[43]

Spurned by the Barnburners, who maintained their party loyalty, the Free Democracy held its independent convention at Pittsburgh and nominated the deposed Senator John P. Hale for president and George Washington Julian (who had temporarily lost his seat in Congress) for vice-president. The convention went on to adopt a platform remarkable for its Democratic pronouncements concerning federal powers and banks.

Conditions seemed to demand an independent antislavery campaign in 1852, but few of those involved in the free-soil movement viewed the Free Democracy as anything other than a temporary means of sustaining a degree of antislavery momentum in national politics. The Free Democracy was not a stable nucleus for a future political party. The absence of the New York Barnburners and the eagerness of Conscience Whigs to position the third party to hurt Pierce and thereby help Scott were obvious weaknesses in the 1852 Free Democratic campaign. With the collapse of the Free Soil–Democratic coalitions, moreover, and the failure of the Democratic reunions in New York and elsewhere to divert the national Democracy from its proslavery course, President Pierce's aggressively proslavery policies in the territories quickly forced antislavery Democrats into the antiadministration camp. With leading antislavery Whigs—notably William H. Seward and Horace Greeley in New York, Thaddeus Stevens in eastern Pennsylvania, Caleb B. Smith in Indiana, and Abraham Lincoln and Elihu B. Washburne in Illinois—still loyal to the national Whig party following the 1852 campaign, there was little chance that northern antislavery unity could be forged on Democratic principles. Accordingly, although Scott's defeat in 1852 encouraged northern Whigs to seek new political associations before the next presidential canvass, there was every reason for them to emphasize the traditional anti-Democratic sentiments of antislavery reformers. Indeed, the dramatic and to many the frightening rise of the Know Nothing movement heightened Conscience Whig fears of mass politics at the same time that it reinforced the anti-Democratic bias of antislavery reform. As antislavery reformers entered the final battle against slavery, they remained confident that the aggressions of the slave power and the excesses of the Democracy were one and the same.

The Limits of Politics

7

"THE North must be united and take control of the Government," Charles Sumner declared privately in April 1854. If the North failed to unite, the Massachusetts senator continued, "we shall slide under the despotism of the slave power."[1] By the early 1850s, Sumner's warning sounded familiar. Antislavery reformers had long argued that the impetus for northern sectional unity lay, fundamentally, in perceptions of an aggressive and consolidated slave power. Sumner's own fears of the slave power stretched back at least a decade to the Conscience Whig opposition to the annexation of Texas. But Sumner's call for unity carried with it a fresh sense of urgency born of radically altered political conditions across the North. Sumner made his remarks to the wealthy abolitionist and political economist Amasa Walker, a figure who combined moral hostility toward slavery with Democratic views on national economic policy. Walker actively supported the Massachusetts Free Soil–Democratic coalition that elected Sumner and Wilson to the Senate. But it was not the fate of the old coalition that concerned Sumner in his call for unity. On the surface of national politics, the congressional debate over the Kansas-Nebraska Act introduced by Senator Stephen A. Douglas in January 1854 and the related territorial crisis disrupted party unity and prompted political realignments along sectional lines. Beneath the surface, however, more complex and in some ways more profound forces reshaped the context of political discourse in the North and in the nation.

The dramatic rise of immigration throughout the 1840s and the equally dramatic nativist reaction culminating in the early 1850s produced political conditions that destroyed the Whig party and left northern Whigs generally eager for sectional unity. Alarmed at the prospect of greater political division in the North and exhilarated by the collapse of the old party system, Sumner and most reformers encouraged sectional unity. To an extent, the collapse of the Whig party and the rise of the Republican party fulfilled the expectations of those antislavery reformers who had followed an independent political course since the Free Soil revolt of 1848. But antislavery agitation alone had not destroyed the Whig party, and the hope of restoring the Whigs to the presumed purity of their original values defined much of the antislavery political behavior of the late 1840s and early 1850s. Wendell Phillips spoke to these sentiments when he characterized the original Whig party as "the natural ally of free labor and free speech." The party died, said Phillips, because it lowered itself to the level of the Democracy, in "servile bidding for Southern fellowship."[2] Although it was the nativist insurgency and not a betrayal of antislavery principle that caused northern Whig loyalists to seek new political associations, an identification of antislavery reform with Whig principles (as Phillips suggested) remained strong in reform ranks.

Whig views dominated the emerging Republican party. Nevertheless, Democratic identities persisted under the Republican banner, and the competing interests that had sustained the two-party system did not disappear. Nowhere did these rivalries find more heated expression than in the reformist response to the nativist movement, in which the leading advocates of antislavery coalitions with Democrats worked to accommodate what they regarded as legitimate nativist goals. As in earlier coalition efforts, it was their intention to identify antislavery reform with popular concerns. Whig-oriented reformers, by contrast, sternly denounced nativists and coalesced with moderate and conservative Whigs in the new Republican party in part to resist nativist political influence. At the same time, however, reformers of Whiggish views showed more sympathy than their Democratic rivals for legislation restricting citizenship and the franchise. For reformers of Democratic and Whig views, it was the political potency of nativism (particularly its appeal to the lower classes) and the movement's capacity to raise new men to public office that seemed particularly impressive or alarming. In both cases, the reformist response to immigrants and nativists underscored mounting liberal suspicions of the laboring poor and advanced a related interest in defining the limits of mass politics.[3]

Always sensitive to the nuances of political maneuverings and sentiments, New York Senator William H. Seward moved cautiously but steadily toward Republican union. Seward's Whig loyalty remained firm through the election of 1852—"no new party will arise," he wrote confidently, "nor will any old one fall"—but by September 1854, he joined the call for unity. Although not yet ready to speak publicly about political reorganization "as relates to parties," Seward no longer denied the need for northern unity outside of the national Whig organization. Within a year, Seward allied himself wholeheartedly with the emerging Republican party and encouraged leading antislavery Whigs to follow. ("I have a letter from Mr. Seward strongly in favor of union," William Jay reported to Sumner in 1855.) Although Seward saw partisan difficulties ahead—"Whigs frightened draw off—Democrats frightened hesitate to come on"—he insisted with as much firmness as Sumner that "this transformation to a new organization has become necessary."[4]

Politics produced strange bedfellows, indeed, as the emerging Republican party offered wider political opportunities to moderates such as Seward and to conservatives whose earlier hostility toward antislavery reform seemed, in the late 1840s and early 1850s, to doom them to political extinction. For the conservative Caleb B. Smith, the rise of the Republican party proved a positive boon. As a loyal Whig, Smith consistently opposed the Conscience element, led in his home state of Indiana by George Washington Julian. Elected to Congress for three consecutive terms from 1842 to 1846, Smith, a native of Boston, shared the New England Whigs' opposition to the annexation of Texas and the Mexican War. Adding marginally to his antislavery reputation, he supported the Whig presidential nomination of Supreme Court Justice John McLean in 1848 (McLean was still respected among northern Whigs for his cautious hostility to slavery) over the war hero Zachary Taylor. But Smith was no friend to antislavery reform. While Julian led the exodus of Indiana's Conscience Whigs into the Free Soil party, Smith campaigned loyally for Taylor's election. For the time being, the enemies of slavery seemed to be the victors. At the forefront of the antislavery insurgency, Julian won election to Congress for one term as a Free Soiler in 1848 and Smith accepted a post on the Board of Commissioners appointed by President Taylor to adjust American claims against Mexico.[5]

To the more zealous foes of slavery, Julian's election and Smith's appointment seemed fitting rewards, indicative of the advancing spirit of reform. "You will not have Caleb to contend against," Gamaliel Bailey wrote Julian after the appointment. "Men who serve the South cannot expect pay at home," Bailey added in scorn, "so they must receive it from their master." Julian's father-in-law and fellow antislavery congressman, Joshua R. Giddings of Ohio, considered Smith to be the prototypical doughface, laying northern interests aside to gain political favor. Joseph Medill, editor of the *Chicago Tribune,* concurred. Medill later recalled that Smith, as a loyal Whig, supported the 1850 Fugitive Slave Law and advocated a "Southern 'Constitutional guarantee'" as a remedy for continued sectional hostilities. Damning as all of this seemed to antislavery reformers, the organization of the Indiana Republican party in the mid-1850s paved the way for Smith's return to political prominence. Understanding that Republican success required united Whig support, Smith left his private law practice in Cincinnati and returned to Indiana in time to lead the state's delegation to the 1860 Republican convention. In Chicago, Smith seconded Lincoln's nomination. With Smith's support, Julian won reelection to Congress in 1860 for the first time since his unsuccessful bid for a second term in 1850. In 1861, as Julian began the first of four consecutive terms in the House, Smith entered Lincoln's cabinet as secretary of interior.[6]

Although antislavery reformers pursued political independence or coalition in the expectation that the two-party system would crumble from its own inconsistencies and contradictions, they were not prepared to respond to the speed with which the Whig party collapsed under nativist pressures. Just as Julian found himself unexpectedly beholden to Caleb Smith, Zebina Eastman of Illinois discovered that the political expediency he deplored seemed to succeed as Whig leaders moved cautiously toward the Republican party. A partner of the pioneering Quaker abolitionist Benjamin Lundy, Eastman settled in northern Illinois in the 1830s as coeditor of Lundy's *Genius of Universal Emancipation.* Following Lundy's death in 1839, Eastman emerged as a prominent antislavery voice in the West, following the line of antislavery reform that led to the Liberty and Free Soil parties. Eastman presided over the publication of the abolitionist *Genius of Liberty,* the *Western Citizen* (a Liberty party journal), and the Free Soil party's *Free West.* With most Free Soilers, Eastman labored in the expectation that his efforts would convert Illinois's moderate Whigs—most notably Elihu B. Washburne and Abraham Lincoln—to consistent and reliable antislavery principles. But Lincoln carefully kept his distance from the third-party movement and, although Eastman offered his editorial support for Washburne's Whig congressional campaign in 1852,

Washburne similarly eschewed the third party and its aims, which Eastman outlines as seeking to leave the Democrats "ruined" and the "old fogy Whigs" isolated.[7]

Like Seward and Smith, Lincoln and Washburne held to the mainstream of northern politics. As the nativist upheaval transformed party politics, their caution proved to be justified. Eastman watched in amazement as nativists altered the conditions of northern politics. More than a decade of third-party agitation had not prepared him for such a rapid shift in political loyalties. It was "astounding," Eastman wrote Washburne, "how the people love to spurn their party ties." In the East, Massachusetts's coalition leader, Henry Wilson, witnessed the same phenomenon with corresponding awe and respect. Nativist insurgents "can carry the state now I think," Wilson reported to Sumner in 1854. "They say that they can carry every city in the state and I think they can," he continued, observing as did Eastman in the West that "Whigs and Democrats are sick of politics" and eager to seek refuge in the semisecret nativist lodges.[8]

With very few demurs, reformers allied themselves in the last phase of the antislavery struggle with men whose caution and Whig loyalty had once seemed a measure of northern subservience to the slave power. William Schouler's transition from Cotton Whig to Republican illuminates this conservative-liberal alliance and the northern political unity it produced. A prominent journalist, Schouler assumed publication of the *Boston Atlas* in May 1847 in time to launch a vehement attack against the bolting Conscience Whigs and to maintain the *Atlas* as an organ of conservative Whiggery. With the collapse of the Whig party, Schouler's career with the *Atlas* temporarily ended and his continued political influence—like Smith's in Indiana—seemed in doubt. Commending Schouler for remaining steadfast "for sense and principle" amid the Conscience revolt, Seward predicted that if Schouler "weathers this storm safely he will soon be wanted." Schouler did indeed weather the storm, serving briefly as editor of the *Cincinnati Gazette,* formerly a Whig journal, which he turned to the support of nativism and the anti-Nebraska cause. In 1858, Schouler returned to Boston to take charge of the *Atlas* once again and to appeal to revived nativist sentiment following the panic of 1857. One of Charles Sumner's closest associates, Edward L. Pierce, thought that "Schouler in the end goes with those whom he meets the most," but there was a consistency to Schouler's career which Pierce missed. As a Cotton Whig and conservative Republican, Schouler understood the continuing political importance of questions affecting currency, trade, and manufacturing. On these matters, antislavery reformers allied with conservatives, not because they always concurred with conservative economic policy but because they wanted the political resolution of such matters insulated from the unpredictable influence of mass politics. It was the proper function of mass politics, in the reform view, to divorce the national government from the slave power and, ultimately, to destroy property in slaves. With this accomplished, as Schouler observed with evident satisfaction in 1869, "the champions of emancipation . . . feel that they have nothing more of a practical character to accomplish." Political leaders could once again concentrate on shaping government policy regarding "Trade, Money, Commerce, [and] Manufacturing."[9]

The willingness of reformers to unite politically with conservatives such as Schouler seemed highly unlikely in the early 1840s, when reformers championed the cause of the immigrant in the same terms that they championed the causes of the slave and of labor in general. Not surprisingly, reformers identified bigotry and violence toward immigrants with the despotic and brutish influence of slavery and the slave power. As the self-conscious defenders of all victims of oppression, reformers resisted with initial success the cultural insularity of their Calvinist New England heritage and justifiably prided themselves on their liberality when they embraced the cause of impoverished Irish immigrants and identified liberty in Ireland and the liberty of the Irish in America with antislavery reform and the universal cause of human freedom.

There were good reasons for reformers to view Irish immigrants with initial favor. Daniel O'Connell and Father Theobald Mathew—Ireland's two most prominent patriots and leaders of the movement to repeal Britain's 1801 Act of Union—issued ringing denunciations of American slavery during the early 1840s and urged Irish immigrants in America to "*cling by the abolitionists*" and join in the struggle to free the southern slaves. Correspondingly, all factions of the American antislavery movement identified Irish repeal with the struggle against the slave power. As reformers shortly discovered, however, it proved to be far easier to establish a rhetorical link between repeal in Ireland and emancipation in America than it was to convince Irishmen in America that their interests as workingmen required them to enlist in a struggle to liberate southern slaves.[10]

Across the North, Irish repeal associations rejected O'Connell's and

Father Mathew's antislavery appeal. Although Mathew soon dropped the slavery issue to focus his attention on temperance, the rebuke of Irish-Americans dismayed O'Connell and frustrated reformers. O'Connell expressed his shame that Irishmen and sons of Irishmen denounced abolitionism in America in the name of Catholicism, constitutional liberty, and the inferiority of the Negro. Such ideas did not spring from the soil of Ireland, O'Connell declared, or from the teaching of the church. On one point, however, O'Connell acknowledged a measure of truth in the repeal associations' antiabolitionist attacks. "You say that the Abolitionists are fanatics and bigots, and especially entertain a virulent hatred and unchristian zeal against catholicity and the Irish," he wrote to the Cincinnati Repeal Association in 1843, adding that he did not "mean to deny, nor . . . conceal" that such sentiments existed. Indeed, O'Connell thought that "there are among the Abolitionists many wicked and calumniating *enemies* of Catholicity and the Irish, especially in that most intolerant class, the Wesleyan Methodists." Even so, "the best way to disarm their malice" was to take the higher ground "of benevolence and charity, and . . . zeal for the freedom of all mankind," rather than to "take the side of Slavery."[11]

O'Connell's plea did not change the antiabolitionist stance of the Cincinnati Repeal Association, but it did coincide nicely with the efforts of Salmon P. Chase and Gamaliel Bailey to broaden the appeal of antislavery reform. As members of a "Committee of the friends of Liberty, Ireland, and Repeal, in Cincinnati," Chase and Bailey issued a public reply to O'Connell that explained the historical process by which slaveholding interests consolidated as a monopoly to subvert the original antislavery policy of the nation's founders. Believing that an earnest struggle for freedom had only just begun, Chase did not despair over the unenlightened views of the repeal associations. Instead, he noted enthusiastically that at the 1843 Liberty party convention in Buffalo, "an Irish Laborer, distinguished by his warm heart and clear understanding," rose to say that he had cast his first vote "for Catholic Emancipation in Ireland" and that he would cast his second "for Liberty in America."[12]

Following O'Connell's death in 1847 and Father Mathew's open break with American abolitionism during his 1849 tour of the United States, disdain replaced optimism in reformist assessments of the Irish. Even in an optimistic mood, William Lloyd Garrison considered it to be his task as a reformer to dismantle "a stupendous conspiracy . . . between the leading Irish demagogues, the leading pseudo-democrats, and the southern slaveholders." As early as 1845, Garrison observed privately that "almost the entire body of the Irishmen in this country are disposed to go with the accursed South for any and every purpose and to any extent." The Irish were misguided, to be sure, and they acted against their own best interests. But, Garrison concluded, they constituted "a mighty obstacle" in the path of progress all the same.[13]

As Irish repeal associations rejected antislavery appeals in the mid-1840s, reformist efforts to win the Irish to their cause faded rapidly and the focus of reform concerns shifted from immigrants to nativists. Reformers found nativism particularly difficult to contend against in part because it attracted support from people they considered friendly to the antislavery cause and in part because its organized political expression—dubbed the Know Nothing movement by a contemptuous Horace Greeley—cut across established party lines with stunning effects. The popular disaffection from the national parties would have been a welcome event among reformers had it not occurred entirely outside of their expectations and control. At a moment when reformers hoped to subordinate what they regarded as the narrow interests of class to a wider struggle for equal rights, nativists identified impoverished immigrant labor as a fundamental threat to republican liberty. Although reformers would soon disagree concerning the proper political response to the Know Nothings, the *National Era*'s editor, Gamaliel Bailey, expressed a generalized reformist sentiment when he denied nativists the right "to disfranchise your brother man, seeking a home in this country." In the same manner, Bailey denied whites the right "to disfranchise your colored neighbor." "In its essential elements," Bailey declared, nativism "is as repugnant to the doctrine of equal rights, as Slavery."[14]

For antislavery reformers of the Conscience group (already deeply suspicious of the direction of mass politics) the Know Nothing upheaval confirmed their belief that mass politics could no longer serve as an agency of reform. For the antislavery coalition leaders (painfully aware that the nativist defections from Whig and Democratic ranks undermined their efforts to build a popular antislavery base for northern politics) Know Nothingism raised a more practical set of concerns.

Eager not to lose their political base, coalitionists urged caution and patience in response to the Know Nothings and attempted to distinguish legitimate reform concerns from excessive efforts to limit citizenship and suffrage. The result was a new wave of reformist disagreement over the limits of politics.

In Massachusetts, reformers divided in their response to nativism along lines established in response to the Free Soil–Democratic coalition. Henry Wilson, the coalition leader, openly accommodated the Know Nothing order and won election to the United States Senate following statewide Know Nothing gains in the fall elections of 1854. "What an election & what a result!" exclaimed Conscience Whig leader Stephen C. Phillips, dismayed by the political turmoil attending the Know Nothing victory. "In such a chaos it is easy to see that much has been overthrown which one desired to see overthrown," he continued, referring to the collapse of the Whig party. Phillips did not lament the passing of the Whig organization, even if it was attributable to nativist rather than antislavery pressures. But what of the Conscience group's independent stance as Free Soilers? "I see nothing which is more completely subverted or abandoned, than our policy, our organization, and even our principles," Phillips concluded gloomily. Needless to say, "the path of duty" remained clear for Phillips, and he took satisfaction in knowing that he would never deviate from it even though he would no longer travel "in a crowd."[15]

In Ohio, Chase followed a course similar to Wilson's and drew similar criticism from his Conscience Whig opponents on the Reserve. Somewhat more cautious toward nativism than Wilson, Chase confessed to feeling uneasy about the "influence of the Order on our movement." He acknowledged that "there is *danger*" that the nativists might push antislavery principles aside. But rather than simply attack the "cayennes" (or KNs), Chase preferred to accommodate them by acknowledging "that there was some ground for the uprising of the people against papal influence & organized foreignism" while opposing "secret organization & indiscriminate proscription on account of origin or creed." Chase remained confident that antislavery principles would prevail among nativists if reformers did not alienate them through harsh criticism. "It is best not to say any thing against them," Chase cautioned Edward S. Hamlin, editor of the *Columbus Ohio Standard*. "Wait until it becomes necessary & it may never become necessary." The "objectionable" aspects of the movement might cure themselves, Chase speculated. The duty of reformers remained, as it always had been, to keep "the antislavery idea paramount."[16]

Chase believed that Wilson's election in Massachusetts would reassure all but the most suspicious Conscience Whigs that an accommodation of the Know Nothing order need not bury the antislavery crusade in an anti-immigrant reaction. Wilson remained firmly identified with antislavery reform—with "the denationalization of slavery & the exercise of the legitimate influence of the Government on the side of Freedom"—and his victory set the stage for a separation of the "North Americans" (the northern Know Nothings) from their pro-slavery counterparts in the slave states. "His election will be a decided triumph of the Anti Slavery element in the K.N. organization," Chase noted with satisfaction. "It may lead to disruption."[17]

Encouraged by Wilson's success, Chase forged an alliance of Know Nothings, anti-Nebraska Whigs, and antislavery Democrats which secured his own election as governor of Ohio in 1855. The success of this coalition required the neutralization of Lewis Campbell, a three-term Whig congressman from Ohio who embraced Know Nothingism and the anti-Nebraska movement in the wake of the national Whig party's collapse. Taking pleasure in the Whigs' disarray, Chase noted that Campbell identified himself in Congress as "a Seward Whig" and found it "curious" that while Seward denounced nativists and coalitionists (such as Chase), who would accommodate them, Campbell emerged as "the Chief of the Western Know Nothings." As Chase understood, of course, it was an unavoidable fact of political life in the 1850s that nativists exerted a powerful independent influence across the North. Partisan rhetoric aside, Seward himself sought nativist support when it became necessary for his own reelection campaign in 1855.[18]

Campbell understood the influence of nativism as clearly as anyone. At the state level in Ohio he appealed jointly to nativist and anti-Nebraska sentiments and believed that the Know Nothings would sweep all opposition before them. Campbell's success in Ohio, combined with his efforts to build a national nativist party out of the wreck of the Whig organization, directly challenged Chase's antislavery goals. Campbell described Know Nothingism as "a formidable organization" in all parts of the country. Its members were "strongly anti-slavery" in the free states, and Campbell believed that hostility to slavery could be subsumed—in the manner of the old Whig party—in a national organization dedicated "to remedy other palpable wrongs besides slavery!" With this conviction, Campbell drafted the 1856 American party platform, announcing the party's opposition to geographical parties, affirming its recognition of congressional authority in matters relating to fugitive slaves, and denying any federal authority over slavery extension. Campbell correctly perceived that nativism and anti-Nebraska sentiment overlapped significantly in the North. But he proved wrong in believing that nativism could be dislodged from the anti-Nebraska movement to provide a political bridge across the widening sectional chasm.[19]

Intending to assert the primacy of nativism over anti-Nebraska sentiments, Campbell planned to hold the Ohio American party convention in Cleveland shortly before the Anti-Nebraska convention already scheduled by Chase to meet in Columbus in July 1855. Campbell expected a united nativist contingent to shape the direction of the Columbus convention and to produce a statewide alliance in harmony with a neo-Whig national nativist party. In response, Chase threatened to bolt the Columbus convention. Chase warned that if the Americans made independent nominations at Cleveland and then tried to control the anti-Nebraska gathering, "*none but Know Nothings will participate in the nomination.*" Certain that "outsiders are an overmatch for insiders now," Chase believed that the Americans would cooperate with the anti-Nebraska forces or be beaten by them. Antislavery candidates, particularly if they did not antagonize nativists, "can poll more votes and will poll more votes" than the Americans campaigning on their own.[20]

Chase's assessment proved to be correct. Antislavery nativists (calling themselves "Know Somethings") divided the Cleveland convention on the Nebraska issue, and Campbell's forces proved to be as malleable as Chase expected when they arrived at the Columbus convention. After Chase's nomination for governor, Campbell threw his support to the anti-Nebraska ticket and helped deliver enough Know Nothing votes to secure Chase's election. In the wake of the Ohio coalition's success, Campbell emerged—together with Nathaniel Banks of Massachusetts (a moderate antislavery Democrat, who supported Wilson's anti-Nebraska–Know Nothing coalition)—as a candidate for Speaker of the House acceptable to anti-Nebraska and Know Nothing forces. Campbell ultimately lost to Banks and in 1858 lost his congressional seat to the proslavery Democrat and future Copperhead leader, Clement L. Vallandigham. Chase blamed Campbell's narrow nativism for his defeat. If he "had only pursued a conciliatory course toward our naturalized citizens," Chase argued, Campbell's American party attachment would have been forgiven by immigrant German voters and Vallandigham could have been defeated. Damned by the antislavery press as a doughface and attacked by the Democrats for "selling-out the K.N.s to the 'abolitionists' and 'wolly heads,'" Campbell blamed his political misfortune on Chase. "My *Americanism* was no great sin when I used it for the triumphs of 1854 and 1855," he complained. "I intend to hold on to it and . . . shall patiently await the resurrection." But emerging Republican leaders had learned to manage nativism, and the movement did not revive as an independent force in antebellum America. Chase deemed it a "pity" that Campbell attached so much importance to nativism as a political creed. "Almost all even of the Americans" regarded the extreme demands of the Know Nothings "as non essentials."[21]

A concern for essentials obliged reformers to place principle before ethnicity as they considered the need to contain electoral politics. For Chase and Wilson, an accommodation of nativism required recognition of the legitimate interests of nativists and opposition to their excessive and indiscriminately proscriptive restrictions on immigrant suffrage. Despite his close identification with Know Nothingism, therefore, Wilson opposed nativist efforts in Massachusetts to prohibit immigrants from voting for a period of fourteen years. Chase urged caution as well. As Chase noted in his reply to Daniel O'Connell, some Irish immigrants identified with the liberal struggle against the slave power even if the mass of Irish-Americans remained hostile to antislavery reform. Chase believed that such liberal sympathies took hold among Germans as well, particularly those who followed the lead of the "Forty-Eighters." "The Germans are bold thinkers & true lovers of liberty," Chase wrote the Garrisonian reformer Sydney Howard Gay in 1854. "It is with the greatest pleasure," he added, "that I see the German mind directed to the subject of slavery."[22]

Most reformers looked at Chase's and Wilson's accommodation of Know Nothingism as foolhardy and potentially dangerous to reform goals. Thus Gamaliel Bailey, who had been allied closely with Chase's coalition efforts in the western Liberty party, looked askance at his alliance with a "corrupt secret combination." Bailey took personal satisfaction in Chase's election as governor of Ohio but "politically" pronounced himself "far more satisfied with the results gained in New York," where Seward spoke against Know Nothings. Specifically, Bailey feared that Chase's accommodation of Know Nothings would help the American party to "occupy pretty much the place of the old Whig Party," with native-born Protestants united in their hostility to immigrants and controlled by conservative Whigs such as Campbell in Ohio and William Schouler in Massachusetts. In such a situation, the "Old Line Democracy" would have free reign among immigrant voters, and the "friends of freedom" would be isolated as the "'third party'" in the manner of the old Liberty party. That outcome, argued Bailey, undermined antislavery goals: it was "precisely the result at which slaveholding tacticians have been aiming."[23]

Shortly before Chase's election, Julian of Indiana expressed much the same concern. Moderately supportive of Chase's coalition efforts in the past, Julian now hoped that Chase would win the Ohio governorship with a sufficiently large majority to dampen the Know Nothings as an independent movement. But Julian also feared "that the Know Nothings on election day will secretly & systematically cut his [Chase's] throat & throw back the anti-slavery men of the north upon their radical doctrines to fight their battle single handed." Julian found "very little soundness" in Indiana's emerging Republican party, a coalition of nativists and anti-Nebraska Whigs. "It is whiggery with a change of name," Julian declared, "reinforced by some office seeking democrats & entirely controlled *by nativism*."[24]

For the old Conscience Whigs—clustered around Charles Francis Adams and Stephen C. Phillips in the East and Joshua R. Giddings and John C. Vaughan in the West—the coalitionists' efforts to accommodate Know Nothings seemed as distasteful as the upstart nativist movement itself. To Francis W. Bird, a leading Massachusetts Conscience Whig, the combined coalitionist appeal to Democrats and Know Nothings threatened to sink antislavery principles in a slough of opportunism and demagoguery. Standing squarely with Adams and Stephen Phillips in opposition to coalition and Know Nothingism, Bird opposed Wilson's coalition efforts from the outset. "We have always professed to believe, that the 'coalition' was a temporary thing," Bird protested to Sumner in 1854. Bird could justify the Free Soil–Democratic coalition only by conceiving it to be a means of bringing new support to the Conscience Whig position, by "indoctrinating the democratic party with our ideas" and bringing "the best part of the party" into the Conscience camp. Now, "the humbug of state reform" together with Know Nothingism possessed a momentum all its own, and Bird (like Stephen Phillips).felt increasingly isolated in his adherence to principle. The spectacle of emerging Republican leaders attempting to appease nativists with their "prejudice against the negro" under a banner proclaiming "Freedom for the White Man" dismayed Bird. "Nationally, everything is black," remarked the wealthy paper manufacturer in 1857: "Pretending freedom for the negro, we united with a party which proscribed the foreigner: & now, without repudiating that union, we are ready to trample on the rights of the negro." Bird foresaw political defeat and, given the new party's lapses of principle, he thought "we deserve it."[25]

As in Massachusetts, the Conscience element in the West denounced cooperation with Know Nothings. John C. Vaughan, who earlier joined with the Conscience Whig leader Joshua R. Giddings to sound the alarm against Chase's coalition with Democrats, led the anti–Know Nothing effort. As a western champion of Free Soil party purity, Vaughan viewed Chase's association with Know Nothings as a natural consequence of his degrading ties with the Democracy. Chase argued that denunciations of the Know Nothings—whether they came from Vaughan or from Chase's former coalition associates, Gamaliel Bailey and Edward S. Hamlin—"make the members of the order less disposed than they would be otherwise to cooperate with outsiders on the Slavery issue." Although Hamlin and Bailey supported Chase over Giddings in the 1849 Senate contest and provided editorial support (in Hamlin's *Columbus Ohio Standard* and Bailey's *Washington National Era*) for the Free Soil–Democratic coalition that elected Chase to the Senate and repealed much of Ohio's black code, on the Know Nothing issue both men found themselves closer to Vaughan and to the Conscience Whigs on the Reserve. "The proscriptive spirit of Know Nothingism, and its disequalizing spirit," Hamlin observed bluntly, "are in sympathy with the spirit of slaveholding."[26]

In Massachusetts, Conscience Whigs looked to Charles Francis Adams as the exemplar of reformist propriety. Although Adams joined with antislavery Democrats in 1848 to run as the Free Soil party candidate for vice-president alongside the Barnburner leader Martin Van Buren, he thoroughly opposed any coalition with Democrats in Massachusetts. Similarly, Adams believed Know Nothingism to be steeped in all of the corruption of mass politics which he associated with the party of Andrew Jackson. The impoverished origins, sudden wealth, and rapid rise to political prominence of Henry Wilson, the coalition leader in Massachusetts, underlay Adams's fear that this aggressive young reformer would "spread disease into the very hearts of our friends." "Wilson," grumbled Francis Bird in agreement, "is still whoring (as Seward says) with every decent-looking strumpet he meets." Wilson regarded Adams's and Bird's social prominence with corresponding contempt. "For one," he wrote Charles Sumner in 1853, "I don't wish the endorsement of the 'best society' in Boston until I am dead—then all of us are sure of it—for it endorses everything that is dead." Wilson understood reform as a fight, not as an exercise in public propriety. Seeking an editor for Boston's leading antislavery journal, the *Commonwealth,* Wilson looked for qualities of combativeness. "We don't want a 'respectable' paper any longer," he declared. "We want a paper that can fling 'Bricks,' this fall and not an imitation of the [conservative Whig] 'Advertiser.'" According to one member of the Conscience group, the intense dislike expressed toward Wilson for his accommodation of Democrats and Know Nothings sprang as much from his "plebian origins" as from his political maneuverings, "or rather his present position adds to the bitter jealousy with which they have always regarded him."[27]

Chase never suffered from the lack of social standing that plagued Wilson, yet he too stood somewhat apart from the typical Yankee reformer. As an Episcopalian in Cincinnati, Chase remained theologically as well as physically separated from the Calvinist traditions and from the revivalist enthusiasms of Western Reserve Yankees. Like Wilson, Chase tended to view respectable New England reformers as culturally insulated from the mass of northerners and, therefore, politically ineffective. When, in 1854, Chase responded to the New York antislavery journalist John P. Bigelow's request for a sketch of his life and antislavery career, he referred (with uncharacteristic sarcasm) to the tendency of all New Englanders to attempt to trace their origins to the *Mayflower.* Chase made no claims of religious dissent among his forebears, although he proudly traced his New England lineage to the mid-seventeenth century. The Yankee tendency to identify all of the nation's virtues with the Calvinist values of the Pilgrim and Puritan fathers clearly rankled Chase. In December 1866, when Chase attended a gathering of New Englanders in the nation's capital to celebrate Forefathers Day, he did so as chief justice of the United States, keenly aware that the assembled guests were "mostly of the Congregational church." Chase noted on one of the food-laden tables two pumpkin pies, one decorated with the words "Landing at Plymouth 1620" and the other with "Negro Suffrage 1866." "I suppose," Chase remarked to his daughter, "that Manhood suffrage is a logical result of the principles of civil & religious liberty." But Chase doubted that the Pilgrims "were *very* zealous for any other civil & religious liberties than their own." "The quakers did not think they were," he concluded, "nor did the negroes & much less the Indians of that day."[28]

For the Conscience element generally, opposition to Know Nothingism coexisted with a genteel hostility toward immigrants and a desire to contain and restrain mass political participation. Reformist efforts to create a nativist shadow movement illustrate the point. While Chase and Wilson worked to harness the Know Nothing insurgency to their Free Soil–Democratic coalitions, the Conscience element attempted to redirect nativist protests through "Know Something" societies that excluded Catholics and endorsed temperance reform together with antislavery principles. As one of Charles Sumner's correspondents observed approvingly, "The members agree by *word and deed* to uphold the interests of Freedom, Protestantism, and temperance." Samuel Gridley Howe, who stood with Adams and Palfrey in opposition to Wilson's Democratic coalition and to his association with the Know Nothings, reported enthusiastically that "the 'Know Something' lodges are increasing." Although Howe himself refused to join such a lodge— he would not be led anywhere blindfolded, he said—he thought the movement would be effective among those who found fraternal associations and rituals appealing: "There are strong indications that the antislavery leaven if it does not leaven the lump of K. Nothingism, will cause great ferment without it." Following the example of the Conscience Whigs in the East, John Vaughan carried the Know Something message from northern Ohio to nativist workingmen "west of the Lakes" and recruited the veteran abolitionist Ichabod Codding to organize lodges in northern Illinois and southeastern Wisconsin.[29]

Despite reformist denunciations of nativist bigotry toward immigrants, reformers feared the potential for political corruption which the impoverished immigrants represented. With characteristic disdain for political realities, Adams underscored this point in 1859— well after the Know Nothings had ceased to be an independent political force—when he supported an amendment to the Massachusetts constitution that would extend the naturalization period for immigrants by two years. A year earlier, Adams had won election to Congress as a Republican. He now advocated the extension despite the solid opposition of his party and defended the amendment as a reasonable restriction on immigrant suffrage in contrast to the Know Nothings' fourteen-year proposal. Wilson, who had resisted the fourteen-year amendment, opposed the two-year rule as well. Even Nathaniel Banks, who earlier sympathized with the Know Nothing movement, remained studiously silent on the new two-year restriction. Undaunted, and doubtless expressing the sentiments of respectable reformers like himself, Adams pressed ahead until the measure met defeat. None could question Adams's fidelity to principle, and none could doubt his conviction that propriety in public affairs demanded a measure of suffrage restriction.[30]

To be Irish in America, noted Garrison in 1857, "is next to being of African extraction."[31] The reason, as William Elder explained a decade earlier, was not hard to find. Irish immigrants and Negro slaves came to American shores, willingly or not, to supply a demand for labor. Critical of the antiforeign prejudices of Yankee reformers, Elder noted that New Englanders historically defended the importation of Negro slaves, as they would later welcome Irish immigrants, as "all right proper & patriotic" as long as they profited from it. "But when we don't want any more for our *own* use," Elder insisted, "why then it is piracy and popery and perdition to welcome any more of the article." Elder thought that the nativist upheaval could produce beneficial results because the Democrats could not effect a platform broad enough to hold the Irish "without making room for *our natives*," the southern slaves, as well.[32]

The presence of the Irish as a propertyless laboring class demonstrated to the satisfaction of reformers the efficacy of emancipation. But the Irish also raised troubling questions for reformers regarding the capacity of the working poor to follow the path reformers blazed toward moral and material progress. When the Unitarian theologian and radical abolitionist Theodore Parker visited the Virgin Islands in 1859, he wrote at length to Wendell Phillips describing life and labor under the new free labor system. Parker also gave free rein to his views of the Irish and the Negro character. Parker compared the plantation overseers and managers (whom he thought to be Scots-

Irish) to the crude and ill-mannered "paddies" of Boston. In contrast, he enjoyed the playful, carefree, and exuberant character of the blacks, whom he found more warmhearted, docile, and emulative of their betters than the Irish, although they were frivolous, improvident, and licentious as well. Parker noted a predominance of large-breasted and wide-hipped women among the former slaves and reported to Phillips that they bore their numerous children with little regard for marriage. Slavery accounted for some of these characteristics, Parker thought, and climate played a role as well. But Parker concluded that the Negro temperament was rooted largely in race. He continued to view blacks as fit objects of moral reform, but he discerned limits to their capacity for advancement. Parker thought that freedmen labored best under benevolent guidance with nonmonetary incentives.[33]

Even as reformers used the Irish-Negro comparison to advance Negro rights, they expressed a mounting hostility toward the working poor. Considering the status of the black "contrabands" during the first year of the Civil War, the prominent antislavery essayist George William Curtis concluded that "we must do exactly what we should do if they were white and not black men. If they will not work, they must starve, like the rest of us: for Government cannot feed the people. If they are willing to work and there is no work in that spot, they must be sent elsewhere, as a thousand Irishmen would be."[34] On the question of Negro suffrage, the negative aspects of the comparison emerged with particular clarity. When the issue of equal suffrage came before the voters of New York in a statewide referendum in 1860, the *New York Independent* (a respected voice of Yankee Protestantism and moral reform) proclaimed the "native colored citizens" as qualified to cast a ballot as the "ignorant, foul, priest-ridden Paddy." Similarly, when the Republican senator from Michigan, Jacob M. Howard, wrote Charles Sumner in 1865 insisting that Negro suffrage in the South "is our *only security* & the only means of making emancipation effectual," he disposed of reformist concerns about the Negro's qualification to vote by noting that the freedman "is as worthy of it as the Irish Copperheads at least."[35]

In the postwar years, as reformers grew increasingly sensitive to issues of political corruption, the negative character of the Irish-Negro comparison served yet another purpose. In the midst of the Liberal Republican campaign to unseat President Ulysses S. Grant and end federally directed Reconstruction, the liberal political economist David A. Wells instructed an uncertain Charles Sumner on the shortcomings of federal policies. Without education or experience in public affairs, the "colored people . . . throw their vote solid,—and like the Irish—perpetuate their caste, and array one political party against them." Bloc voting in the South, in Wells's view, permitted "carpetbag rule" and produced "state prostration," which, in turn, sustained "the assertion that the Negro is incapable of self-government."[36]

Wells's fears of the political effects of ethnic and class divisions characterized the late nineteenth-century Mugwump style of liberal reform. But these liberal concerns were rooted in the antebellum era of antislavery reform. Wells's concerns were those of reformers who endeavored to lead a northern struggle against slavery within bounds of public propriety established in their political and economic battle with the slave power. In political behavior as well as in economic relations, liberalism required a distinction between public duty and private interest—between adherence to objective principles of political economy and the pursuit of personal gain. For the liberals, this distinction defined morality in public affairs. In its absence, when the public and private spheres converged, corruption and eventually despotism occurred. Here lay the danger of Irish (and later Negro) voting behavior and the political threat of the Know Nothing reaction. Here, too, lay the danger of the slave power, which insisted with increasing bluntness during the 1850s that the authoritarian and paternalistic foundations of its domestic institutions must be recognized and secured in the public sphere of national politics and economic policy.

Slavery in Its Property Aspect

THE reformers' public expressions of sympathy for the southern slaves did not preclude private uncertainties regarding the moral character and material aspirations of the laboring classes. In fact, moral hostility to slavery encouraged reformers to objectify the condition of labor as they identified freedom and the moral foundations of progress in terms of individual autonomy and self-control. Freed of traditional political accommodations of slaveholding and of the constraints of paternalism in relations between masters and laborers, the moral sentiments of antislavery reform advanced the utilitarian ethic of liberal capitalism. As Wendell Phillips explained in 1862, it was the common pursuit of "liberty" and "business" that generated the "boundless energy of New England and New York." This energy, Phillips predicted—the energy of men free to rise according to their individual abilities and fortunes—would soon sweep aside the despotism of slavery and secure the American nation for freedom.[1]

By the mid-1840s, with its moral sympathies encompassed by a utilitarian concept of progress, the antislavery struggle entered a new and aggressively political phase. Contributing to the sense of urgency that animated antislavery politics were political upheavals across the North and the challenges of proslavery ideologues (notably George Fitzhugh) from the South. In both cases, labor's productive relationship to capital assumed greater prominence in antislavery discourse. Fitzhugh touched a particularly sensitive point when he denounced the oppressive character of free labor relations. When reformers described labor and capital as equal partners in production, Fitzhugh argued that they simply permitted the weak to perish in competition with the strong. Fitzhugh's central contention, that slave labor fared better by moral and material measures than free labor, transformed traditional southern defenses of slavery into a radical critique of liberal capitalism. Recognizing that the reformers' concern with the plight of the slave defined the moral elements of freedom, Fitzhugh reminded his readers of the degradation of the North's laboring poor. Recognizing as well that the principle of utility defined (to the reformers' satisfaction) the means by which individual striving produced the greatest good for the entire society, Fitzhugh called attention to the human suffering that attended the northern struggle for economic advantage and gain.[2]

The critique of free labor that Fitzhugh advanced could not be answered directly by antislavery reformers for the same reason that the defenders of slavery could not directly respond to the utilitarian critique of slavery. In both cases, to do so would introduce a dangerous and perhaps fatal element of doubt. Thus reformers acknowledged the strength of capital relative to labor, but they posited a greater cooperation between capital and labor—not the overt subordination of labor to capital—as the remedy. Slaveholders for their part acknowledged inefficiencies and inconveniences in slave labor as they pressed toward a more perfect paternalism and a more absolute authoritarianism.

By the mid-1850s, a northern perception of slavery as an increasingly authoritarian system undermined the older arguments of Henry C. Carey that the South would pass through slavery to free labor. This perception also brought conservative Whigs definitively into antislavery ranks. In this sense Fitzhugh's proslavery challenge strengthened the North's antislavery resolve. As the Pennsylvania ironmaster and railroad builder Stephen Colwell noted, it was the South's defense of slavery as a "moral industrial institution" that required its complete destruction.[3] This concern with the condition of labor in industrial society (termed the "labor question" in late nineteenth-century liberal discussions) assumed central importance as the antislavery struggle entered its final phase. Raised in the 1830s in conjunction with antislavery claims that slavery sapped northern prosperity, robbing laborer and employer alike, the labor question reemerged in the 1840s and 1850s in reformist explanations of the benefits of emancipation. The writings of Amasa Walker, whose career in business and reform seemed to Wendell Phillips to exemplify the restless energy of the North, illustrate the manner in which the moral sentiments of abolitionism meshed with utilitarian doctrines of political economy to produce an increasingly objective and sweeping rejection of slavery.

As a shoe merchant, a Garrisonian abolitionist, a railroad builder, and eventually a professor of political economy, Walker united a robust pursuit of business with moral perfectionism and liberal theories of social and economic progress. Denied admission to Amherst College as a young man, Walker shifted his early ambitions from scholarship to business and during the 1830s emerged as a prosperous retailer of boots and shoes in the Boston area. While still building his fortune, Walker embraced Garrisonian abolitionism and universal reform. His enthusiasm ranged across the spectrum of antebellum reform. An advocate of international peace, temperance, unrestricted commerce, and the "abolition of all institutions and customs which do not recognize and respect the image of God and a human brother in every man of whatever clime, color or condition of humanity," Walker served as a member of the Board of Directors of the American Peace Society, as vice-president of the 1848 International Peace Congress in England, and as a delegate to the 1849 Paris Peace Conference. He assumed an active role as well in the American temperance movement (he was elected president of the Boston Temperance Society in 1839) and lent his support to public schools, cheap postage, and the abolition of capital punishment. By 1840, at the age of forty, Walker had acquired a sufficient fortune to retire from active business and to devote his energies to public affairs and the study of political economy. A founder of Oberlin College, Walker lectured there during the 1840s on the subject of political economy; during the 1850s he lectured on political economy at Harvard; and, by the 1860s, he had gained national prominence as a liberal economist and professor of political economy at Amherst.[4]

In politics, Walker displayed the anti-Masonic tendencies of many reformers and served in 1832 as a delegate to the Massachusetts State Anti Masonic party Convention. But Walker deviated from the ranks of conventional reformers when he championed the laissez-faire and equal rights principles of the Jacksonian Democracy. In 1834 and again in 1836, Walker stood for election to Congress as a Democrat whose hostility to slavery nonetheless won him the public support of Garrison and Wendell Phillips. Opposed to slavery and to monopolies, suspicious of banks and corporations, Walker associated antislavery reform in the 1830s with what he hailed as the advancing status of labor. In the face of an aggressive slave power, Walker considered the interests of capital and labor to be equally insecure. With Democrats of antislavery views across the North, Walker joined the Free Soil coalition of 1848. An active participant in the Free Soil–Democratic coalition in Massachusetts, Walker took a leading role as well in the formation of the state Republican party. Throughout his political career, he expressed "a deep reverence for the rights of man" and linked his political activities to the "highest moral and religious sentiments of our nature."[5]

Despite the diversity of his interests and activities, Walker focused his reform energies on two related goals: the emancipation of black labor. in the South and the steady improvement of the condition of white labor in the North. Because slavery denied laborers the means to improve their condition, the struggle for emancipation advanced the interests of all who labored by promoting harmonious and productive relations between capital and labor. In Walker's view, antislavery reform relieved class tensions in the North by promoting a "perfect harmony and reciprocity of interests" between labor and capital. Antislavery reform demonstrated that conflicts between labor and capital were not "necessary" and that one class "ought" not to be "arrayed in hostility" against the other. Like William Elder, who earlier attached antislavery principles to Henry C. Carey's doctrines of political economy, Walker understood that though labor and capital were not "antagonists," they were "active and increasing competitors for the profits of industry." In that competition, Walker acknowledged that capital "has greatly the advantage," and he pledged to workingmen, as a principle of antislavery politics, to seek "in our legislative acts to guard with strict fidelity against any encroachment upon the rights and interest of the weaker party." In his own view of the superintending and sustaining functions of the state, Walker presented the Free Soil political agenda to northern workingmen as the platform of the true Democracy, severed "from its unrighteous copartnership with the slave propagandists of the South." By advancing the cause of freedom in the South, antislavery politics promoted "just and equal laws" in matters affecting labor and capital in the North, "with no exclusive legislation for the one [class] at the expense of the other."[6]

As Walker explained the logic of antislavery politics, reformers were "bound to regard the interests of the not overpaid laborer of the north as truly as those of the entirely unpaid laborer of the South." "While we are striving to emancipate labor in the other states," Walker announced in 1861, "we should be equally solicitous to ameliorate and elevate its condition in our own." Free men must destroy slavery and with it that "hybrid oligarchy, a cross between sham democracy and slaveholding despotism," which, beneath the banner of the Democracy, spread its blighting influence across the land. It was the Democracy's anti-Negro and antiabolitionist appeal to white workingmen which Walker conceived to be the essence of slave power despotism. "Our democracy especially must learn that this is not a 'nigger question,' but a white man's question," he insisted at the outbreak of the Civil War. "It is their own safety and welfare that demand the extinction of slavery." Therefore, "the great question with all liberal minds, is not what the general interests of the colored men require, but what the general interests of the white people demand."[7]

Beyond slavery loomed the wider labor question which Walker had attached to the slavery issue in his antebellum political appeals. Although Walker projected "the gradual amelioration of our human condition . . . by wiser use of wealth, for kind purposes," he and liberal economists generally became progressively more vague on details. Walker looked to a liberal state to ensure that "the rights of man as a holder of property are sacred" and that "his rights as a laborer equally so." With equal rights thus secured, Walker expected that all the efforts of capital and labor, "even in the severest assertion of their individual claims," would work to the common good. Walker acknowledged that "there are certainly other and higher considerations than the greatest production and accumulation of wealth." Similarly, "the greatest wealth is not logically coincident with the highest economic good." These points had been made clear in the utilitarian critique of slavery. But Walker remained confident in the aftermath of emancipation that the highest good would follow from the pursuit of the greatest wealth and that concerns about the "social and moral results" of such a quest could be placed, confidently, in "the domain of sociology" for scientific examination and resolution. With moral reform sentiments comfortably contained within a utilitarian analysis of progress, the way had been cleared for the emergence of scientific reform and for objective analyses of suffering humanity, which, assisted by Walker's writings in political economy, advanced apace with liberal theories of state action and social control.[8]

During the 1850s, the utilitarian analysis of slavery that Walker helped to popularize became commonplace in the North. When, for example, the New York city free-soil Democratic leader George Opdyke published his *Treatise on Political Economy* (1851), he concluded in the increasingly confident manner of antislavery reformers that the "average degree of wealth" in the North was "at least double that of the southern freemen, including the market value of their slaves." Looking beyond the comparative poverty of the South, Opdyke noted that only governments founded on "the principle of equality" could remain stable and effective. Effective government provided "an equal distribution of benefits" and endeavored to "elevate the masses . . . by increasing the aggregate of benefits." With William Cullen Bryant and David Dudley Field, Opdyke soon led the Democratic faction of the New York Republican party.[9] In like manner, the former Liberty party organizer Elizur Wright insisted that emancipation would increase "the aggregate wealth of the country." Convinced of the utility of emancipation, Wright and other reformers moved easily to the conclusion that uncompensated emancipation destroyed no value. "No intelligent political economist can believe," Wright asserted in 1861, "that any considerable amount of real wealth would be destroyed by non-chattelizing the black people." Instead, by elevating the condition of all who labored, emancipation would produce wealth.[10]

The antislavery journalist and political economist Daniel R. Goodloe developed the era's most elaborate and sophisticated analysis of the broad benefits reformers anticipated from emancipation. Associated with Joshua Leavitt and Gamaliel Bailey in the publication of the *National Era,* Goodloe analyzed the political economy of slavery in an attempt to reach beyond the "common opinion" of political economists—Goodloe cited Henry C. Carey and John Stuart Mill—that the South was inferior to the North in wealth because slavery as an inefficient labor system retarded economic progress. Goodloe found this analysis misleading because it implied that rational capital investment decisions necessarily favored the hiring of free labor over the ownership of slaves. If this were so, it followed that slaveowners were persistently and universally irrational in their economic decisions, or that slavery itself would wither away with economic progress, in the manner described by Carey. Goodloe undertook to demonstrate that slaveholders were in fact rational economic men, and that they were, nevertheless, unlikely to exchange slavery for free labor without political and economic pressures from the free states.

Goodloe believed that writers of all of the standard works of political economy erred when they considered slavery only as an abstract problem in capital investment and thereby concluded that it was less advantageous for planters to own slaves than to hire free labor. For Goodloe, a native of North Carolina familiar with the practical benefits of slaveholding, this analysis did not account for the historical fact that in the South "wherever agriculture was sufficiently profitable to induce large investments of capital the labor of slaves was preferred, and it was only the small farms of the south which were worked by free labor." Goodloe traced this "universal preference given to slave labor" to the original availability of slaves. Thereafter, "the very existence of slavery . . . produced a condition of things, and generated manners and habits which made it more profitable to employ slaves than free laborers." Slavery did indeed breed a dangerous spirit of masterdom, Goodloe argued, and he joined with the abolitionists to oppose the evil. But he insisted that "the chief evils of slavery to the body politic resulted from principles more stubborn and powerful than its moral effects upon the people."[11]

The distinctive point which Goodloe pursued specifically challenged the optimistic assumption of earlier political economists, particularly Carey, that slave labor would inevitably be displaced by the more efficient and profitable free labor system. Goodloe argued that slavery "absorbs the chief part of the accumulated wealth of the people." The progressive forces that produced prosperity in the North simply did not operate in the South. "It is the necessary tendency of a slave country to grow poor," Goodloe write in 1849. "This is a necessity, and not a bad habit, as some suppose." As "the great capitalists of the South," slaveholders regarded slaves as "the most valuable property in the South." Slavery, then, became "a monopoly which benefits the few at the expense of the many." To explain the profitability of slavery, Goodloe offered as an example two one-hundred-acre farms identical in every way save the status of their laborers. In the example, Goodloe held constant the value of the cotton produced by the slave and free laborer and the expenses incurred by the free and slaveholding farmers for their personal needs and the needs of their laborers. Thus, the free farmer would spend $1,000 in excess of wages for his own needs, food for his ten laborers, and provender for horses and cattle; the slaveholder would spend $1,000 in excess of the capital he had invested in his ten slaves to provide for his own needs and those of his slaves and provender for horses and cattle. When these costs were deducted from the $4,000 worth of cotton produced on each farm, the two systems of labor were precisely the same. The only difference was that the free farmer paid an additional $1,440 in wages (at $12 per month). Consequently, the slaveowner's net profit for the season was $3,000; the free farmer's only $1,560.[12]

Of course, Goodloe's example was far too simple to resolve the debate over the profitability of slavery. The historian Ulrich B. Phillips found Goodloe superior to all other American writers on the political economy of slavery but concluded in his treatment of the business aspects of slavery that "plantation slavery . . . was less a business than a life." In Phillips's famous analysis, the planters' deductions for food, clothing, medical care, and other costs associated with slaveholding frequently exceeded the value of the goods produced by the slaves. Although Phillips enthusiastically embraced Goodloe's conclusion that slavery distributed wealth but did not produce it, he rejected the notion that slavery was directly profitable as a business venture for the planters. Nevertheless, Goodloe's conclusion that slaveowning farmers enjoyed a net profit of "9 3/5 percent upon the capital invested in slaves" fits nicely with the most recent scholarly assessment of the profitability of slavery.[13]

Goodloe believed that he had corrected the mistaken assumption that southern planters "could always more safely employ free than slave labor." He also challenged the optimistic assumption that the incentives of free labor would generate greater productivity than that which could be extracted by the stimulus of the lash. If slavery were measured against free labor only in profits, it must be judged a success, Goodloe argued. "The economic evil of slavery lies deeper" than profits. "It is not that individuals or capitalists may not make money out of it," he concluded, "but that society in the aggregate, cannot make money out of it." For though the slaveowner could successfully expropriate much of the product of his slave's labor, the capital necessary to carry on a slave labor enterprise vastly exceeded (by the market value of the slaves) the capital necessary to produce the same product with free labor. In this fashion, slavery "absorbs the chief part of the accumulated wealth of the people," leaving little capital available for "investment in the manufacturing arts, commerce, &c."[14]

Goodloe's arguments provided a utilitarian justification for uncompensated emancipation. Because, as he had labored to demonstrate, "property in slaves has nothing to do with production," it followed that the wealth individual slaveowners accumulated in their slave property "has added nothing to the resources of the State or Nation." The slave's value as property "cannot contribute any thing to production, for the reason that the destruction of the property by the liberation of the slave would in no degree destroy the efficiency of his labor." Therefore, although emancipation without compensation would bring "much individual loss" to slaveholders, it "would destroy none of the resources of the country." As Goodloe later explained to Charles Sumner, "capital invested in slaves is unproductive, because unnecessary. In other words, the abolition of slavery destroys no value because nothing is destroyed but titles."[15]

Goodloe's analysis represented an extension of familiar "creative destruction" arguments, in which conservative Whigs as well as abolitionists and antislavery reformers found a secure and objective framework for an attack against the slave power. Perhaps the clearest expression of this new antislavery tone—and certainly a prominent and influential example of it—came from Frederick Law Olmsted, whose antebellum writings about slavery and the South won the praise of conservative Whig-Republicans (particularly Henry Raymond, the editor of the *New York Times,* in which Olmsted's work first appeared) as well as Garrison and other reformers. Olmsted based his commentaries on personal observations made during extensive tours of the South ranging from the Atlantic seaboard to the Texas frontier. The immediate impact of his experiences, together with his consistent concern with the relationship between order and efficiency in the South's productive enterprises, lent particular authority to his work. Olmsted's accounts were written first as installments for the *Times* and then collected and expanded into three lengthy books and finally condensed into a single volume, *The Cotton Kingdom* (1861), dedicated to John Stuart Mill and to "the cause of moral and political freedom" in America.[16]

Although Olmsted came to regard his work as a systematic indictment of slavery, he undertook his southern journeys as an adventure consistent with his still youthful eagerness for experience in the world and for the means to make his mark in it. With a restlessness characteristic of his generation, Olmsted had already sailed before the mast to China, traveled widely in Europe and Britain, and published modestly successful accounts of his adventures. In his late twenties, he had turned his attention to scientific farming—his letters to the *Times* from the South would bear the signature "Yeoman"—and wrote enthusiastically on the techniques and virtues of efficient husbandry. While still engaged in his writings on the South, Olmsted assumed principal responsibility for the design and construction of New York's Central Park. Later, as general secretary of the United States Sanitary

Commission during the Civil War, Olmsted applied his administrative and organizational talents to the care of sick and wounded Union soldiers. In the postwar era, he secured a lasting reputation as America's leading landscape architect.[17] The range of his activities and interest contributed to the comprehensive character of his writings on slavery and to their success as an expression of northern utilitarian values.

Although Olmsted cannot be termed an abolitionist or an anti-slavery reformer, his circle of friends and acquaintances included both groups, and he clearly absorbed much of the progressive spirit of the age. Yet his penchant for detachment kept him apart from the era's causes. He remained skeptical of his generation's enthusiasm for moral certitude and cast a suspicious eye as well on claims of political principle. ("Reason," he insisted, "has mighty little to do with politics.") He judged his own loyalty to conservative Whig values to be based on nothing more lofty than a distaste for the "pretended" laissez-faire principles of a "besotted" Democratic "Loco Focoism." Because Whigs and Republicans paid lip service to the virtues of order in public affairs in their protectionist policies and in the sponsorship of internal improvements, and the Democracy did not, the former received Olmsted's support.[18]

Despite his personal quest for objectivity and his tendency to observe the political and social transformation of his era with scientific detachment, Olmsted's practical nature grew increasingly impatient with slavery. "I most want to have a talk with you about Abolitionism &c.," he confided to a friend in 1847. "I never have discussd or spoken upon the subject with a single man," he continued, "but I keep thinking occasionally and I don't know but I am growing into an Abolitionist." Encouraged by Raymond to travel through the slave states and report his observations on southern life and labor for the *Times,* Olmsted began the task with a well-developed sense of the proper methods of husbandry and with corresponding doubts about the efficiency and productivity of slave labor. Olmsted's accounts of southern life attracted a wide readership in the 1850s largely because he took care to construct a portrait of the South that satisfied the already firm northern conviction that the moral and economic defenses of slavery could not bear close scrutiny. At the same time, in sharp contrast to the polemical tone of earlier abolitionist literature, Olmsted wrote in a tolerant and inquisitive style. He appeared to portray the slave South with understanding, free of the outraged sentiment that animated abolitionism. The effect, following two decades of abolitionist agitation, was striking. After reading *A Journey in the Back Country* (1860), the last of Olmsted's trilogy, the antislavery essayist George William Curtis (soon to be the influential editor of *Harper's Weekly*) joined the chorus of praise. Curtis thought that Olmsted's volume "shows conclusively what a blight slavery is," although he thought that it suggested as well "how difficult and distant the remedy seems to be."[19]

With the outbreak of the Civil War, when the remedy for slavery's blighting effects seemed difficult but no longer quite so distant, Olmsted issued *The Cotton Kingdom* with the editorial assistance of Daniel Goodloe, now editor (following Gamaliel Bailey's death) of the *National Era*. Goodloe hoped to retain as much as possible of Olmsted's economic focus and especially admired *A Journey in the Seaboard Slave States, with Remarks on Their Economy*, the first of Olmsted's volumes, published in 1856. "I have thus far found scarcely a page which could be dropped without injury to the picture you give of the South," Goodloe wrote Olmsted in 1861. Despite his praise for Olmsted's insights, Goodloe proposed (unsuccessfully) to add an extensive introduction to *The Cotton Kingdom* for the purpose of recasting Olmsted's recurring perception—derived from Carey and Mill—of the inefficiency of slave labor. Goodloe wanted to present Olmsted's material in *The Cotton Kingdom* in a way that sustained his own contention that it was the unproductive concentration of wealth in slave property (not the inefficiency of slave labor) that retarded progress in the South. Denied a lengthy introduction, Goodloe nevertheless approached his task as editor with the conviction that Olmsted's observations offered an "implicit illustration" of his own economic arguments.[20]

In the chapter entitled "Slavery in Its Property Aspect," adapted from *A Journey in the Back Country*, Olmsted's observations and Goodloe's editorship combined to demonstrate that slavery, even at its most efficient and profitable, could only degrade labor and those associated with it. The chapter is particularly noteworthy for its description of the severe flogging of a slave girl, the only example of extreme cruelty witnessed by Olmsted during his southern tours and the only discussion in his writings of what abolitionists earlier decried as the true nature of slavery. Neither Olmsted nor Goodloe intended to revert to the sentimental abolitionist appeals of the 1830s. Rather, they focused on the lash as the authoritarian essence of slavery. It was not the regimentation of the slave's labor, the close supervision of the overseer, the long hours of labor, or the physical condition of the slave that rendered slavery barbarous. Instead, the necessity of the lash and the related spirit of domination and submission made slavery far too frightening a spectacle to persist alongside the new forces of regimentation and discipline taking hold in the industrializing North.[21]

As always, Olmsted chose his scene carefully. He isolated the property aspect of slavery by considering the operation of the "most profitable" plantation he had visited in the South. On such large plantations, Olmsted insisted, slaves were treated most consistently "as mere property, and in accordance with a policy calculated to insure the largest pecuniary returns." Here he found an ideal arena in which to test the proslavery proposition that slavery as an industrial system was morally superior to free labor. Olmsted observed at the outset that in some respects large plantations functioned like northern factories. The large plantations enjoyed "advantages which are possessed equally by large manufacturing establishments in which free laborers are brought together and employed in the most effective manner." Indeed, Olmsted assumed that small cotton plantations were doomed to extinction "for the same reason that hand-loom weaving has become unusual in the farm houses of Massachusetts." That these large plantations "pay a much larger percentage on the capital invested in them than smaller ones" was the "only plausible economical defense of slavery." On the large plantation which Olmsted described, there existed none of the squalor and mean-spiritedness he had found and earlier described elsewhere in the South. Here he found tidy buildings, well-tended crops, a manager who "was himself a gentleman of good education, generous and poetic in temperament." Olmsted described the overseers in terms northerners associated with Yankee merchants— they were "frank, honest, temperate, and industrious" men. The physical needs of the slaves were well provided for. Most blacks lived in "well built cottages," kept their own chickens and pigs, tended their own vegetable gardens, and trapped a good deal of game for the master's and their own tables.[22] Yet it was on this prosperous, well-managed, orderly plantation that Olmsted recorded an episode of cruelty (which Goodloe retained in its entirety) that brought his readers face to face with slavery's blighting effects.

After publishing it in the *Times* in 1853, Olmsted expanded his account of the violent episode and in *A Journey in the Back Country* made it the center of his analysis of the property aspect of slavery. In the expanded account, Olmsted described a cotton plantation located on "a tributary of the Mississippi" and recalled that he had toured the estate in the company of an overseer and a "young gentleman of fifteen." Traversing the plantation on horseback, Olmsted's party descended into a deep ravine and suddenly came upon a slave girl hiding in the bushes. The overseer questioned the girl briefly, judged her excuses for being away from work false, dismounted, and "struck her thirty or forty blows across the shoulders with his tough, flexible, 'rawhide' whip." The overseer again questioned the girl and, hearing the same excuses, ordered her bluntly: "Pull up your clothes,—lie down." The girl, whom Olmsted judged to be eighteen years old, unhesitatingly obeyed, and the overseer proceeded to beat her with his whip "across her naked loins and thighs." Olmsted described the overseer's face as "passionless," "grim," and "business-like." And the young gentleman of fifteen, with the girl "writhing, grovelling, and screaming" before him, exhibited "an expression only of impatience at the delay." Olmsted's passions were inflamed. Although he concealed his reaction, the scene was more than he could bear, and he spurred his horse ahead: "We plunged into the bushes and scrambled fiercely up the steep aclivity. The screaming yells and the whip strokes ceased when I reached the top of the bank. Choking, sobbing, spasmodic groans only were heard. . . . My companion met me there, and immediately afterward the overseer. He laughed as he joined us, and said: 'She meant to cheat me out of a day's work and she has done it too.'" [23]

In *The Cotton Kingdom,* Goodloe framed the description of the beating with two short but significant passages. The first suggested that Olmsted observed this plantation with particular care: "I do not compare it with others noticed in this chapter, my observations of which were too superficial to warrant a comparison." The second passage, inserted at the close of the account, explored the meaning of the event. The flogging had been a "red-hot experience for me," Olmsted's narrative continued. The memory of it remained "a fearful thing." Precisely why his moral sensibilities should have been aroused so furiously also concerned him. He understood that physical punishment was common on southern plantations, and he had witnessed milder examples of such discipline earlier in his travels without such unsettling effects. Indeed, the narrator reasoned, "accepting the position of the overseer, I knew that this method was right." It was the correctness of the overseer's behavior, together with the reaction of his young companion—a "delicate and ingenuous lad," who had not betrayed "the slightest flush of shame"—that demanded attention. This, together with Olmsted's effort at the time to suppress "the least expression of feeling of any kind," supported the conclusion that southern whites could not "retain the most essential quality of true manhood" while they were subjected repeatedly to such casual violence. In such a world, elevating moral instincts were stifled. And if, on the most prosperous and well-managed of plantations, labor must be so brutalized, the managers of that labor must themselves be rendered brutes from contact with what Olmsted earlier described as "a hopelessly low and immoral class."[24]

It was the lash, then, and not the overseer's decision to use it, that made slavery in its property aspect fundamentally abhorrent. In this expression of antislavery principle, Olmsted and Goodloe offered conservative northern Whigs a means of transcending the narrow calculation of profit and production that dominated the thinking of the Cotton Whigs.[25] In this context, Wendell Phillips anticipated the tendency of antislavery reform when he observed in his introduction to the first edition of Frederick Douglass's *Narrative* (1845) that Douglass's account of his servitude demonstrated the true "wretchedness of the slave, not by his hunger or want, not by his lashes and toil, but by the cruel and blighting death which gathers over his soul." It was not by measuring the material condition of the slave or the relative efficiency of slave labor that one properly passed judgment on slavery: "Those who stare at the half-peck of corn a week, and love to count the lashes on the slave's back are seldom the 'stuff' out of which reformers and abolitionists are to be made. . . . A man must be disposed to judge of emancipation by other tests than whether it has increased the production of sugar,—and hate slavery, for other reasons than because it starves men and whips women,—before he is ready to lay the first stone of his antislavery life."[26] Olmsted's sensitivity to the "essential quality of true manhood" echoed Phillips's concern with slavery's "blighting death." From both perspectives, there was nothing wrong with the operation of the slave system if the goal was to maximize profits and production for planters. Coercion and brutality worked on this level, but slavery's productive capacity required a degree of domination and obedience which the liberal North, emphasizing the incentives of freedom and the ameliorating effects of autonomy and self-control, fundamentally opposed. The image from which Olmsted and his readers shrank in his portrayal of plantation discipline was one of authoritarianism.[27]

Allied with liberal fears of authoritarianism were reformist warnings that the slaveholders and their northern supporters—the cotton merchants and textile manufacturers—might strengthen their alliance in the face of antislavery attacks and establish a brutal despotism in industrializing America. For some enemies of slavery, such an alliance already seemed to exist. As one abolitionist put it, "the Wealth of the South and the Wealth of the North are combined to crush the liberal, free, progressive spirit of the age." Olmsted offered a similar warning in a chapter of *The Cotton Kingdom* titled "The Danger of the South." If the "capitalists of labour" in the South were to gain the national economic and political security which their regime required, they would reverse the last fifty years of "Northern history" and impose slavery on workingmen in the North. In the face of such an aggressive slave power, warned the antislavery journalist James S. Pike (whose liberal fears later produced a famous denunciation of Reconstruction in South Carolina), "the war of freedom has to be a war against centralization and against federal power."[28]

The revival in the 1850s of discussions concerning compensation reflected similar antislavery concerns about the economic consequences of emancipation. During the 1850s, the antislavery Whig leader William H. Seward frequently spoke of the virtues of compensation. Still intent on maintaining the Whig organization as the anti-Democratic party of northern principles, Seward urged that the proceeds of western land sales be devoted to compensation of southern masters so that America's greatest asset could offset its greatest liability.[29] Seward was not alone. Daniel Goodloe, notwithstanding his argument that emancipation destroyed no value, supported compensation to avoid social dislocation. Compensation would maintain the planters as the capitalists of the South and permit them to lead their section out of economic stagnation. When Congress approved compensated emancipation for the District of Columbia in 1862, President Lincoln appointed Goodloe chairman of the commission charged with administering the bill's provisions. Within the maximum average value of three hundred dollars set by Congress, and with a Baltimore slave dealer employed to set market values, Goodloe was to "appraise and apportion" the relative value of slave property, a task he undertook with the intention of arriving at a classification of the slaves according to their "intrinsic utility to their owners." Shortly before the passage of the District's emancipation act, Chase (then secretary of the treasury) commented that the great danger of compensation was that the valuation might be set too high. Like Goodloe, Chase noted that slaveholders would continue to profit from the labor of their former slaves even when they had lost title to them as property. And because Chase believed that with the stimulus of freedom the former slave's labor would be "more valuable than before," he worried lest emancipation increase the wealth and power of the planter class.[30]

Although Chase later concurred with Goodloe's cautious approach to compensation, he saw nothing but danger in Seward's proposals. As early as 1850, he predicted that slaveholders themselves would shortly acknowledge the inevitability of emancipation, seek a firmer alliance with northern business, and demand compensation for their investment in slave property. "In this," Chase added, "they will probably have the sympathy of the capitalists who always favor the creation of a national debt."[31] In Chase's mind, Seward's call for compensation portended continued life for the long-standing alliance of northern business and southern planters, an alliance he believed to be the heart of Whiggery. Chase feared that Seward's fondness for compensation would breathe new life into the old Whig party. "Seward's scheme is antislavery movement begun, carried forward and finished in the Whig Party and by a series of Whig measures," wrote Chase. "He would like to connect a scheme for emancipation with a scheme for a high Tarriff," Chase continued, "founded upon the creation of an immense National debt for the means of purchasing the slaves from their masters." Such a scheme would make free men "slaves of capitalism" and turn the emancipated slaves "into paupers."[32]

Chase predicted that "the influences of capital in the Whig party, and of that conservatism which is the offspring of capital, will forever prevent the Whig Party from adopting a consistent line of action in opposition to the pretensions of Slavery." The divorce doctrine assumed greater importance, he thought, as a means of preventing an alliance of "Capital in mills and shops and stocks and Capital in men[,] women and children." The day was swiftly "drawing on" when slavery would cease. As Americans considered the means by which emancipation would occur, "the difference between the Whig & Democratic view is likely to be as great as it is in respect to any question of finance or trade."[33]

The necessity of emancipation did not dictate the terms or the pace of social progress in the South. Similarly, liberal sensitivity to the authoritarian character of slavery did not resolve long-standing antislavery concerns with the consequences of emancipation and the future of the freedmen. If slavery could only debase slaves and masters, reformers wondered what they might expect of slaves without masters and of masters without slaves. Olmsted offered his conservative judgments in this regard when he observed in 1860 that he did not expect former slaves "in one generation or two" to overcome the "effects of centuries of barbarism and slavery." He thought progress could be achieved after "an intermediate period of systematic pupilage, restraint, and encouragement." Whether progress was swift or slow, however, it rested "on these accepted facts": "that a negro's capacities, like a horse's, or a dog's, or a white man's, for all industrial purposes, including cotton-growing and cotton-picking, must be enlarged by a voluntary, self-restrained, self-urged, and self-directed exercise of those capacities."[34]

Reformers had wrestled with these issues for some time. Opponents of emancipation traditionally complained that blacks would not labor as freedmen and that emancipation in the absence of colonization would fasten upon the nation a class of dangerous vagabonds and paupers—a class potentially as dangerous to the North as to the South. Opponents of slavery traditionally responded, in the manner of Henry C. Carey and Olmsted among others, with projections of a gradual transition from slavery to an independent peasantry tied to the planters by bonds of paternalism and by economic necessity. As early as 1762, the Philadelphia abolitionist Anthony Benezet suggested that following emancipation small tracts of land could be set aside for the former slaves. Freedmen not hired by planters would thereby maintain themselves. At the same time, "both Planters and Tradesmen would be plentifully supplied with chearful and willing-minded Labourers . . . [and] the Produce of the Country greatly encreased."[35] The American Convention of Abolition Societies endorsed a similar plan in 1821 when it pondered the question, "What are the means by which this evil slavery is to be removed consistently with the safety of the master and the happiness of the slave?" The answer the convention agreed upon required that "the slaves be attached to the soil." With "an interest in the land they cultivate," the southern slave would be put in the position of the serfs of Russia. In the convention's plan, each slave family would rent a cottage and a small parcel of land from the master. Slaves would then work for wages, with deductions for maintenance and for the time they devoted to the cultivation of their plots. Finally, with the introduction of "wise and salutary laws" to provide education and to prohibit harsh treatment or removal outside of the master's community, a new generation of freedmen would emerge.[36]

In certain respects, agitation for immediate abolitionism during the 1830s temporarily diverted attention from the future of the freedmen by eschewing discussions of detail and denouncing slavery purely and simply as sin. For some abolitionists, freedom meant individual autonomy and nothing more. "Loose the cord that binds the slave," observed Parker Pillsbury, and the details of the freedmen's existence would sort themselves out "in parallel with the curves and circles of the moral universe."[37] But for those who concerned themselves with the political economy of slavery and focused their attention on the proper relationship between capital and labor, the future of the freedmen continued to be a matter of genuine interest. In 1831, the elder Theodore Sedgwick outlined the consequences he foresaw of an immediate shift from slavery to freedom. Because the slaves already produced enough to support themselves as well as a substantial surplus for their masters, Sedgwick considered it absurd to contend that they could not support themselves "with the stimulus of liberty." Moreover, assuming that emancipation would be immediate and without direct compensation to the masters—or "allotment of lands" for the freedmen—Sedgwick concluded that "the present masters or employers of slaves would probably continue to employ them after they were emancipated." In short, "wages would be substituted for maintenance," and the former slaves would contract to labor for their former masters: "The natural course of things would be for the proprietors of estates or their agents, to make contracts with the negroes who were already tenants upon their estates."[38] Similarly, in Garrison's draft of the "Declaration of Sentiments" of the American Anti-Slavery Convention in December 1833, abolitionists generally linked opposition to compensation for masters with the observation that the former slaves would continue to labor for the planters. "Emancipation would only destroy nominal, not real property," Garrison wrote. "It would not amputate a limb or break a bone of the slaves, but by infusing motives into their breasts, would make them doubly valuable to the masters as free laborers."[39]

During the 1840s, Joshua Leavitt, Salmon P. Chase, and Gamaliel Bailey tied these projections to their efforts to divorce the national government from the interests of the slave power. The fundamental problem with American civil government, Leavitt argued in 1840, was its attempt "to make slave labor and free labor prosper under the same policy," which seemed to him to be "just as absurd as perpetual motion." Slavery, he insisted, "adds nothing to the wealth of the country, but is a continual tax upon the products of free industry."[40] The fruits of slavery, Chase added in his influential *Address of the Southern and Western Liberty Convention* (1845), impoverished the South and weakened the nation. Each of the negative effects slavery produced implied expectations for the future of the blacks after emancipation. If slavery prevented public education, paralyzed industry and enterprise, corrupted religion, and destroyed morality, its eradication would mark the beginning of a steady progress in the virtue, intelligence, and industry of the South. In short, the characterization of slavery as an excrescence upon the body politic carried with it the assumption that with emancipation former slaves and slaveholders would shed their distinctiveness and become elements in the general interaction between labor and capital.[41]

Eli Thayer's Virginia colonization project offered an ambitious antebellum expression of this progressive faith as well as a model for wartime and Reconstruction "experiments" in free labor. Active in the New England Immigrant Aid Society's efforts to people Kansas with antislavery settlers, Thayer soon embraced a wider field of labor. He turned from Kansas to Virginia, where his North American Immigrant Aid and Homestead Company proposed to settle New England farmers in slave states, introduce the wage system, and "exterminate slavery on this continent in less than twenty years." "The slave power," Thayer proclaimed confidently "has no strength to control against a monied organization which will be sure to pay its stockholders twenty percent per annum."[42] The pursuit of business and liberty, as Wendell Phillips predicted, rang the death knell of slavery.

The True Interests of the Freedmen

ANTISLAVERY reformers' expectations for the future of the freedmen reflected a developing distinction between the public and private spheres of middle-class social consciousness. The utilitarian focus of antislavery reform effectively distinguished a private sphere of social welfare and missionary activity from public discussions of the proper and productive relationship between capital and labor. In the late nineteenth century, the tender moral sentiments and romantic yearnings for perfection that once swelled the hearts of reformers, raised them above the constraints of tradition, and placed them at the vanguard of progress persisted as private expressions of domestic virtue and good works. In the dominant public sphere, by contrast, competition reigned and individual success belonged to those whose vigor, determination, and will prevailed. Reviewing the progress of the century in his 1893 Phi Beta Kappa address at Harvard College, the political economist Francis A. Walker—son of the political economist and abolitionist Amasa Walker—celebrated the competitive spirit of the age and welcomed "the vast change in popular sentiments and ideals" that brought it to the fore. A Union officer during the Civil War, the younger Walker returned to academic life (as professor of political economy at Yale and, later, as president of Massachusetts Institute of Technology) convinced that the discipline of war had foreever subordinated "the transcendentalism and sentimentalism" of the early nineteenth century to the "strength of will, firmness of purpose, resolution to endure, and capacity for action" that shaped the public character and guided public conduct in the late nineteenth-century.[1]

To Francis Walker, the transcendentalism and sentimentalism of his father's generation seemed inappropriate to the public challenges of the new industrial age. Certainly the aggressiveness with which the younger Walker praised competition stood in contrast to the transcendental "yearnings," "aspirations," and "intellectuality" which he mocked. But the moral concerns of antebellum reform had not simply evaporated in the heat of war. As Amasa Walker explained in *The Science of Wealth*, first published in 1866, the science of political economy refused to look at any question "in a purely moral light," and yet moral sentiments were never "widely or permanently" separated from its concerns: "Political economy has for its end the common good of society on the whole, and in the long-run." Utilitarianism, then, defined morality, and Amasa Walker transferred earlier perfectionist quests for a moral social order to the "domain of sociology." Francis Walker did not break with his father's social and intellectual concerns; he simply extended them. But the ridicule he heaped on transcendentalism and sentimentalism clearly intended to turn his father's enthusiasm into an orthodoxy. Francis Walker told the young men of Harvard to dismiss as silliness an era of ethereal and sometimes radical musings in which men of his father's stamp unequivocally rejected the inequalities of the past and sometimes projected an equality of condition for the future.[2]

Walker spoke at the end of an era, at a time when the radical individualism and perfectionist tendencies that had once prompted reformers to resist the authority of the state had come to define the legitimacy of the new order or to find expression in private efforts to guide, instruct, and uplift meek and suffering humanity. As the abolitionists themselves displayed in their almost universal acceptance of state violence to preserve the Union, it was not a theory of state power which the reformers opposed but its antebellum applications. Abolitionists, too, valued the capacity for action, and a spirit of martyrdom consistently brought them into conflict with the state. This was Wendell Phillips's point when he linked William Leggett and John Brown in a common pursuit of the "democratic principle." It was William Lloyd Garrison's point when he damned the "mere animal indulgence" of conventional patriotism and called on men to imitate the heroism of the Revolution. But as soon as the secession of the slave states made it possible to invoke state powers to maximize individual autonomy and the liberty to pursue material gain, reformers acted with all of the energy and determination of Francis Walker's ideal man of action. The Civil War, with its capacity to free the national state from the corrupting influence of slavery, brought the abolitionists' martyr spirit to the defense of the Union. "War is indeed terrible," Garrison conceded to Phillips in April 1861 as Massachusetts troops rushed to answer President Lincoln's call to arms. The fate of a sinful nation continued to rest with a just God. Nevertheless, Garrison cheered the North's willingness to defend "'the Union and the Constitution.'" "I do not hesitate, non-resistant as I am, to say, that I am glad to witness this uprising of the Northern people." "I am glad," Garrison concluded, that the North joined the conflict "with at least all the courage and manliness that pertain to war." Lydia Maria Child concurred, rejoicing that "the spirit of our fathers is not quite dead, as I have sometimes feared."[3]

Reformers welcomed and encouraged the North's war spirit, but they were aware as well of an absence of moral concern in the popular will to fight down the rebellion. The Garrisonian abolitionist Lydia Maria Child lamented after nearly a year of war that the "entire absence of a moral sense" in the war effort threatened to rob the war, and even wartime emancipation, of any significance: "Even should they be emancipated, merely as a 'war necessity,' everything *must* go wrong, if there is no heart or conscience on the subject." The conservative antislavery essayist George William Curtis concurred. Writing to fellow conservative Charles Eliot Norton in 1861, Curtis observed that "there is very little moral mixture in the 'anti-slavery' feeling of this country." Beyond "abstract philanthropy" (by which he seemed to refer to the philanthropy of traditional churchmen, uninformed by principles of political economy), Curtis ascribed northern antislavery sentiments to a popular "hatred of slaveholders" and a "jealousy for white labor." "Very little," he concluded, "is consciousness of wrong done and the wish to right it." As the Republican party expanded its political base in the North during the war, Curtis thought that it appealed to "all mankind except the abolitionists." As always, in Curtis's view, advances in public morality came from the direction and example of a cultivated elite. A veteran of two years at Brook Farm during the 1840s and a respected journalist throughout the last half of the nineteenth century, Curtis propounded social views that combined the pensive elitism of transcendentalism with the staid realism of New England Federalism to produce a public demeanor familiar in late nineteenth-century liberalism. As Curtis explained in his 1856 address to Connecticut's Wesleyan University, it was the duty of educated citizens—men and women of refined moral sensibilities—to elevate politics above the corrupting influence of the masses. He later identified women's suffrage and civil service reform as two means of doing so. As for the moral issues embedded in the Civil War, Curtis saw vast new fields of labor open before him, particularly among the freedmen of the South. With other reformers, he took an active role in the New York City Port Royal Relief Commission to relieve the suffering and improve the moral condition of the former slaves under federal control in the South Carolina sea islands. The work of moral reform continued, not in confrontation with the authority of the state or with the laws of political economy but among those—as one reformer described the "contraband" in his care—whose "docile and affectionate" natures seemed to welcome and to benefit from the vigor, thrift, and industry of "Saxon . . . civilization."[4]

As Lydia Maria Child demonstrated with striking clarity, the increasingly female-centered sphere of moral sentiment and domestic guidance reinforced the utilitarian principles of political economy that defined public discussions of land, labor, and production in the postemancipation South. The daughter of a "mechanic" and the wife of a socially prominent lawyer, David Lee Child (a Garrisonian and a Whig), Lydia Maria Child wrote extensively on the wrongs of slavery and the wisdom of emancipation. Yet her success as an author rested on the popularity of *The Frugal Housewife*, which appeared in thirty-five editions between 1829 and 1870, and *The Mother's Book*, which she published in six editions between 1831 and 1846. Somewhat earlier, Child launched the *Juvenile Miscellany* (published between 1826 and 1834), a journal which John Greenleaf Whittier credited with being "probably the first periodical in the English tongue devoted exclusively to children." In the same style, and with similar motives, Child published *The Freedmen's Book* in 1865 to instruct the former slaves through the elevating example of exemplary black men and women. "It is intended to encourage, stimulate, and instruct them," she wrote privately shortly after the volume appeared. To do so, she took care "to have everything very simple, clear, and condensed for them."[5]

Child's concern with domestic life and with public policy regarding free labor rested on perceptions of class relations derived from her celebration of middle-class values. Child addressed *The Frugal Housewife* and *The Mother's Book* to women of the "middling class," who, if sales of the volumes provided an accurate measure, welcomed advice on methods of maintaining respectable households within modest means. Child identified individual virtue and self-restraint as essential elements of domestic life, particularly in the rearing of children. Accordingly, *The Mother's Book* advised women to guide their children—as Child would later seek to guide the freedmen—through an unseen influence emanating from a pure "heart and conscience" and from the suppression of passions. "The first rule and the most important of all, in education," Child wrote, "is, that a mother govern her own feelings." In "developing good affections in a child," therefore, it was essential that the child "never be allowed to see or feel the influence of bad passions even in the most trifling things." To this end, Child admonished her readers, "you must divorce evil passions out of your own heart."[6]

The elevating influence of good example extended to missionary efforts as well, and Child drafted *The Freedmen's Book* to facilitate this good work. Child pursued moral reform out of sympathy for the "wronged and weak" but also in pursuit of broadened domestic influence for women and a broadened social influence for the middle class generally. In her understanding of class relations, Child defined a middle class composed of "farmers and mechanics," those "who work with their *hands* [and] own a house." By "mechanics" she meant shopkeepers and small manufacturers (her father, whom she called a mechanic, had been a baker) as well as artisans. Most important, Child perceived no significant barriers, social or economic, dividing this middle class from the "genteel" class, which she defined as those whose wealth permitted them to live "in mansions of their own," freed of daily concerns with business and production. Child intended her explorations of domesticity to help middle-class women assert and expand a moral influence in their families. A principal goal of this influence was to enhance those elements of social intercourse (most notably marriage) that linked the middle and genteel classes. As for the laboring class, which Child defined as those who owned no property and, consequently, "subsist upon the proceeds of their labor upon the premises of other people," Child perceived a growing economic and social chasm insulating them from the middle and genteel classes. Child did not welcome this class distinction, but by the late 1870s, she viewed "an increasing tendency toward a strong *demarcation of classes* in this country" as a social reality that cut across racial and ethnic lines. Indeed, she took it to be a universal tendency among all who acquired property—the Negro "'furst families'" and the Irish "shop-keeper, or provision-dealer," as well as the native white middle class—to shun social ties, especially marriage, with the laboring class.[7]

The social distance which Child perceived between the laboring class and the middle and genteel classes paralleled and reinforced the distinction between private moral sentiments and the utilitarian principles that guided public discussions of the conditions and rewards of labor. Like most reformers, Child repeatedly proclaimed herself to be "warmly" in sympathy with the strivings of workingmen, and she looked forward to *"co-partnerships"* that would promote a harmony of interests between workingmen and their employers. A similar sympathy encouraged middle-class reformers in the antebellum decades to support the ten-hour-day movement as a moral reform akin to child labor laws, which, collectively, enchanced the influence of family, church, and school. There were demurs, particularly from conservative Whigs, including William Schouler, who headed a committee appointed by the Massachusetts legislature in 1845 to report on the feasibility of a ten-hour law. Labor needed no special protective legislation, Schouler's committee reported. "Labor in Massachusetts is on an equality with capital and indeed controls it," the committee concluded. "Labor is intelligent enough to make its own bargains." Although Child remained silent on the ten-hour issue, a number of reformers—most notably Henry Wilson and Amasa Walker in Massachusetts—sided with the workingmen. In the postwar struggle for the eight-hour day, however, reformist sympathy divided sharply.[8] George Washington Julian and Wendell Phillips supported the eight-hour movement, but Lydia Maria Child joined with a growing number of reformers who now concurred with Schouler that workers must be left free to bargain as individuals for the duration and compensation of their labor. Thus Child denounced proposals for an eight-hour day as "utterly impracticable" because they would lower profits and, inevitably, wages as well. If such legislation could be secured, Child wrote Charles Sumner in 1870, it "would prove very injurious to employers, without securing any real benefits to the employed." Matters of trade, currency, "and the relations of labor and capital, ought to be left free to find their own level," she concluded. A year later, writing to Julian, Child insisted even more forcefully on the importance of allowing the law of supply and demand to determine hours and wages: "For one party to bargain to fix his own price on what he has to sell, and to fix it above the market value, and to attempt to compel the other party, by *legal force*, to pay it, seems to me to have an element of tyranny in it. . . . There is an eternal law of supply and demand, by which [labor] *will* keep returning to their level, whatever may be done to prevent it."[9]

The principle that utilitarian considerations alone determined the

proper relationship between capital and labor applied to the freedmen of the South as well as to the workingmen of the North. In December 1862, anticipating the promulgation of the promised Emancipation Proclamation, Massachusetts's abolitionist governor, John A.
Andrew, observed that "we are now working out of the sentimental
and political periods of the history of Anti-Slavery effort." The justice
and practicality of emancipation no longer required demonstration.
All that remained to be settled was the best method of restoring the
productivity of capital and labor in the South:

> The main question—to which all others is tributary—is How to
> establish in the best way,—as a practical matter—just and nor-
> mal relations between the labor of so many poor men without
> capital and so much capital needing laborers to render it pro-
> ductive. This economical question,—regarding it from the point
> of view of mankind . . . is How shall these poor laborers, con-
> tribute to the production of wealth to mankind. Any just solu-
> tion of this question is the best for the owners of the land and
> the capitalists who possess the floating resources.[10]

As a general proposition, reformers agreed that the eradication of
slavery permitted free market relations to operate in the South. No
one asserted this proposition with more confidence than the antislavery political economist Daniel R. Goodloe. "The destruction of
slavery," Goodloe explained at the close of the war, "forever dissolved
[the] common interests" that bound slaveholders together as a class.
Because "the whole structure of southern society was founded on slavery," emancipation produced "a revolution more complete and radical
than any of which history furnishes a record." Goodloe acknowledged,
and reformers generally concurred, that successful reconstruction required the suppression of the old slaveholding spirit. Goodloe also acknowledged (as he had not in his antebellum discussions of the transition to free labor) that it was only "human" for the former slaves to
"indulge in a protracted holiday" immediately following emancipation. But Goodloe believed that this period of dislocation would be
brief and that the benefits of freedom which he had detailed in his
antebellum writings would quickly become clear to all. With blacks
freed of slavery's restraints, "all of the nobler impulses" of labor—the
"desires and hopes, and aspirations for knowledge, for wealth and
power [which] are illimitable"—would induce the freedmen to labor

reliably and productively for wages. "The negroes," Goodloe concluded "will become an industrious, thrifty, and law-abiding people, eminently docile, and emulous of improvement." Once the planters received the truth that capital invested in slaves was wasted because it was unnecessary, they too would prosper as employers of free labor, even if they remained utterly "blind . . . to the moral wrong of slavery." Confident that the "great economical problem" which emancipation posed subsumed the long-standing abolitionist concern with the "conscience and morals" of the slaveholders, Goodloe endeavored to allay reformist fears about the slaveholders' lingering prejudices. Goodloe characterized the planters as efficient and productive managers of land and labor whose desire to make money and grow rich was as well developed as that of any northern capitalist. "Now that slavery is overthrown," Goodloe concluded, the former masters "will exert their energies in methods promotive of the general as well as of their own particular welfare."[11]

Goodloe spoke for all reformers when he projected the triumph of free labor relations in the postemancipation South. But not all reformers were as quick as he to lay their moral concerns aside in the public discussion of labor relations. Indeed, because the transition to free labor occurred amid what Goodloe described as the "derangement and disorganization" produced by civil war, many reformers were less than certain that the spirit of masterdom and the habits of subservience died with the institution of slavery. The Philadelphia abolitionist William Henry Furness expressed a common reformist concern (a concern particularly strong among Garrisonians like himself) when he voiced his fear that former masters accepted only the necessity rather than the virtue of emancipation. A "voluntary" abolition of slavery by the slaveholders would have been preferable because it "would have been preceded by the destruction of the prejudices by which it was supported." This, of course, had been the original aim of the abolitionists' moral appeal. As it happened, however, slavery had been "swept away by events, and of course it has left its roots behind."[12]

With similar concern, reformers scrutinized the attitudes of the freedmen themselves. Their doubts about the ability of the freedmen swiftly to shed the habits of slavery were not new. In 1836 and again in 1862, for example, Lydia Maria Child reviewed for her American audience the experience of emancipation in the British West Indies.[13] Despite the difficulties that she acknowledged to exist in Jamaica, where freedmen in substantial numbers withdrew their labor from the sugar plantations, Child dismissed as groundless the contention that blacks would not labor productively as freedmen in America. It was the "clumsy apprentice system" (initially delaying full emancipation in Jamaica) which, in 1836, accounted for the difficulties encountered by some planters. Apprenticeships removed the "old stimulus of the whip," Child observed, without permitting "the new and better stimulus of wages." She believed that wages, however modest, inevitably elicited faithful labor: "Even the low price of a penny an hour operated like magic upon them, and inspired them to diligence." As the United States prepared for emancipation in 1862, Child continued to blame the apprentice system for Jamaica's loss of productivity, although she added that prejudice and bankruptcy among planters inhibited the payment of reliable wages after the end of the apprentice system. Without reliable wages, Child thought it was understandable that blacks preferred "to raise produce on a few acres of their own" as opposed "to working on plantations without wages." With reliable wages and a willingness among planters to rent garden plots to their laborers, both the freedmen's desire for independence and the planters' demand for labor could be met and the alienation of labor that plagued Jamaican planters would be avoided in America. "That the negroes will work, if modestly compensated, no candid man can doubt," Child concluded in 1862: "Their endurance for the sake of very little gain is quite amazing . . . and they are very desirous to provide for themselves and families as large a share as possible of the comforts and decencies of life."[14]

Child was not alone in noting the withdrawal of freed labor in Jamaica. Writing in 1842, John Jay (like Child) emphasized "the perfect safety and practicability of immediate emancipation." Labor problems, Jay believed, derived entirely from the failure of planters to provide reliable wages. "Whenever wages were regularly paid," Jay insisted, "no difficulty was found in obtaining work." Indeed, free labor exceeded slave labor in productivity when employers treated their workers fairly. Implicitly acknowledging a decline in production, however, Jay noted that "on a few plantations," where managers treated their workers "kindly and judiciously," production "far exceeded that performed in slavery." It was of particular importance to Jay that the labor "was done cheerfully."[15]

Despite the problems they recognized in Jamaica, most reformers retained their optimistic view that, ultimately, self-interest and a desire for self-improvement produced the strongest incentive to exchange leisure for labor. If white planters chose to abandon their plantations rather than adopt more enlightened methods of managing free labor, Senator Salmon Chase of Ohio saw an alluring opportunity for enterprising American black emigrants. "If I were a colored man," Chase insisted in 1850, "I would gather a colony—go to Jamaica—buy one of the deserted plantations—sugar mill and all." With the land divided among the colonists and the mill available for all, Chase thought that free labor in Jamaica could resemble free labor farming in Ohio.[16] At least obliquely, however, reformers faced the possibility that declining sugar production in Jamaica resulted not from the unenlightened response of planters but from the recalcitrance of the freedmen themselves. Thomas Carlyle, the English sage of the Romantic era, faced this issue squarely in 1849 and dramatically broke with the prevailing optimism of free labor advocates. Carlyle insisted bluntly that the progress of civilization demanded continued staple production regardless of the inclination of the laboring population. Carlyle warned that in the Caribbean, and wherever a warm climate made it easy to supply a man's basic wants, proponents of progress could not rely on the fundamental fear of hunger and cold to induce productive labor. If the wealth of the tropics were to be harnessed for the advancement of mankind, Carlyle insisted that laborers in those regions would require active supervision enforced by the state.[17]

Concerned with the withdrawal of the labor of freedmen in Jamaica and alarmed by the implications of Carlyle's response, John Bigelow visited the island in 1850 "to explain the causes of the stricken and prostrate condition of one of the most productive islands in the world." Bigelow was co-owner and coeditor with William Cullen Bryant of the *New York Evening Post,* and his advocacy of free labor and free trade aligned the *Post* with the free-soil Democracy and with the early Republican party. Bigelow blamed Jamaica's economic decline on the persisting "moral influence of slavery." As a result, white landowners held to their aristocratic ways and looked upon black laborers as degraded beings. It followed, "with the average sequence of negro logic," that the freedmen "infer that if gentlemen never work, they have only to abstain from work to be gentlemen." Although the financial fortunes of the sugar planters declined sharply after emancipation, Bigelow found that capital continued to dominate labor and that planters continued to resist "the union of capital and labor" that characterized "politico-economical conditions" among "small proprietors, so common throughout the northern part of the United States."[18]

Bigelow saw no hope for economic and social progress in Jamaica until conditions there began to encourage the emergence of a middle class, by which Bigelow (like Lydia Maria Child) meant property owners who labored. In this regard, Bigelow was surprised and pleased "to find how general was the desire among the negroes to become possessed of a little land." He noted that a small freehold of four or five acres permitted the freedmen "to live in comparative ease and independence" and, at the same time, left them free to labor for wages on the sugar plantations, which could secure their willing and reliable labor by paying adequate wages and treating them with dignity. In Bigelow's view, the steady increase in this class of "colored proprietors" disproved Carlyle's lamentable charge that in lands like Jamaica, where soil and climate sustained life with little exertion, the law of supply and demand would not prompt energetic labor. On the contrary, Bigelow protested, small landholdings permitted freedmen to "raise supplies for their immediate wants" and to produce a surplus for market. Ultimately, by the "laws of nature and of trade," Bigelow believed that these small proprietors would purchase portions of the large estates and, in some undefined manner, restore the island to its "ancient prosperity and wealth."[19]

The withdrawal of freed labor from Jamaica's sugar plantations clearly troubled American antislavery reformers although, as at least one of their number, Richard Hildreth, observed, the alleged "'ruin'" of Jamaica amounted to nothing "more dangerous than the gout." Hildreth admitted that the island's sugar planters undoubtedly found the conditions of free labor "painful." But the planters' former prosperity rested solely on their brutal exploitation of enslaved labor, and the decline in sugar production hurt no one but the former masters. "In spite of this protracted and reiterated ruin of the sugar planters," Hildreth concluded, most of the island's inhabitants "are vastly better off in every respect—socially, politically, intellectually, religiously, physically, and morally—than at any former period."[20]

More typically, however, reformers responded to the decline in sugar production in Jamaica by attempting to identify the conditions necessary for maintaining staple crop production under a free labor system. As Hildreth and Carlyle understood, a utilitarian faith in progress could not resolve the conflict between liberty and production which reformers sensed in Jamaica. Although most reformers remained unwilling to abandon their optimistic expectation that liberty and production could be harmonized through the incentive of wages and the effect of fair treatment, conditions in Jamaica certainly alerted them to the possibility that an alienation of plantation labor might accompany emancipation in the United States. Visiting a large sugar plantation in Louisiana in the 1850s, Frederick Law Olmsted noted that his planter host viewed with distaste and suspicion the neighboring Acadian farmers, who "owned small farms, on which they raised a little corn and rice." Olmsted noted that the planter "described them as lazy vagabonds, doing but little work, spending much time in shooting, fishing, and play." Whenever possible, the planter bought the Acadians' land, forced them to move away, and quickly "destroyed their houses and gardens, removed their fences and trees, and brought all their land into his cane-plantation." Explaining his actions to Olmsted, the planter insisted that the Acadians "demoralized" his slaves. The planter believed that his slaves, seeing the Acadians living in comparative comfort, sustained by very modest landholdings "and without steady labour," could not help but conclude that "if they were free they would not work."[21]

Olmsted had the opportunity to test the planter's opinion on one of his slaves, a servant named William, who drove Olmsted some twenty miles in a buggy at the end of his plantation visit. Finding the slave "inclined to be talkative and communicative," Olmsted listened carefully, asked neither leading nor intimidating questions, and recorded the conversation immediately after his ride. William talked of many things, but Olmsted directed the conversation to the slave's expectations of freedom. When Olmsted asked William what he would do if he were free, the slave replied that he would first "go to work for a year, and get some money for myself." Then he would buy "a little house, and a little lot land," marry, and "raise things in my garden, and take 'em to New Orleans, and sell 'em dar, in de market." When Olmsted's carriage passed a cluster of Acadian cottages, he tempted William to "sneer at their indolence and vagabond habits." But William refused to do so, insisting, as Olmsted reported, that the Acadians worked "as hard as they ought for their living." Olmsted warned William that freedom required everyone to take care of himself and that those who worked no more diligently than the Acadians would remain as poor as they. What would happen, Olmsted asked William, if all of the blacks suddenly were set free: "You don't suppose there would be much sugar raised, do you?" William's reply answered Olmsted's immediate concern but left him more deeply uncertain about the black man's potential response to emancipation. Blacks would continue to raise sugar, William said, because they had no choice. "De wite people own all de land—war dey goin' to work?" he asked. William said that freedmen would work harder than slaves "to get more wages." "I dont own any land," William explained, "I hab to work right away again for massa, to get some money." In the end, however, Olmsted doubted that William "would keep to his word" if the opportunity to live like the Acadians presented itself. "Such an apparent mingling of simplicity and cunning, ingenuousness and sly-ness," Olmsted concluded, "detracted much from the weight of his opinions and purposes in regard to freedom."[22]

Reformist efforts to account for the alienation of freed laborers in Jamaica, together with the broader concerns expressed by Olmsted regarding the capacity of the freedmen fully to internalize the utili-tarian work ethic, lent particular significance to the wartime discus-sion of wage scales and labor policies among the "contraband" blacks under Union control. Reformers understood that the artificial condi-tions created by war distorted market conditions and made it difficult to determine the true value of labor. Difficulties in the management of contraband labor, ranging from apparent laziness to open recalci-trance among the blacks, troubled reformers. But their conviction that emancipation created the necessary conditions for a smooth tran-sition to free labor remained firm. Union victory and reliable wages would solve all of the problems encountered during the war. The difficult task during the war was to approximate as closely as possible the postwar value of the freedmen's labor. As Secretary of the Trea-sury Chase cautioned his agent in the South Carolina sea islands early in 1862, it was important that reformers not set wages artificially high. Forty cents a day (regarded by contemporaries as the prevailing wage for agricultural labor in the North) might be too much: "We must not expend more than is absolutely necessary," Chase insisted. It was in the freedmen's interest to keep wages low rather than to make them too high, "the practical result of which will be to encourage expecta-tions which cannot be gratified in the long run."[23]

The question of wages attracted a good deal of attention during the war as federal officials tried to improve the efficiency of government-directed plantation operations. But beneath the surface of wage discussions lurked issues reformers could not easily resolve. Throughout the occupied South, federal authorities noted reluctance on the part of the freedmen to labor in the production of staple crops. Some blamed the unreliability of wages, others thought wages should be raised, still others blamed the cruelty of former masters and the greed of northern leasees. Thomas W. Conway, superintendent of freedmen in Louisiana, reported to the New York Chamber of Commerce in 1866 that "cotton will never come from the South in such quantities as our condition need until the labor that produces it has as much justice and protection as the capital which employs that labor." The reluctance or unwillingness of former masters to appreciate the virtues of free labor and to accept the responsibilities of employers plagued reformers throughout Reconstruction.[24]

So, too, did the willingness of former slaves to labor productively for wages. Touring the Mississippi Valley in 1865 at the request of Secretary of War Edwin M. Stanton, Republican Congressman John Covode noted both problems. He found a widespread unwillingness among former masters to pay wages for the labor they once commanded. Covode shared the reformers' assumption that fair wages reliably paid would secure faithful labor from the freedmen, but he also noted a strong desire on the part of the freedmen to raise livestock, together with food and fodder crops for their own consumption: "The Freedmen are willing to work at growing corn where they don't expect to be paid for their labor while the[y] are unwilling to grow cotton & sugar as they expect to get enough to eat from the former while the latter will be sold and passes out of their hands." "All things considered," Covode concluded that it would be wise for a freedman "to have a small piece of land . . . [because] it teaches him to rely on his own exertions and management." John Jay recalled the experience of planters in Jamaica and likewise recommended that blacks receive title to garden plots. The problems in Jamaica "arose from the extortional rents demanded by the old masters for the huts & gardens occupied by the slaves," Jay commented privately to Charles Sumner. To avoid this injustice and the resulting alienation of plantation labor, Jay urged Congress to "secure to every slave a few acres." In this way, the freedmen would be content to stay on or near the plantations, and, with the security of owning a garden plot added to the incentives of free labor, the "practical effect" of emancipation would be "to develop the industrial faculties of the freed slaves—& assist in the rapid procurement of cotton."[25]

The vision of the freedmen as proprietors of garden plots near the large plantations held a special appeal for antislavery reformers and constituted, in a collective sense, the single most coherent plan for agricultural reform in the postemancipation South. Elizur Wright, one of the original abolitionist supporters of Gerrit Smith's Liberty party, hoped in 1860 that North and South would adopt a "feasible scheme" for voluntary and compensated emancipation so that the destruction of slavery would be accompanied by continuity in economic relations. In Wright's view, the planters would act as the "*friend and Protector*" of the freedmen, and harmonious relations among former masters and former slaves would promote tranquillity and prosperity in the land. Specifically, Wright thought that a former master should hire the labor of his former slaves, paying wages for at least half of their time. In addition to laboring for wages, each black family would be given "the use of a truck patch and use of the cabin rent free." In this way, the planter would secure the loyal labor of his former slave, and the freedman, when not laboring for wages, would be free to "build his school house, dress out his garden, go to market & go to church and a Merciful God . . . will bless both parties." Looking back on the Reconstruction era in 1879, Lydia Maria Child blamed the planters for doing "everything to discourage and alienate" freedman labor. Under the best of circumstances, Child insisted, "it would naturally take generations for the poor dwarfed souls to develope to the size of ours." The planters had been "impolitic" as well as unfair in refusing to guide and help the freedmen "through their transition state."[26]

Wright's view on agrarian reform in the South expressed longstanding antislavery concerns with the need for equity and harmony in relations between labor and capital. Wright expressed as well a growing tension between the agrarian doctrine embraced by the antebellum Liberty party that every man enjoyed a natural right to own enough land to support himself and his family and the increasingly dominant utilitarian emphasis on the productive capacity of free labor. Agrarian doctrines proposed to free men from dependence on market relations at the same time that utilitarian values identified the discipline of the marketplace with a transcendent social morality. In their discussions of postemancipation economic and social relations in the South, reformers earnestly (albeit briefly) struggled to harmonize these diverging standards of freedom.

The notion that former slaves, as independent owners of small plots of land, would tend their gardens, build homes, schools, and churches, and also desire to hire their labor to neighboring planters had been endorsed by the American convention of Abolition Societies as early as 1821. The same idea dominated wartime land reform discussions and experiments. Francis W. Bird, Joshua Leavitt, John Jay, and John Murray Forbes, among others, offered essentially the same plan for agricultural reform in the postemancipation South. Leavitt's plan combined agricultural reform for blacks with measures designed to encourage an infusion of northern men and methods into the South. Leavitt proposed that the government offer confiscated lands as bounties to Union soldiers. Officers would receive 320 acres from the "conquered lands," company officers would get 160 acres, and privates 80 acres. Such a policy would bring to the South the "intelligence, personal influence, capital, labor &c, which are essential to prosperous society." As for the freedmen, Leavitt considered it essential that the "hope of *permanent* advantage" accompany the transition to free labor. "The problem is *not* . . . whether these negroes will work for wages," Leavitt insisted in response to the wartime discussion of the proper level of wages. "They will mostly give a fair day's work for a fair day's pay." But if reformers also hoped to demonstrate the superior productive power of free labor, they needed to generate an added enthusiasm among the freedmen. "We need all the interest & energy of labor & care & contrivance, in order to make free labor compete with slavery in the production of cotton." The ownership of land—Leavitt suggested 40 acres—would demonstrate to the blacks the utility of free labor because their own desires to acquire the resources to make their land more productive would induce them to labor for wages on the large estates.[27]

With slight variations in detail, reformers saw land reform as essential to instilling in the freedmen the incentive to labor for wages in the production of staple crops. Governor Andrew of Massachusetts remarked to Secretary Chase shortly after the issuance of the final Emancipation Proclamation that the successful reorganization of southern society required that "the freedmen shall have an interest in the soil, so that they shall become a self supporting and worthy class of citizens, and that cultivation of the great staples of that district shall be kept up by experienced hands." As one northerner involved in the sea islands experiment in free labor observed in 1862, freedmen without land lacked the security and independence upon which free labor rested. If blacks remained landless, they would be subject to "the most pressing conditions that the capitalist can lay upon the laborer." Blacks needed modest homesteads of "ten to twelve acres for each married man" to make them "independent for their mere living." Such an arrangement would leave "a portion of their labor to be accorded to whom ever will give them fair wages." When President Andrew Johnson excluded all large landowners from his first Amnesty Proclamation, Quartermaster General Montgomery Meigs expressed a similar view of land reform to Senator Sumner. The time was right, said Meigs, to make it a condition of the planters' pardon that they provide five to ten acrs of tillable land to each family of former slaves.[28]

As many of the land reform recommendations suggested, redistribution of land to blacks often seemed to require punitive confiscation of rebel estates. Some proposals of this variety were conservative in spirit and colonizationist in character. This was true of Francis P. Blair's suggestion that blacks be colonized on "vacant territories . . . protected by our flag." It was true as well of General William Tecumseh Sherman's confiscation plan for the Mississippi Valley and his famous Field Order Fifteen affecting South Carolina. In a similar vein, United States District Court Judge John C. Underwood of Virginia proposed that the cotton states of the deep South "should be set apart for the loyal colored men." Underwood would place the former slaves under the military direction of black leaders such as Frederick Douglass, transfer to them "title of the rebel lands," and permit them to organize new states for admission to the Union. A native of upstate New York, Underwood married into a Virginia family before the war and (until his free-soil and Republican views forced him to move north in the late 1850s) farmed eight hundred acres in northwestern Virginia. Returning to the state as district judge in 1864, Underwood presided over the Radical Republican constitutional convention of December 1867 and thereafter acquired several thousand acres of land. In Underwood's view, postwar land reform in the South could combine confiscation from rebel planters with racial separation. "Douglas & his people would immediately take care of the cotton states," Underwood observed, "& we white men I think would take care of the residue."[29]

Elizur Wright, who had earlier supported compensated emancipation as a means of smoothing the transition to free labor relations in the South, turned to confiscation out of frustration with the tenacity of the slaveholders' rebellion. "There is no practical way of ending this war," Wright wrote Secretary Chase, "but to single out the real foes & rebels[,] the slaveholding class[,] and let them and the world understand that not only their slaves are to be free, but their lands are to be divided among those who help conquer them." By the close of the war, Wright proposed the passage of an "agrarian law," which would not divide lands equally among all citizens but would endow "all the laborers whom slavery utterly deprived of land, with suitable Homesteads, out of the great estates which the slaveholders have forfeited" through rebellion.[30]

Other plans tied confiscation to war reparations. Thaddeus Stevens's suggestions for the wholesale confiscation and redistribution of southern estates rested on the slogan, "THE PROPERTY OF THE REBELS SHALL PAY OUR NATIONAL DEBT, *and indemnify freed-men and loyal sufferers.*" By confiscating all estates worth more than ten thousand dollars or exceeding two hundred acres, seventy thousand individual planters would be dispossessed and nearly 400 million acres together with substantial town properties would be available for sale and redistribution. Senator Charles Sumner's confiscation plans similarly linked war reparations and land bounties for soldiers with agrarian reform. Like Stevens in the House, Sumner urged "indemnity for the past and security for the future" as the principal benefits of confiscation. If the large plantations were dismantled, they would never again serve as "nurseries of conspiracy or disaffection." Divided into small estates, these lands would provide homes for the planters' "poor neighbors" as well as for the "brave soldiers who have left their northern skies" and who would, Sumner hoped, "fill the land with northern industry and northern principles." Although these plans clearly intended for the freedmen to benefit from their masters' defeat, northern investors were the obvious source of the revenue for indemnification which Stevens's and Sumner's plans proposed to raise.[31]

Strong as the desire to punish the rebel planters was, the association of confiscation with land bounties for Union soldiers and land sales for the benefit of the federal treasury raised problems for reformers who embraced agrarian reform as an expression of middle-class anti-monopoly sentiments and as a palliative for the discontents of wage earners. It had long been a cardinal principle of middle-class land reform proposals that opposition to land monopoly promoted social order and thereby protected property rights. Middle-class land reformers had long insisted that their advocacy of agrarian reform did not amount to a leveling doctrine. As Lydia Maria Child noted in praise of George Washington Julian's record as an advocate of land reform, the opponents of homestead legislation—particularly the slaveholders—characterized all reformers as "'agrarians,' 'revolutionists' and 'levelers.'" In reply, reformers such as Julian took care to emphasize the utilitarian virtues of their proposals. Julian prefaced his defense of his pioneering homestead bill in 1851 with the disclaimer that "I am no believer in the doctrines of Agrarianism or Socialism." He would not disturb "the laws of property" or "the vested rights" of citizens. His was not a "*leveling* policy" but a practical plan to make independent citizens of the propertyless poor. "Give homes to the landless multitudes," Julian argued, "and you snatch them from crime and starvation, from the prison and the almshouse. . . . Instead of paupers and outcasts, they will become independent citizens and free holders." If the availability of homesteads on public lands did not provide a safety valve for discontended wage laborers, Julian, Child, and others believed it did. Hostility to land monopoly went hand in hand with this notion of agrarian reform and interlocked firmly with antislavery reform. "Slavery only thrives on extensive estates," Julian contended. "In a country cut up into small farms, occupied by . . . independent proprietors . . . it would be impossible." Slaveholders monopolized the land and threatened to extend their monopoly into the West and thereby deprive workingmen of the opportunity to become independent farmers.[32]

At the same time, reformers generally recognized the freedmen's strong "instinct" (as John Murray Forbes put it) to own land. Although the Freedmen's Bureau Bill of March 1865 authorized the bureau to provide freedmen with small homesteads, it was well understood in reform circles that the bureau had no authority to grant the freedmen permanent title to the land. Moreover, as Forbes noted, the freedmen "do not yet find their way to the public homesteads to any extent." With former masters resolutely opposed to the "acquisition of land by Blacks—whether from the public or private Domains," Forbes continued to press for federal intervention. But reformers could not unite on a policy of confiscation. Federal intervention—in the confiscation acts of 1861 and 1862 as well as in the land redistribution provisions of the Freedmen's Bureau Bill—was fatally circumscribed by constitutional prohibitions against bills of attainder and by the swift restoration of the planters' property rights.[33] Even George Washington Julian viewed his Southern Homestead Act of 1866 as an extension of the antimonopoly goals of the western homestead act and resisted the political appeal of confiscation as a means of providing land bounties for Union veterans. Julian denounced such policies as an invitation to speculation and monopoly. In all previous American wars, he noted, veterans had been rewarded with land bounties. Political pressures were strong during and immediately after the Civil War to maintain that tradition. Julian opposed such measures, arguing that bounties inevitably fell into the hands of speculators and promoted monopoly. The threat of monopoly represented as great a danger in the South as in the West. In the South, Julian feared that the horrors of slavery would be surpassed by "the grasping monopolists of the North, whose domination over the freedmen and poor whites will be more galling than slavery itself." Lydia Maria Child concurred, fearing that northern speculators would produce a land monopoly in the South more complete and oppressive than that of the slaveholders. "I have observed with anxiety," Child wrote Julian early in 1864, "that large tracts of southern confiscated lands were being bought by Northern capitalists." Child believed that the large southern estates "ought to be mainly distributed among the emancipated slaves; and the poor whites who will consent to become loyal citizens of the U.S." Confiscation for sale to northern investors must be resisted. Child had "almost as strong an aversion to Land Monopoly, as I have to Slavery," believing it represented "another phase of Slavery; another form of the absorption of Labor by Capital, which has tormented and degraded the world from the beginning."[34]

With leading advocates of agrarian reform opposed to land bounties for soldiers and land sales to northern investors, the early political momentum behind confiscation proposals faded. Several reformers thought it was just as well. As Lydia Maria Child later noted, "it is more salutary to all classes of people to *earn* a home than to have it *given* to them." The same notion led the Boston textile manufacturer Edward Atkinson to oppose "any general measure of confiscation." A devotee of Henry C. Carey and one of the original backers of Edward L. Godkin's *Nation*, Atkinson invested substantially in sea islands land sold under the terms of the federal Direct Tax Law. Land reform would occur by natural processes, he argued, through "death and taxes" and the introduction of northern farming methods. In addition, Atkinson thought that it would "about ruin freedmen" to give them "*improved* land."[35]

Nevertheless, some blacks—particularly in the Southeast—gained and held title to small parcels of land. To an extent this resulted from federal action. Adolph Mot, collector of the port of Fernandina, Florida, during federal occupation (and later Reconstruction major of the town) reported to Secretary Chase in 1867 that a number of freedmen occupied land allocated to them by Sherman's order and by the wartime provisions of the Treasury Department. In the same year, Chase's longtime friend, Reverend Mansfield French, reported from the South Carolina sea islands that he had divided "nearly 400 acres of good land . . . into the hands of the freedmen." But lasting change in land tenure in this low-country region of South Carolina and Georgia came with the postemancipation collapse of the rice industry. In this region, despite the best efforts of Yankee reformers to maintain or increase production of staples, subsistence agriculture replaced many of the plantations of the old regime.[36]

Reformers viewed land reform as part of a larger process of social transformation involving every facet of southern society. It was in this context as well that they measured the success and necessity of Reconstruction policies. The restoration of the South's productive capacity under a free labor system required a good deal more than giving land to blacks. As Daniel R. Goodloe observed at the close of the war, progress in the South required planters to become "habituated" in their planting operations and in the conduct of their households "to the idea that their late slaves are freedmen."[37] John Murray Forbes thought that the attitudes of the nonslaveholding whites were equally important. Assessing the cost of the war for the South after two years of war, Forbes concluded that "the available wealth of the South has now been exhausted." Among the "*future* resources" upon which the rebels could draw, Forbes placed "the labor of the Blacks" first in importance. Beyond that, the rebels could draw only upon "the *thin squeezings* that can be wrung by the Provost Marshals, from the daily labor or small accumulations of . . . the poor whites." All of this suggested to Forbes the military wisdom of an emancipation policy combined with government-sponsored free labor operations. Since "any disturbance of the labor of the slaves is going to bring the pressure of the war upon the poor Whites" and thereby demonstrate to them the despotic class relations which slavery produced, "wherever we can, by [emancipation] or any other means, bring this class to a realising sense of the fact that the war is really made by the planters against *them* & against free labor every where, we shall see the end of the war & a basis for reconstructing a Democratic Republic North & South."[38]

Reformers justified Reconstruction measures, including land reform and the introduction of northern men and methods, as ways of facilitating this transformation. Reformers generally agreed, as Forbes admitted in 1872, "that the time has *got to* come when the 4 million [freedmen] must do without guardianship & learn to take care of themselves." But Forbes hoped that the national government would retain authority in southern labor relations until all of the freedmen acquired security in small landholdings. Without that security, they "will never be safe from something like Peonage," he concluded. For many reformers, particularly those less committed to land reform than Forbes, the time to let the freedmen, planters, and white yeomen work out their own salvation had long since arrived. When the American Freedmen's Inquiry Commission (composed of the utopian reformer Robert Dale Owen and two abolitionists, Samuel Gridley Howe and James McKaye) recommended the creation of the Freedmen's Bureau to facilitate the transition to free labor, they warned that too much intervention would postpone or prevent the very changes they hoped to promote. As Howe remarked privately to Charles Sumner, the commission intended to establish "that emancipation means *wages for work!*" But Howe wanted federal labor policies to be based "upon the ordinary principles of demand and supply for labour, so as to dispense with machinery." Howe later reported that the inquiry commission divided on the issue of "enforced protection." McKaye "insists upon *protection*—and compelling the blacks to receive it," he wrote, adding that "Owen & I vote him down." Intervention denied freedom: "Give to the blacks as to the whites the privilege of starving if he prefers that to work." If black refugees needed federal rations, Howe continued, "insist that he shall work before he can eat." As one of Henry Wilson's correspondents noted early in 1862, "if we can in any proper way manage to keep oppressive hands off them, I have no fear that we can leave them, where the rest of us are, in the hands of God, and subject to the great law which feeds the industrious and sometimes lets the idle starve."[39]

The harsh tone of Social Darwinism, which increasingly invaded

liberal rhetoric in the last half of the nineteenth century, did not con-
tradict or abandon the social optimism of antebellum reform, but it
did reveal the degree to which liberal considerations of public policy
gradually excluded substantive discussions regarding the distribution
of economic benefits. If emancipation had not completely freed the
former slaves from the oppressive legacy of bondage—and reformers
agreed in the postwar years that it had not—the remedy lay in the restoration of civil liberties and in the expanding influence of market relations. Reformers continued to advocate and support private efforts
to uplift the freedmen in morals and in education, but by the early
1870s, public discussions regarding land and labor in the South had
ended. In the debate that accompanied the Liberal Republican campaign in the presidential election of 1872, it mattered less that reformers differed over the wisdom of continuing federal intervention in the
South than that they agreed that at some point the artificial conditions
of Reconstruction must end. Contradictions inherent in the reformist
idealization of small proprietors and in their middle-class faith in the
productive capacity of free labor—indeed, in the moral imperative of
free labor's productive capacity—foreshortened agitation for land reform and hastened a reconciliation of the northern middle class with
the former master class of the South. As champions of utilitarian values and liberal principles of public propriety, antislavery reformers
led the northern reaction against Reconstruction in the name of reunion and the restoration of republican government to the South.

A Spirit of Magnanimity

10

I N the summer of 1872, in the last year of his life, Chief Justice Salmon P. Chase recorded in his diary the sketchy outlines of a "singular dream." In Chase's dream, President Lincoln and Confederate President Jefferson Davis struggled in a climactic battle leaving Davis "beaten & [a] prisoner." Lincoln, as victor, resigned and Davis assumed the responsibilities of the presidency. Congress, consisting only of eleven members of the former Confederate legislature, met and amended the Constitution to provide for emancipation and universal suffrage. With these fundamental reforms secured, Davis resigned and Lincoln returned to the presidency to proclaim universal amnesty and to restore the insurgent states to the Union amid "General harmony & reconciliation." It was a dream of victory, to be sure, but it revealed uncertainties about Reconstruction as well. Chase, who had been at the forefront of the antislavery struggle, dreamed that a reformed South led the way to national reunion.[1]

In certain respects, nothing appeared more inconsistent in the reformist response to the postemancipation South than the desire to seek reconciliation with the former master class. Indeed, a spirit of magnanimity toward the defeated slave power directly challenged northern desires to punish rebels and to gain for the Republican party a secure bastion in the vanquished slave states. General John W. Phelps of Vermont, a man of strong antislavery and antisouthern sentiments (who earlier embarrassed his commander, Benjamin F. Butler, when he began arming and drilling contraband slaves in Louisiana in 1862), expressed these northern desires for control in the South when he added his support to Thaddeus Stevens's confiscation plans and when he urged Charles Sumner to think "beyond the elements which are stirred up by revolutionary violence" in the South to ensure the security of "republicanism." Phelps insisted that "when the old institution (of slavery) has been removed, we must introduce something else in its place." In Phelps's view, "what the actual condition of the South demands is a despotism." As Chase's dream of harmony and reconciliation suggested, however, such radicalism toward the defeated South did not sustain reformist views of progress. Phelps himself opposed Negro suffrage, for example, and joined other colonizationists to recommend a policy of resettling blacks abroad as the entering wedge of expanding American influence in Africa and Central America. "The African race," Phelps wrote Sumner in 1865, can no more "be made a component part of American nationality than the mistletoe and other parasites can be of the oak, which they load down and destroy."[2]

As long as northerners such as Phelps identified national security with the suppression of the southern spirit of rebellion, the stern policies espoused by the Radical Republican opponents of Andrew Johnson enjoyed substantial public support. As Secretary of War Edwin M. Stanton noted in 1866, until the South demonstrated a "reciprocity in forgiveness," federally imposed sanctions would continue to be necessary. For a time a number of reformers enthusiastically concurred. "The Government is solemnly bound to be omnipresent, omniscient and omnipotent" in the South, William Lloyd Garrison insisted in 1866. Garrison thought that southerners "are full of the spirit of revolt . . . and are not to be trusted in any promises they make for the future." Security for the Union required that the rebel states remain under military rule until "the actual spirit, design and condition of the South" determined otherwise. "The South is an old covenant-breaker," Garrison intoned, "she is . . . rotten with perfidy, and still demonized by her old slave system."[3]

Some old abolitionists, including Francis Gillette of Hartford, Connecticut, who had been deeply saddened by his son's battlefield death, could never forget the suffering the despised slave power had caused them. "In the name of God and Humanity," Gillette asked Charles Sumner in anguish in 1870, "why did not Congress hang or banish the whole brood of the chief conspirators and murderers of our sons and brothers and confiscate their estates to pay the money cost of the war?" Gillette feared that the national government now fell victim to "the distemper of 'magnanimity,' so prevalent among white men from H.[enry] W.[ard] Beecher, H.[orace] Greeley and Gerrit Smith," down through the compromise-seeking politicians. After touring the South during the summer of 1872, the Boston financier John Murray Forbes saw a continued need for federal intervention and urged support for

President Grant and the Republican party in the coming presidential contest. The only security for the North lay in the suppression of the former slaveholders, "under a united Republican north until the colored population are strong enough to protect themselves." In a similar spirit, Lydia Maria Child denounced the "sickly sentimentality" apparent in some reformers who expressed sympathy for the defeated South. Were Confederate General Nathan Bedford Forrest to be tried as a murderer for his role in the massacre of blacks at Fort Pillow, Child would be sorely tempted to set aside her moral hostility to capital punishment. "There is a right and a wrong in this matter," she insisted, "which ought not to be confounded by a desire to exhibit magnanimity."[4]

Despite such angry assertions, the spirit of magnanimity enjoyed a growing popularity among the former foes of the slave power. In part, this spirit expressed the reformist drive for national unity. With slavery gone, many reformers thought it was time to forget the past and rely on the old planter class to develop productive habits as employers of free labor and to lead the freedmen down the path of moral and material progress. As John Jay observed late in 1863, with "Slavery abolished I am ready to forgive & forget & fraternize to an extent that now seems impossible." With emancipation, "the last stumbling block between the North & South will vanish—& then we can afford to be magnanimous." In a similar mood, Salmon P. Chase observed in April 1864 that "the great objects for which I entered political life . . . are now accomplished." The war had destroyed the "oligarchical Slave Power," and the Republicans had severed the federal government from any ties to slavery. Once a constitutional amendment recognized emancipation, "nothing would remain for patriotic labor but reconstruction on the new and solid foundation."[5] At the close of the war, Governor John Andrew of Massachusetts added his voice to this spirit of reconciliation. Andrew agreed with Senator Sumner and other congressional leaders that the rule of law in the South required a period of federal intervention, particularly in the form of the Freedmen's Bureau. Although intervention carried dangers, as a temporary measure Andrew preferred to risk the excesses of bureau agents (whose actions "can be remedied or appealed") rather than to permit "neglect or failure" to harm "the poor blacks" for whom "no appeal can afford a remedy." At the same time, however, Andrew urged Sumner to pursue reconciliation with the "educated," "enlightened," and "superior persons of the South. We have dealt a death blow to one barbarism by the arm of another," Andrew observed. "Now we have Civilization, Reason, Religion—all of these to work with."[6]

As Andrew's comments suggested, it was primarily the political economy of slavery, not the landed wealth of the South, which reformers attacked as unproductive and immoral. At the outset of the war, when Charles Sumner returned to the Senate after recuperating from a beating inflicted by South Carolina Representative Preston Brooks, his old friend Dr. Samuel Gridley Howe reminded him that "you should denounce Institutions but spare men." Howe thought that Sumner might well satisfy a "rude sense of justice" by launching a "furious onslaught upon slaveholders," and "the multitude will rejoice savagely." But Howe held Sumner to a higher mark. "You should not fall into the common error of dividing men into righteous & wicked," Howe insisted. "Slaveholders are what the Institution of slavery makes them." It was the institution of slavery that had launched the South on its "hopeless, desperate, fatal voyage" of secession. "Let the Gulf Fleet sail away under the black flag," wrote Howe during the secession winter. "It is not an 'irrepressible conflict' that we should talk about," he added, "so much as an irrepressible development of humanity." Howe, who as one of the secret supporters of John Brown did not shrink from visions of violence, suspected that in time the North would respond to secession with a larger version of Brown's raid on Harpers Ferry. He envisioned a force of twenty to forty thousand volunteers "backed by the money & power of the U.S." to "plough through the South, & be followed by a blaze of servile war that would utterly & forever rout out slaveholding & slaveholders." By the spring of 1861, however, Howe accepted the necessity of war as opposed to insurrection—as did virtually all reformers, including Garrison and the nonresistant abolitionists—believing that the slaveholders had brought the conflict upon themselves by attacking Fort Sumter. With some trepidation, Howe sanctioned state violence as a means of self-defense. Under the circumstances he thought that reformers would be "false to humanity if we did not use every means which our enemies have put into our hands to save this country for freedom." In any case, through war or the "irrepressible development of humanity," Howe believed that he would live to "be the citizen of a real republic; & to rejoice in the political equality of all men."[7]

During the war, as public opinion seemed to be advancing swiftly to antislavery ground, increasing numbers of reformers concluded that emancipation combined with constitutionally secured equal rights accomplished their essential goals. In New York, the old Liberty party leader Elizur Wright noted of conservative Democrats that "some of the worst & biggest hunkers here now acknowledge that nothing but 'nigger equality' will save us." As the Union war effort continued, George William Curtis saw a similar advance toward antislavery principles among conservatives of Whig antecedents. As the notion of immediate and uncompensated emancipation became commonplace, Curtis remarked to Charles Eliot Norton, editor of the Loyal Publication Society, that "you and I are superannuated fogies." The goals of antislavery reform had advanced far faster than anyone could have expected, Curtis thought, and Wendell Phillips's continued cries of alarm seemed artificial and forced: "Wendell Phillips, I hear, is coming to tell us that the rebels have conquered & that twice two this time makes only three." As the South moved to adopt the Republican constitutional amendments in 1869, Curtis saw—"for the first time in my experience"—the end of sectional hostilities.[8]

It was in this spirit of sectional reconciliation that Gerrit Smith posted bond to secure Jefferson Davis's release from prison. In the same spirit, Henry Wilson secured more comfortable quarters for the imprisoned Confederate Vice-President Alexander H. Stephens. Early in 1870, Joseph R. Hawley, a former Liberty and Free Soil party leader in Connecticut, declared flatly that "the fight is done." As a second-generation abolitionist (his father supported Gerrit Smith's Liberty League), Hawley endorsed a wide range of moral and political reforms in the 1840s and 1850s. Now a Union veteran directing Reconstruction in Wilmington, North Carolina, Hawley felt the need for reconciliation. (With a distinguished war record, he soon returned north to take a leading role in Republican politics for the rest of the century.) Hawley loyally supported Grant during the Liberal Republican bolt in 1872, but he concurred with the Liberal Republican call for a restoration of the Union "in full harmony, & [with] the fifteenth amendment crowning the whole work."[9]

For Horace Greeley as well, 1870 marked not only the beginning of a new decade but of a new era of national harmony. Greeley insisted that "nearly every old fashioned, long-time Abolitionist . . . has long since evidenced a kindly, generous, magnanimous disposition toward the beaten, broken-down Rebels." A number of abolitionists continued to oppose reconciliation, but there was more than wishful thinking involved in Greeley's observation. As the aging abolitionist poet John Greenleaf Whittier concluded in 1871, the time had come to forgive the wrongdoing of the past. "Let us begin anew," Whittier urged Senator Sumner, "and punish if need be all new offenders." Whittier lamented the contentious spirit associated with the Liberal Republican campaign of 1872, although he agreed with the Liberals that something approaching a general amnesty would "take away a pretext for disturbances" in the South, the "suffering of which falls on the colored people." Whittier concluded that nearly all that could be done through legislation and protection for the freedmen had been done. "We can now only help them to help themselves," he wrote. "Industry, economy, temperance, self-culture, education for their children— these are things indispensable to their elevation and progress, [and] are in a great measure in their own hands."[10]

Reformers were not entirely pleased with the South's progress in the wake of emancipation, but they did recognize that the region's landed elite had become the reluctant ally of a dominant industrial order. As this realization took hold, Reconstruction lost its positive meaning and became (first among reformers but shortly for the nation as a whole) synonymous with corruption. Liberal principles had not triumphed in the South as reformers had once believed they would. Instead, the legacy of slavery dissipated unevenly and, in the heart of the plantation South, very slowly. Nevertheless, liberalism did triumph at the national level and the South as a dependent region could be safely left to forge its own relationship (however reactionary it might be) to the new industrial order.[11]

Liberal fears of corruption in public affairs were not new. Throughout the antebellum decades, reformers discussed the importance of controlling popular passions and of insulating government and the public sphere generally from the influence of mass politics. In this endeavor, it was the responsibility of the civilized and educated classes to exert a restraining and guiding influence. Although most reformers believed at the end of the war that an influx of northern men into the South would contribute to the stability of the region, neither the presence of northerners nor the interjection of federal authority produced the expected results. Instead, the violent disorders that characterized Reconstruction confronted reformers with an unexpected and uncomfortable reality. Although some reformers continued to look to executive authority and the federal army to maintain order in the South, many began to link sentiments of magnanimity toward the former slaveholders with fears of the corrupting influences of Reconstruction.

Daniel R. Goodloe, who returned to his native state of North Carolina in 1865 as a United States marshal, concluded by 1868 that federal efforts to suppress the legacy of slavery simply created opportunities for corruption. At the beginning of his Reconstruction career, Goodloe had been more hopeful. When he first returned to North Carolina he believed that whites in the state would soon grant blacks civil and political rights, if only to avoid confiscation and other harsh Reconstruction measures at the hands of their conquerors. Although appointed to office by President Andrew Johnson, Goodloe soon joined the Radical Republican opposition to the president's lenient Reconstruction policies and supported congressional opposition to the pro-Johnson forces in North Carolina. By 1868, however, Goodloe believed that Reconstruction had become a hindrance to progress and a great boon to demagogues and untutored rascals of every stripe. Reconstruction policies enhanced the influence of men "inferior in intelligence and character" to many of those who had been disfranchised. Instead of protecting the rights of blacks as Goodloe originally hoped, Reconstruction perpetuated political corruption at the hands of "'carpet-baggers' and rebel demagogues."[12]

In social relations as well as in politics, reformers judged Reconstruction to be an obstacle to progress. The brief period of federal protection and intervention, which reformers initially supported, threatened to become a way of life during Grant's first administration, not only for political opportunists in the South but also for northern politicians profiting from perennial instability in the South. Although Grant and "Grantism" became the focal point of the reformist break with Reconstruction, there was more at stake in the Liberal–Stalwart Republican schism of 1872 than questions of political personality or party factionalism. Increasingly after 1868, reformers identified federal Reconstruction as the cause rather than the cure for continued social disorder in the South. From this perspective, the Kentucky abolitionist Cassius M. Clay urged Henry Wilson to adopt a "liberal course" toward the South. By continuing a "policy of *repression*," Republican leaders could only prolong the turmoil in the South and, eventually, bring about their own political defeat. The "evils of an-archy" in the South could only be cured by southerners, those "who are most of all interested in good government there."[13]

Salmon P. Chase, whose position as chief justice of the United States did not dissuade him from continuing to seek a reformist coalition with the Democracy, emerged as an early advocate of self-determination as the best solution to disorder in the South. Throughout the war, Chase argued that the federal government's policy toward the rebellious South should be based on the principle that "the loyal citizens of a State constitute the State." He defined as loyal those "who desire the suppression of the rebellion, and consent to the means which the Gov-ernment has found necessary for its suppression." Loyal citizens in-cluded virtually all of the black population together with those whites who accepted emancipation and Negro suffrage. Chase thought it was vital that the federal government make "no distinctions between colored and white loyalists," and he attributed the shortcomings of Lincoln's efforts in Louisiana, where Chase believed "the old secession element is rapidly gaining the ascendancy," to the exclusion of blacks from the ballot. Chase believed that universal suffrage, incorporating the principle of equal suffrage for blacks, would provide the founda-tion necessary for universal amnesty and for the final reconciliation of North and South. Touring the South in May 1865, Chase wrote to Sec-retary of War Stanton that "*universal suffrage* is essential to *thorough pacification.*" Most important, he believed, "the white population will acquiesce in this policy without any serious opposition if it is clearly announced, & firmly but kindly pursued."[14]

Like most reformers, Chase believed that full citizenship and equal-ity under law flowed naturally from emancipation. Whereas many re-formers viewed a broadened franchise with suspicion, Chase placed his entire faith in universal suffrage as the "surest guarantee and most powerful stimulus of individual, social and political progress." Chase also regarded universal suffrage as a means of facilitating sectional harmony. Universal suffrage, he insisted, is "the best reconciler of the most comprehensive leniency with the most perfect public security and the most speedy and certain revival of general prosperity." With the right to vote secured, Chase urged the freedmen to demonstrate to whites through "economy," "industry," "sobriety," and "patient Per-severance" that they recognized that the "peculiar conditions" under which they were given the vote imposed on them "special obligations as to the discharge of common duties." Like all reformers, Chase accepted the necessity of a period of military reconstruction and, indeed, insisted as chief justice that "military control must be supreme" until civil order and civil law could be fully and safely restored. Similarly, although Chase agreed with Gerrit Smith that it would be impractical for the federal government to press charges of treason against the rebels, he stood with most reformers in opposing Smith's dictum that the rebels' loyalty to the de facto Confederate government could not be distinguished morally from unionist loyalty to the federal government. "If the rebels waging war against the government are not traitors," Chase responded, "secession was a valid act; and our war was one of conquest." Finally, although Chase supported the Liberal Republican party in 1872, he favored Grant's initial victory in 1868 because he expected the Republicans to enforce Negro suffrage in the South and thereby relieve "the better sort" among the southern whites from the "social ostracism" that otherwise would accompany indigenous efforts to secure Negro suffrage.[15]

By 1868, Chase insisted that the "complete restoration of peace and union" required only that the "proprietary class" in the South recognize that blacks and whites were equal as citizens. With this principle established and Negro suffrage secured, northerners could expect "justice and good will [to] give to the educated classes of the South the lead of the Colored masses." The freedmen's votes "would be given to the members of this class whom they knew to be competent by intelligence & character to give them the needed security." As Reconstruction ended, "the educated classes would naturally & almost necessarily [be] restored to lead."[16]

Carl Schurz soon associated the same sentiments with the Liberal Republican movement. By 1871, Schurz believed that the time for a general amnesty had arrived. "If we do not find the means to control public opinion," Schurz warned, all of the legislative efforts to suppress the Ku Klux Klan and similar outrages would be futile. In the South as in the North, the educated and responsible elements of society must assume responsibility for the administrative functions of government. Schurz believed that Reconstruction hindered progress in this regard by continuing to suppress the political influence of the educated classes. "A great many men of property and enterprise in the Southern states," he argued, "begin to feel that they must protect the equal rights of all citizens, put down disturbances, in one word maintain the new order of things, in order to protect their own interests." Schurz organized the Liberal Republican movement to encourage these interests. "Far from intending to give up or to compromise a single principle we ever contended for," he insisted, "this is the way in which their triumph can be permanently secured."[17]

Chase's and Schurz's emphasis on universal suffrage as the *quid pro quo* for universal amnesty and sectional reconciliation confronted long-standing reformist doubts regarding the wisdom of a broadened popular franchise. In New York, where reformers continued to press for equal suffrage until the ratification of the Fifteenth Amendment settled the matter, John Jay looked back on the granting of "free suffrage" among whites in the 1820s as a "blunder." Because he belived that blacks, North and South, needed "some degree of political power" to protect their fragile rights, Jay supported Negro suffrage in New York and in the South. But it was not an ideal solution, and Jay hoped to restrict the vote in the South "to negroes who could read and to those *who have served creditably in the army.*" Theodore Tilton, editor of the *New York Independent* (which earlier championed equal suffrage for blacks in New York while regretting the political influence free suffrage gave to the Irish), urged a similar literacy restriction in the South. "It is frightful to think how many persons in the Southern States cannot spell their own names," Tilton observed to Wendell Phillips. Tilton acknowledged that blacks as well as whites would be barred from the polls by his proposal, but he believed that a literacy requirement "would disfranchise *far more whites than blacks*—because more whites than blacks are unable to read." Amos Tuck, New Hampshire's old Free Soil party leader, argued that such an "educational test" would have "a practical influence leveling *up* the masses." For these reformers, Negro suffrage made sense only as a counterbalance to the baneful influence of mass politics.[18]

During the late 1860s, reformist sensitivity to corruption in public affairs began to overshadow frustrations with continued violence in the South and cast federal intervention into the civil affairs of the southern states in a negative light. As the young reformer Moorfield Storey noted to Charles Sumner in 1873, corruption in public affairs assaulted the sensibilities of honest men in every corner of the nation and at every level of government: "All over the country and in every form corruption seems to be spreading, or rather perhaps we are waking up to acknowledge of its existence and the importance of reform."[19] Reformers identified much of this corruption with the tendency toward "personal" government on the part of politicians adept at turning popular passions to political advantage and eager to subordinate public duty to private gain. As early as 1867, Edward Atkinson warned Sumner that the combined influence in Massachusetts of Benjamin Butler and Nathaniel Banks—two antebellum Democrats who continued in the postwar years to align themselves with a variety of popular issues and causes—threatened to force honest men out of the Republican party. In Atkinson's assessment, both men possessed "little or no character, for truth, integrity, honor or military skill." Butler, who would shortly join the Greenback movement, could not be trusted in matters concerning the currency. And Francis W. Bird thought Banks's "sole aim is to keep himself up no matter who goes down." "Gentlemen," observed Atkinson, considered both men "an incubus upon the party with whom it would be better to break than to keep unanimity." Atkinson shortly added Benjamin Wade of Ohio to his list of unprincipled schemers and dreaded the prospect that, with the possible dismissal of Andrew Johnson, Wade might become president. Atkinson certainly harbored no affection for Johnson, but he feared that the impeachment proceedings played into the hands of demagogues like Wade. Moreover, by giving up the entire legislative session to the impeachment trial, Congress turned its back on what Atkinson considered "the great economic problems which in their real significance are moral questions second only to that of the destruction of slavery."[20]

Atkinson's fears that unprincipled politicians would cater to popular sentiments in critical economic decisions were not unique. Edward L. Pierce, Elizur Wright, John B. Alley, Amasa Walker, and John Murray Forbes among others also urged Sumner to speak out on the currency issue. In their view, the resumption of specie payment emerged as a moral issue equivalent to slavery. "Just as the Constitution ensured the equal rights of all men," observed Elizur Wright, "it likewise demanded that the government pay its debts in gold." Atkinson argued that anyone who opposed resumption intended to rob capitalists like himself. Amasa Walker took the same ground and urged an immediate contraction in the currency as a first step toward getting "currency on a par with gold." When Sumner finally took the Senate floor in July 1868 to speak on the currency issue, he drew Walker's congratulations for linking "the questions of repudiation and slavery." In a later speech, however, when Sumner linked immediate resumption of specie payment with immediate emancipation, the Lynn shoe manufacturer and abolitionist John B. Alley joined Atkinson and others to urge caution. Atkinson warned that the "natural laws of trade" could not be "controlled by statute." Alley argued that the government should adopt gradual resumption as its goal to avoid the dislocations a sudden contraction would produce. As in the struggle against slavery, the goal was not to control trade and money or to direct the relations of labor and capital but to remove the state (and thereby blunt the pernicious influence of self-seeking politicians) from any corrupt or obstructive interference with the free interaction of economic forces.[21]

Although corruption permeated every facet of public life, it was President Grant's penchant for "personal government" that caused reformers to denounce "Grantism" with a zeal they had once reserved for the slave power. Early in 1871, Austin Willey, a former Liberty party abolitionist from Maine, looked with alarm on the "already historic tendency to presidential Imperialism." It had been an article of the Liberty party's faith that military men ought not to be elected president, and Willey regarded Grant's "usurpation" with alarm. "The office is but little more than simply executive," he insisted, "and to that it must be held with all the tenacity with which we cling to the life of the Republic." When, in March 1871, Grant's supporters removed Senator Sumner as chairman of the Foreign Relations Committee, a number of reformers saw the heavy hand of presidential despotism reminiscent of Andrew Jackson. "Have we a Senate of the United States?" asked James M. Stone of Boston. "Or has that which was once a Senate humbled itself & gone down under the heel of executive usurpation?" Stone insisted that the dangers of presidential despotism outweighed the lingering difficulties in the South:

> This movement towards executive concentration of power is alarming. Individuals & their wrongs sink into insignificance in view of this march of power over the prostrated senatorial independence. The Ku-Klux outrages are less dangerous. If the Senate consents to an enforced abdication of its independence the People must be summoned to the preservation of the constitutional principles of the government.
>
> It is useless longer to talk of the preservation of the Republican party. The party is already in its shroud.[22]

Elizur Wright added his voice to the chorus of protest. "I spent a fortnight in the South last fall," Wright wrote Sumner in July 1872, "and became fully convinced that an administration which could not prevent *its friends* from robbing these poor states . . . cannot long maintain itself there by any fair means." It was true, Wright admitted, that President Grant used federal troops to suppress the Klan, "but what is the use of keeping people's throats from being cut, if they are to be perpetually robbed?" Wright concluded that the federal government had "done what it ought to *in some places*" to suppress the Klan. But it had done nothing to hinder the spread of "Tweedism in the states." The former Conscience Whig editor William S. Robinson dismissed continued federal intervention as nothing more than "a political doup to keep this disgusting incapable who is now President, in the foreground for another 4 years of disgusting personal government." Local government, in Robinson's view, not consolidated federal power, offered "the best security for the liberties of the people—in the long run—and *the best education of the people, also for government.*" Robinson saw Sumner's removal as chairman of the Foreign Relations Committee as "the culmination of the era to which we have been tending for years—personal government, instead of political & legal." In this view, political government—whether Democratic or Republican—"is comparatively pure" because it adheres to political principles. Personal government "inevitably tends to corruption" because it was rooted in nothing but self-interest.[23]

David Wells Alvord, a prominent Massachusetts lawyer and former Free Soiler, joined with his friend Francis W. Bird and others to denounce Grant's despotism. Early in 1871, Alvord announced his support for the course charted by the Missouri Liberal Republicans led by Carl Schurz and B. Gratz Brown. Although Alvord had earlier supported Sumner's "conquered territories" doctrine for Reconstruction, he insisted in January 1871 that the rights of the southern states must be respected. A defense of the rights of the states against intrusions by the federal government had been at the core of the Free Soil party's doctrine, Alvord recalled. The same principle which Free Soilers drew upon to criticize the 1850 Fugitive Slave Law applied to Reconstruction: the national government exceeded its constitutional authority when it circumvented or undercut a state's authority over its own civil affairs. "Indeed," Alvord continued, "the principle is sound or that [fugitive] 'bill' was Law." Moreover, to concede to the general government the power to determine when "the State encroaches upon the rights of the individual . . . would enable Congress to set aside our School Laws, our Pauper Laws . . . our Liquor Laws, on the pretence that such laws violated private rights." In the name of suppressing rebels and defending freedmen, Reconstruction policies under Grant potentially undermined all of the social legislation won by reformers in the antebellum decades. "In my judgement," Alvord concluded, "the war has taught most clearly and forcibly the fearful, crushing, overshadowing, power of the General Government [and] that its power must be curtailed."[24]

Although Sumner voted in favor of the continued suppression of the Klan and pressed forward his Civil Rights Act, he too denounced the tendency toward "personal" government. In Sumner's view, Grant perceived the presidency as his personal office and the cabinet as his personal "family." All of the "safeguards of constitutional government," Sumner feared, "were subordinate to the personal pretensions of One Man." The Republican party had been organized to oppose "the *Oligarchs* of Slavery." A "coalition of Free-Soilers and Democrats," Sumner remembered, had elected him to the Senate in 1851 and laid the foundation for the Republican party. Reformers had then held "Principles Above Party," and they must do so again in 1872. "Higher than party," Sumner concluded, "are country and the duty to save it from Caesar."[25]

When Sumner announced his support for Horace Greeley in July 1872, he insisted that the interests of the former slaves as well as those of Americans generally demanded Grant's defeat. Answering a letter from a prominent group of "citizens of color" residing in the District of Columbia, Sumner publicly considered the issues of the impending presidential election and demonstrated the directness with which his antislavery convictions led him into the Liberal fold. Sumner insisted that Grant's career, beginning with his military commission at West Point, was the product of patronage. Grant's training as a soldier conditioned him to "enlist" in the proslavery Democracy and to "fortify" with his vote all of the usurpations of the slave power, including the infamous Dred Scott decision. Except through the "terrible accident of war," Sumner insisted that Grant had done nothing to oppose slavery or to advance the cause of liberty. The president had always put patronage before principle and never showed "any sympathy with the colored race, but rather indifference, if not aversion." Greeley, however, had been born in poverty and had made his way in the world

assisted only by his "industry and character." Throughout the antebellum years, Greeley had carried himself as a "Reformer and Abolitionist," who, "full of sympathy with the colored race and always fore-
most in the great battle for their rights," had "earnestly desired that
colored citizens should vote, and ably championed impartial suffrage."
Such were the "antecedents" of the two candidates between whom
black and white Americans must choose. The true interests of the
freedmen demanded Grant's defeat and Greeley's victory. Although
Wendell Phillips and others denounced Sumner's letter as a betrayal of
the freedmen, Chief Justice Chase joined other antislavery veterans
to support it. "It is good advice," wrote Chase, "and as an earnest
friend of the race for more than thirty years I sincerely hope it will be
followed."[26]

A number of abolitionists, including the "magnanimous" Gerrit
Smith, vehemently opposed the Liberal Republican break with Grant
because they feared a resurgent "proslavery" Democracy. Nevertheless, they fully shared in the Liberal reformers' distaste for Grant and
"Grantism." Notwithstanding his opposition to the Liberal movement,
William Lloyd Garrison expressed outrage at Stalwart Senator Oli-
ver P. Morton's heavy-handed efforts to damn Sumner as a friend of
the proslavery Democracy. Long the political rival of George Washington Julian, Morton led the Stalwart Republican attack against the Liberal defectors. "Nothing could be more contemptible," thought Garrison, than Morton's sneering reference to Sumner as "a friend of
liberty" and a friend of "the colored man" whose opposition to Grant
now offered positive support to the old proslavery Democracy. "What
personal bitterness and defamation is this," wrote Garrison. "What
shameless denial of the right of conscientious dissent and senatorial
independence! What servile acquiescence in Executive dictation without check or limit." Nor did Garrison dispute Sumner's charge that the
president represented "caesarism." Rather, if Grant continued to enforce Reconstruction and suppress the slaveholding virus, Garrison
would support him. Garrison supported Grant not because the president possessed "any special qualifications for so high a station" but because he thought it a matter of "commanding importance" to preserve
"the unity and thereby ensure the success of the Republican party, as
against its Democratic rival, at the next Presidential struggle." The
nomination of any other candidate would "prove abortive" and "would
lead to a break in the Republican ranks." Garrison found such a pros-

pect unacceptable, though he entirely agreed with Sumner's estimate of Grant's character. "The paucity of his mind is truly surprising," Garrison acknowledged, "and with his coarse habits and utter lack of culture, it is no wonder that men of high intelligence and refinement find much occasion for deep disgust and profound regret."[27]

Gerrit Smith similarly combined a distaste for Grant and the corruption he represented with support for the Stalwarts in 1872. Smith shared Sumner's hostility to Grant's aggressive San Domingo policy and worried lest the stories of the president's heavy drinking prove true. Yet Smith continued to hope that Grant would "cordially" embrace the reformers' position on the "great (greatest of all) question of equal rights for all men," and he agreed with Garrison that Grant deserved support simply because the alternative to a Republican president—any Republican president—was a revived Democracy and a restored slave power.[28]

An overwhelming fear of the Democracy kept Smith loyal to the Republican party in 1872. However distasteful Grant might be, Smith could not bring himself to believe that the president's faults were as dangerous to the nation as the threat of Democratic victory. Grant's reelection "can alone save us from the ruin of coming under the sway of the Democratic party," Smith insisted. Smith thought Sumner exaggerated Grant's personal failings and through "long and continued & intense brooding" had unfairly turned the president into "a weak-brained monster." Sumner judged Grant to be intellectually and morally inferior to all of the nation's presidents; Smith rated him intellectually superior to Harrison and morally ahead of Pierce. Smith feared, however, that the stories of nepotism were true and asserted that if the stories of the president's excessive drinking proved true as well Grant would be "most unfit for the Presidency." But Smith would not permit himself to believe the worst. "Oh, it cannot be!" he exclaimed in reference to Grant's drinking. "What are we to do?" The "popular current" ran toward Grant, and the conditions of the country demanded that the popular will be sustained. A vote for Greeley, Smith concluded, equaled a vote in favor of "some Ku Klux Pro Slavery Democrat."[29]

These differences among reformers produced some very angry exchanges during the 1872 presidential election. But the divisions did not run very deep in reform ranks. Thus, though Edward Atkinson and John Murray Forbes briefly parted company during the Liberal bolt, they remained closely allied in their reform views. Forbes remained steadfast in his conviction that conditions in the South demanded a continued federal presence. Atkinson, by contrast, became one of the principal organizers of the Liberal Republican party in Massachusetts. "I have not the least fear," he wrote Sumner in 1872, that the approaching Liberal convention in Cincinnati "will be untrue to the colored race." Disgruntled with the Liberals' nomination of Horace Greeley over Charles Francis Adams, Atkinson returned to Massachusetts once more loyal to the Grant regime. "I should feel safer with Grant by far," he concluded. Whether they joined the Liberal bolt or not, however, at some point during the late 1860s and early 1870s, national issues involving the currency, trade, good government, and labor supplanted the problems of the freedmen and the South.[30]

In their most optimistic mood, the Liberal bolters projected a rebirth of independent reform politics. "In my political principles, I stand exactly where I stood twenty years ago," insisted George Washington Julian shortly after the 1872 elections. Despite Grant's victory, Julian judged the Republican party to be doomed: "Its very rottenness will kill it." With the Liberal bolt Julian thought that "the source of its life has departed." Since the Democracy had ceased to be "the party of slavery & caste," the emergence of a new party system seemed "certain." Julian moved from the Liberal Republican party into the hard money ring of the Democracy. As a "gold" Democrat, Julian enjoyed the company of the former Conscience Whig leader Francis W. Bird as well as the former Barnburner leader Hiram Barney. In Barney's view, the Republican party had been formed for "the sole purpose of breaking down the slave power," and with that goal accomplished, he concluded in 1872, "no man is bound to stay in it." With the old Barnburner leaders John D. Van Buren and Samuel J. Tilden eager to "sink . . . in oblivion" the antebellum Democracy's proslavery record, Barney (once more) proclaimed the party of Jackson to be the party of reform.[31]

In one way or another, all reformers shared the urge to pursue an independent course, if only as disgruntled Republicans of the Mugwump variety. In this fashion, Elizur Wright, having left the regular Republican party to join with Barney and other Liberals to vote for Greeley in 1872, returned to the Republican fold to support Rutherford Hayes in 1876, convinced that the Democracy could never embrace reform. Expressing interest successively in a third party based on free thought principles, the Greenback issue, and the Populist insurgency, Wright expressed the restlessness and uncertainty of liberal reformers in the Gilded Age. By 1884, when Republican Senator George F. Hoar's support for James G. Blaine brought a stinging rebuke from Mugwump leader E. L. Godkin, Wright (calling himself a "mugwump") expressed his support for the veteran liberal senator and for the right to dissent even from Godkin's orthodoxy.[32]

Erratic as the political course of liberal reform appeared in the late nineteenth century, a common thread connected a wide variety of individual experiences. Beyond Grant and Reconstruction, the labor issue continued to loom large on the reformists' horizon. Looking to the future, Chief Justice Chase cast the familiar antebellum reform concern with the dignity of labor in terms that epitomized the developing Victorian glorification of the union of man and machine: "Labor is now ill dressed, dingy, ignorant. Labor should be well dressed, clean, intelligent. I would have even laboring machines handsome, shining, ornamented. The engines which do man's work should be as rich in art as in use. How much more the workers! Let industry be beautiful & beautifully clad. Let work be handsome & handsomely addressed. Let man's labor like God's be glorious in show as well as in power."[33]

For those who had been sensitive to the plight of wage earners before the war, the legacy of antislavery reform led to cooperative movements as the best means of harmonizing the interests of capital and labor. In varying degrees, the cooperative principle attracted the support of William Elder, Amasa Walker, Elizur Wright, and George Washington Julian, as well as Wendell Phillips. By contrast, those reformers who had been most fearful of the corrupting influence of propertyless laborers sought refuge within the laws of political economy, which alone defined, to their satisfaction, the duration and compensation of labor. Samuel Gridley Howe expressed these concerns with particular vigor during the war, and he spoke for his old Conscience Whig companions, including Charles Francis Adams, Francis W. Bird, and John Gorham Palfrey, when he did so. In the postwar setting, the same theme attracted the enthusiastic support of George William Curtis, Edward Atkinson, and E. L. Godkin as a newly arrived advocate of free labor and utilitarian values.

Above all, however, the generalized reformist hostility to the corrupting effects of "personal" government signaled a broadened middle-class concern with the unruly character of industrial society. Reformers opposed the consolidation of presidential power because it seemed to enhance personal government. They also wholeheartedly endorsed what William Elder referred to as the supervising and sustaining role of the state. For all, progress entailed an expanded and professionalized bureaucracy and an expanded role for the state in the regulation and control of the social ills reformers first identified in relationship to slavery. "Great cities are nests of great vices," Wendell Phillips noted in his advocacy of a professional metropolitan police force in 1863. It should come as no surprise, he added, that he joined with Edward L. Pierce and other leaders of the antislavery cause to demand that the police force no longer "represent the voters of Boston." This sensitivity to the corrupting tendency of mass politics contributed as well to the transcendent importance of civil service reform in the late nineteenth century. And "civil reform," as the New York City lawyer and former Barnburner leader Hiram Barney insisted in 1872, "is a work second in importance to the destruction of the Slave Power."[34]

By the early 1880s nearly all of the reformers whose careers stretched back to the 1830s and 1840s were dead or retired from public life. From the perspective of their declining years, the 1870s marked the end of an era. In an outpouring of histories, biographies, and memoirs reformers busied themselves with recollections of past victories in the cause of freedom and human progress. In this nostalgic spirit, the Chicago abolitionist Zebina Eastman planned an antislavery reunion in 1874 to celebrate the triumph of the cause and to pay homage to fallen comrades. Among the honored dead whom Eastman planned to memorialize was Myron Holley of New York, one of the founders of the Liberty party. As Eastman's plans advanced, he appealed to Holley's daughter Sallie to provide a biographical sketch of her late father.

As it happened, Sallie Holley was in no mood to reminisce. The freedmen's school she directed in Virginia had just been sacked by vandals and with her school's furnishings and equipment destroyed, the spirit of southern rebellion seemed to her to be very much alive. "I have been so closely engaged in a hand to hand conflict with the remains of the old Slave Power," she replied to Eastman's request, "that I have found no hour to devote to any congratulations or review of the past triumphs of the Anti-Slavery cause and the brave part bourne in the struggle by my sainted Father." With continued financial support from Wendell Phillips and other old abolitionists, she soon reopened her school and presided over it for another twenty years. For the time being, however, her mood was bleak. "This, at present, breaks up our good school of nearly six years constant progress," she told Eastman. With no help to be expected "in this semi barbarous community," she necessarily relied on the support of northern reformers: "Surrounded as we are by such evidences that the spirit of American Slavery still lives, I am not yet ready to celebrate the completion of the Anti Slavery work—Tho' I greatly rejoice with every old abolitionist that so much of the holy and grand work has been accomplished—Let us work to the end."[35]

Sallie Holley did not lack in filial piety or in a desire to contribute to celebrations of past victories. Within a few years, she began to provide the New York abolitionist Elizur Wright with material for his biography of her father. Rather, as a second-generation abolitionist, Holley illustrated the legacy of antebellum reform in the new struggles for education for the freedmen and black civil rights, struggles, which— closely allied with the cause of women's suffrage and anti-imperialism —continued into the twentieth century. Holley's effort to remind Eastman that the struggle against southern barbarism continued may well have struck the sensitive nerve she aimed for. But "the remains of the old Slave Power," against which she continued to struggle, no longer laid claim to national power. In this sense, Eastman and his generation of reformers had good reason to celebrate the triumph of anti-slavery reform and to mark the end of an era.[36]

Notes

Abbreviations

The following abbreviations appear in the notes to designate the depositories of frequently cited manuscript collections:

HL   Houghton Library, Harvard University, Cambridge, Massachusetts
HSP   Historical Society of Pennsylvania, Philadelphia, Pennsylvania
LC   Library of Congress, Washington, D.C.
MHS   Massachusetts Historical Society, Boston, Massachusetts

Introduction

1. The outburst of antislavery reform in the antebellum decades is described and analyzed in Louis Filler, *The Crusade against Slavery, 1830–1860* (New York, 1960); James M. McPherson, *The Struggle for Equality: Abolitionists and the Negro in the Civil War and Reconstruction* (Princeton, 1964); Eric Foner, *Free Soil, Free Labor, Free Men: The Ideology of the Republican Party before the Civil War* (New York, 1970); Gerald Sorin, *Abolitionism: A New Perspective* (New York, 1972); James Brewer Stewart, *Holy Warriors: The Abolitionists and American Slavery* (New York, 1976); and Ronald G. Walters, *The Antislavery Appeal: American Abolitionism after 1830* (Baltimore, 1978).

2. David Brion Davis, *Slavery and Human Progress* (New York, 1984), 109, 335 n. 121; Eric Foner, *Politics and Ideology in the American Civil War* (New York, 1980), 63; Howard Temperley, "Capitalism, Slavery, and Ideology," *Past and Present* 75 (May 1977): 94–118; Thomas L. Haskell, "Capitalism and the Origins of the Humanitarian Sensibility, Part I," *American Historical Review* 90 (April 1985): 339–61.

3. On the utilitarian aspects of antislavery thought, see David Montgomery, *Beyond Equality: Labor and the Radical Republicans, 1862–1872* (New York, 1967), 78, 80, 446–47; and David Brion Davis, *The Problem of Slavery in the Age of Revolution, 1770–1823* (Ithaca, 1975), 350–56. On the ideological significance of utilitarian theory, see Karl Marx and Friedrich Engels, *The German Ideology*, in David McLellan, ed., *Karl Marx: Selected Writings* (New York, 1977), esp. 185–89; foreword by Elizabeth Fox Genovese and Eugene D. Genovese to Allen Kaufman, *Capitalism, Slavery, and Republican Values: American Political*

Economists, 1819–1848 (Austin, 1982), ix–xx; and Kaufman, *Capitalism,* 3–17.

4. See Stuart M. Blumin, "The Hypothesis of Middle-Class Formation in Nineteenth-Century America: A Critique and Some Proposals," *American Historical Review* 90 (April 1985): 299–338.

5. Louis Hartz, *The Liberal Tradition in America: An Interpretation of American Political Thought since the Revolution* (New York, 1955), 3–32; Richard Hofstadter, *The American Political Tradition* (New York, 1948), esp. v–xi.

6. Alan Dawley, *Class and Community: The Industrial Revolution in Lynn* (Cambridge, Mass., 1976); Paul E. Johnson, *A Shopkeeper's Millennium: Society and Revivals in Rochester, New York, 1815–1837* (New York, 1978); Anthony F. C. Wallace, *Rockdale: The Growth of an American Village in the Early Industrial Revolution* (New York, 1978); Paul Faler, *Mechanics and Manufacturers in the Early Industrial Revolution: Lynn, Massachusetts, 1780–1860* (Albany, 1981); and Sean Wilentz, *Chants Democratic: New York City and the Rise of the American Working Class, 1788–1850* (New York, 1984).

7. Similarities in the social origins of entrepreneurs and abolitionists are stressed in James M. McPherson, *Ordeal by Fire: The Civil War and Reconstruction* (New York, 1982), 42–45. Davis, *Slavery and Human Progress,* 109, warns against the "temptation to reduce the rise of abolitionism to the interests of an entrepreneurial class."

8. Striking as well is the capacity of antislavery reformers to press their cause while maintaining respectable social ties. See John R. McKivigan, *The War against Proslavery Religion: Abolitionism and the Northern Churches, 1830–1865* (Ithaca, 1984), esp. 69.

9. Foner, *Politics and Ideology,* 76, contends that a "labor-oriented" antislavery tradition reaching back to the artisan republicanism of Thomas Paine remained independent of middle-class reform in the antebellum decades and "rose like a pheonix from the ashes of the Civil War, to inspire the great crusades" of the late nineteenth-century labor movement. See also Foner, *Tom Paine and Revolutionary America* (New York, 1976), 43–50. Bruce Carlan Levin, "Free Soil, Free Labor and Freimanner: German Chicago in the Civil War Era," in Hartmut Keil and John B. Jentz, eds., *German Workers in Industrial Chicago, 1850–1910: A Comparative Perspective* (DeKalb, Ill., 1983), 164–78, concurs that antislavery reform advanced the interests of German workingmen. Jentz, "The Anti-Slavery Constituency in Jacksonian New York City," *Civil War History* 27 (June 1981): 101–22; and Edward Magdol, "A Window on the Abolitionist Constituency: Antislavery Petitions, 1836–1839," in Alan M. Kraut, ed., *Crusaders and Compromisers: Essays on the Relationship of the Antislavery Struggle to the Antebellum Party System* (Westport, Conn., 1983), 45–70, identify artisan signers of abolitionist petitions. Betty Fladeland, *Abolitionists and Working-Class Problems in the Age of Industrialization* (Baton Rouge, 1984), describes the sympathy of British abolitionists for wage earners.

On the other side of the debate, Faler, *Mechanics and Manufacturers,* 197, 199–200, 211–21; and Dawley, *Class and Community,* 100–102, 238, find antislavery reform in Lynn, Massachusetts, to be increasingly closely tied to the interests of the employers and conclude that the Civil War sidetracked the workingmen's struggle. Wilentz, *Chants Democratic,* 263, 263n., 395, finds in New York City, "little evidence to support the contention that the fight for the Union cooled working-class resistance," but also discerns a broad "popular anti-abolitionism" among journeymen and small masters and identifies "evangelical master artisans" as the source of the most consistent artisan support for antislavery goals.

10. Hofstadter, *American Political Tradition,* 138.

11. John W. Blassingame, ed., *The Frederick Douglass Papers, Series One: Speeches, Debates, and Interviews,* Vol. 1, 1841–46 (New Haven, 1979), 206; [Frederick Douglass], *Life and Times of Frederick Douglass Written by Himself: His Early Life as a Slave, His Escape from Bondage, and His Complete History,* Collier Books ed. (London, 1962), 619. The emergence of the modern concept of race in nineteenth-century America is the subject of George M. Frederickson, *The Black Image in the White Mind: The Debate on Afro-American Character and Destiny, 1817–1914* (New York, 1971). For a useful overview of the relationship between the concept of race and the developing industrial order in America, see Barbara J. Fields, "Ideology and Race in American History," in J. Morgan Kousser and James M. McPherson, *Region, Race, and Reconstruction: Essays in Honor of C. Vann Woodward* (New York, 1982), 143–77.

12. John W. Blassingame, ed., *The Frederick Douglass Papers, Series One: Speeches, Debates, and Interviews,* Vol. 2: *1847–54* (New Haven: 1982), 433. The publication of the Douglass Papers and of the Black Abolitionist Papers—C. Peter Ripley, ed., *The Black Abolitionist Papers,* Vol. 1: *The British Isles, 1830–1865* (Chapel Hill, 1985)—demonstrates the need for detailed study of the interaction and divergence of the dominant antislavery movement and the black struggle for freedom. That topic involves discussions that move well beyond the scope of this study, although the two concerns—white reform and black liberation—cannot be divorced from the social developments that shaped them both. Illuminating in this regard are Vincent Harding, *There Is a River: The Black Struggle for Freedom in America* (New York, 1981); and Nathan Irvin Huggins, *Slave and Citizen: The Life of a Frederick Douglass* (Boston, 1980).

Chapter 1

1. Howard A. Ohline, "Republicanism and Slavery: Origins of the Three-Fifths Clause in the United States Constitution," *William and Mary Quarterly* 28 (Oct. 1971): 563–84. On the importance of liberal as well as classical republican values in American revolutionary thought, see Joyce Appleby, "The Social Origins of American Revolutionary Ideology," *Journal of American History* 64 (March 1978): 935–58; and Appleby, *Capitalism and a New Social Order: The Republican Vision of the 1790's* (New York, 1984), esp. 79–105.

2. John C. Miller, *Alexander Hamilton: Portrait in Paradox* (New York, 1959), 122.

3. Wendell Phillips, *Speeches, Lectures, and Letters,* Negro Universities Press ed. (New York, 1968), 369.

4. McDuffie is quoted in William W. Freehling, *Prelude to Civil War: The Nul-*

lification Controversy in South Carolina, 1816–1836 (New York, 1965), 330; Eric Foner, *Free Soil, Free Labor, Free Men: The Ideology of the Republican Party before the Civil War* (New York, 1970), 301–17.

5. On the *Somerset* case generally, see Sir William Holdsworth, *A History of English Law*, 5th ed., 16 vols. (London, 1966), 2:508; David Brion Davis, *The Problem of Slavery in the Age of Revolution, 1770–1823* (Ithaca, 1975), 469–522; William M. Wiecek, "*Somerset:* Lord Mansfield and the Legitimacy of Slavery in the Anglo-American World," *University of Chicago Law Review* 42 (Fall 1974): 86–146; and Wiecek, *The Sources of Antislavery Constitutionalism in America, 1760–1848* (Ithaca, 1977), 20–39.

6. The relationship between slavery and changing attitudes toward unfree and involuntary labor is treated in Edmund S. Morgan, *American Slavery, American Freedom: The Ordeal of Colonial Virginia* (New York, 1975), esp. 319–26, and in Davis, *Problem of Slavery,* 264. On the liberal character of British antislavery reform, see Howard Temperley, "Capitalism, Slavery and Ideology," *Past and Present* 75 (May 1977): 94–118.

7. Davis, *Problem of Slavery,* 394–95, 482–84.

8. Holdsworth, *History of English Law,* 3:7–8; 6:265; 12:282. The civil actions in question were assumpsit, an action to recover damages for breach of contract, and trover, an action to recover the value of property wrongfully converted.

9. Mansfield's actual language in *Somerset* is the subject of controversy. The passage quoted above, from Helen Tunnicliff Catterall, ed., *Judicial Cases Concerning American Slavery and the Negro,* 5 vols. (Washington, D.C., 1926–37), 1:4–5, 15, reflects what American jurists understood to be the language of Mansfield's decision.

10. Quoted in Arthur Zilversmit, *The First Emancipation: The Abolition of Slavery in the North* (Chicago, 1967), 97; see also Bernard Bailyn, *The Ideological Origins of the American Revolution* (Cambridge, Mass., 1967), 239–40.

11. Granville Sharp to Lord North, 18 Feb. 1772, in Charles Stuart, *A Memoir of Granville Sharp* (New York, 1836) [Published by the American Anti-Slavery Society], 12–13; Sharp to Anthony Benezet, 21 Aug. 1772, in George S. Brookes, *Friend Anthony Benezet* (Philadelphia, 1937), 418–22, as cited in Zilversmit, *First Emancipation,* 89.

12. Emory Washburn, "Extinction of Slavery in Massachusetts," in *Proceedings of the Massachusetts Historical Society, 1855–1858* (Boston, 1859), 100, 103–4.

13. Catterall, ed., *Judicial Cases,* 4:481; Eric Foner, *Tom Paine and Revolutionary America* (New York, 1976), 43–50; Mary Stoughton Locke, *Anti-Slavery in America from the Introduction of African Slaves to the Prohibition of the Slave Trade, 1619–1808* (Boston, 1901), 80–82; Zilversmit, *First Emancipation,* 113, 117, 205; Jeremy Belknap, "Queries Respecting the Slavery and Emancipation of Negroes in Massachusetts . . . ," *Collections of the Massachusetts Historical Society,* 1st ser., 4 (1795): 191–211; Howard A. Ohline, "Politics and Slavery: The Issue of Slavery in National Politics, 1787–1815" (Ph.D. dissertation, University of Missouri, 1969), 298–303.

14. Saul K. Padover, *The Complete Jefferson: Containing His Major Writings, Published and Unpublished, Except His Letters,* Books for Libraries Press ed. (Freeport, N.Y., 1969), 319; Julian P. Boyd, ed., *The Papers of Thomas Jefferson,* 20 vols. (Princeton, 1950–82), 9:70, 71; 11:523; 13:649.

15. The instrumental function of equity jurisprudence is stressed in Morton J. Horwitz, *The Transformation of American Law, 1780–1860* (Cambridge, Mass., 1977), esp. 18; see also Appleby, "Social Origins of American Revolutionary Ideology," 935–58.

16. Catterall, ed., *Judicial Cases,* 4:53–54. For Martin's earlier opposition to slavery as a threat to the "genius of republicanism," see Wiecek, *Sources of Antislavery Constitutionalism,* 76.

17. The Kentucky case is *Rankin* v. *Lydia* (1820), summarized in Catterall, ed., *Judicial Cases,* 1:294–95. The Mississippi cases are *Harry et al.* v. *Decker and Hopkins* (1818) and *State* v. *Jones* (1820), summarized in ibid., 3:283–84. The Georgia case is *Cleland* v. *Walters* (1855), summarized in ibid., 3:46. Cobb developed a systematic legal defense of slavery in 1858 to avoid all reference to English common law. See Thomas R. R. Cobb, *An Inquiry into the Law of Negro Slavery in the United States of America. To Which is Prefixed, an Historical Sketch of Slavery,* Negro Universities Press ed. (New York, 1968). See also Mark V. Tushnet, *The American Law of Slavery, 1816–1860* (Princeton, 1981), esp. 44–77.

18. Ohline, "Republicanism and Slavery," 563–84; Robert E. Shalhope, "Toward a Republican Synthesis: The Emergence of an Understanding of Republicanism in American Historiography," *William and Mary Quarterly* 29 (Jan. 1972): 49–80; and Shalhope, "Thomas Jefferson's Republicanism and Antebellum Southern Thought," *Journal of Southern History* 42 (Nov. 1976): 529–56.

19. *Annals of Congress,* 1st Cong., 2d sess., 1197–1205; Locke, *Anti-Slavery,* 114; Ohline, "Politics and Slavery," 97.

20. *Annals of Congress,* 1st Cong., 2d sess., 1182–91; U.S. Constitution, Art. I, sec. 9; Davis, *Problem of Slavery,* 155.

21. Locke, *Anti-Slavery,* 106; Ohline, "Politics and Slavery," 173–74; Shalhope, "Jefferson's Republicanism," 529–56; Davis, *Problem of Slavery,* 155.

22. Warner Mifflin, *A Serious Expostulation with the Members of the House of Representatives of the United States* (Philadelphia, 1793), 13, 20. The convention's petition is quoted in Locke, *Anti-Slavery,* 101–6.

23. *Annals of Congress,* 5th Cong., 2d sess., 1306, 1309–10; Locke, *Anti-Slavery,* 127, 158–59; Ohline, "Politics and Slavery," 298–303.

24. Granville Sharp, *Letter from Granville Sharp, Esq. of London, to the Maryland Society for Promoting the Abolition of Slavery, and the Relief of Free Negroes and Others, Unlawfully Held in Bondage* (Baltimore, 1793), 2–5.

25. John Parrish, *Remarks on the Slavery of the Black People; Addressed to the Citizens of the United States, Particularly to Those Who Are in Legislative or Executive Stations in the General or State Government; and also to Such Individuals as Hold Them in Bondage* (Philadelphia, 1806), 32–33; Locke, *Anti-Slavery,* 163, 175.

26. Parrish, *Remarks,* 8–9, 15, 48. See also James D. Essig, *The Bonds of*

Wickedness: American Evangelicals against Slavery, 1770–1808 (Philadelphia, 1982), 73–96.

27. King quoted in Glover Moore, *The Missouri Controversy, 1819–1821* (Lexington, 1953), 307–8.

28. *Annals of Congress,* 15th Cong., 2d sess., 1192; George Dangerfield, *The Era of Good Feelings* (New York, 1952), 199–245; Ohline, "Republicanism and Slavery," 578–79.

29. Dangerfield, *Era of Good Feelings,* 195; Richard H. Brown, "The Missouri Crisis, Slavery and the Politics of Jacksonianism," *South Atlantic Quarterly* 65 (1966): 15–72.

30. R. Kent Newmyer, *Supreme Court Justice Story: Statesman of the Old Republic* (Chapel Hill, 1985), esp. 208–9, 307, 348–50, 370–79; Jay quoted in Bayard Tuckerman, *William Jay and the Constitutional Movement for the Abolition of Slavery* (New York, 1893), 28–29; Gerald T. Dunne, *Justice Joseph Story and the Rise of the Supreme Court* (New York, 1970), 194; Daniel Webster et al., *A Memorial to the Congress of the United States on the Subject of Restraining the Increase of Slavery in New States to Be Admitted into the Union* (Boston, 1819), reprinted in *The Nebraska Question* (Boston, 1854); Claude M. Fuess, *Daniel Webster,* 2 vols. (Boston, 1930), 1:271; *The Antelope,* 10 Wheaton, 105–6 (1825).

31. William Birney, *James G. Birney and His Times: The Genesis of the Republican Party with Some Account of Abolition Movements in the South before 1828* (New York, 1890), v, 41, 55; Richard H. Sewell, *John P. Hale and the Politics of Abolitionism* (Cambridge, Mass., 1965), 11; David H. Donald, *Charles Sumner and the Coming of the Civil War* (New York, 1960), 30; Richard H. Abbott, *Cobbler in Congress: The Life of Henry Wilson, 1812–1875* (Lexington, 1972), 16–34; Chase to Thomas Sparhawk, 10 Nov. 1828 and 20 Apr. 1829, quoted in Arthur Meier Schlesinger, "Salmon Portland Chase: Undergraduate and Pedagogue," *Ohio Archaeological and Historical Quarterly* 28 (1919): 119–61; Chase to Joseph A. Denison, 14 Nov. 1828, Salmon P. Chase Papers, LC.

32. Quoted in Tuckerman, *Jay,* 52.

33. Foner, *Free Soil,* 73–102; Richard H. Sewell, *Ballots for Freedom: Antislavery Politics in the United States* (New York, 1976), 43–79; Wiecek, *Sources of Antislavery Constitutionalism,* 202–48.

Chapter 2

1. [William Lloyd Garrison], *Selections from the Writings and Speeches of William Lloyd Garrison,* New American Library ed. (New York, 1964), 142.

2. On the transcendental and anti-institutional character of American abolitionism, see Stanley M. Elkins, *Slavery: A Problem in American Institutional and Intellectual Life* (Chicago, 1959), esp. 175–93; John L. Thomas, "Romantic Reform in America," *American Quarterly* 17 (Winter 1965): 656–81; and Lewis Perry, *Radical Abolitionism: Anarchy and the Government of God in Antislavery Thought* (Ithaca, 1973). On the absence of direct political and economic competition between North and South, see Eric Foner, *Politics and Ideology in the*

Age of the Civil War (New York, 1980), 57–76; and Gavin Wright, *The Political Economy of the Cotton South: Households, Markets and Wealth in the Nineteenth Century* (New York, 1978), 130–39. The influence of classical republican ideology in the antebellum South is treated in Kenneth S. Greenberg, "Revolutionary Ideology and the Proslavery Argument: The Abolition of Slavery in Antebellum South Carolina," *Journal of Southern History* 42 (Aug. 1976): 365–84.

3. Wendell Phillips, *Speeches, Lectures, and Letters,* Negro Universities Press ed. (New York, 1968), 531.

4. [Garrison], *Selections,* 149.

5. Ibid., 45.

6. Ibid., 46, 48, 49, 58–59.

7. Marcus Cunliffe, *Soldiers and Civilians: The Martial Spirit in America, 1775–1865* (Boston, 1968), 215–35.

8. [Charles Sumner], *Charles Sumner: His Complete Works,* 20 vols., Negro Universities Press ed. (New York, 1969), 1:11. On the antebellum peace movement generally, see Merle E. Curti, *The American Peace Crusade, 1815–1860,* Octagon Books ed. (New York, 1965) esp. 67–102. On the importance of pacifism in abolitionist thought, see Perry, *Radical Abolitionism,* 55–91.

9. John L. Motley to Charles Sumner, 17 Apr. 1861, Sumner Papers, HL; David Levine, *History as Romantic Art: Bancroft, Prescott, Motley, and Parkman,* AMS Press ed. (New York, 1967), 31, 72. See also George M. Fredrickson, *The Inner Civil War: Northern Intellectuals and the Crisis of the Union* (New York, 1965), 161–65; and Ernest L. Treveson, *Redeemer Nation: The Idea of America's Millennial Role* (Chicago, 1963), 34, 144–47.

10. Salmon P. Chase to John P. Bigelow, 23 Sept. 1854, John P. Bigelow Papers, HL; Lewis Tappan to Gamaliel Bailey, 23 Nov. 1843, letterbook copy, Lewis Tappan Papers, LC.

11. William E. Baringer, "The Politics of Abolition: Salmon P. Chase in Cincinnati," *Cincinnati Historical Society Bulletin* 24 (Summer 1971): 86; Leonard L. Richards, *"Gentlemen of Property and Standing": Anti-Abolition Mobs in Jacksonian America* (New York, 1970), 92–100, 139–44; James Brewer Stewart, *Holy Warriors: The Abolitionists and American Slavery* (New York, 1976), 50–73.

12. William M. Wiecek, *The Sources of Antislavery Constitutionalism in America, 1760–1848* (Ithaca, 1977), 195–96; Leonard W. Levy, *The Law of the Commonwealth and Chief Justice Shaw* (Cambridge, Mass., 1957), 62–67.

13. Helen Tunnicliff Catterall, ed., *Judicial Cases Concerning Slavery and the Negro,* 5 vols. (Washington, D.C., 1926–37), 4:506–8.

14. Morton J. Horwitz, *The Transformation of American Law, 1780–1860* (Cambridge, Mass., 1977), esp. 25, 34–35, 207–10; Levy, *Shaw,* 166–82.

15. [Salmon P. Chase], "Life and Character of Henry Brougham," *North American Review* 33 (1831): 227–61.

16. [Salmon P. Chase], *Speech of Salmon P. Chase, in the Case of the Colored Woman, Matilda, Who was Brought before the Court of Common Pleas of Hamilton County, Ohio, by Writ of Habeas Corpus; March 11, 1837* (Cincinnati, 1837); Chase, *A Sketch of the History of Ohio,* published as an introduction to the *Statutes of Ohio and the Laws of the Northwest Territory* (Cincinnati, 1833), 10, 40.

17. Wiecek, *Sources of Antislavery Constitutionalism,* 191–93. Chase's arguments are in *James G. Birney* v. *The State of Ohio* (1837), 8 Ohio Reports, 230–39; and Chase, *Speech in the Case of the Colored Woman, Matilda.*

18. Richard Hildreth, *Despotism in America: An Inquiry into the Nature, Results, and Legal Basis of the Slave-Holding System in the United States* (Boston, 1854); Phillips, *Speeches, Lectures, and Letters,* 348–49, 370.

19. Joshua R. Giddings to Salmon P. Chase, 7 Apr. 1848, Salmon P. Chase Papers, HSP; David Hackett Fisher, *The Revolution of American Conservatism: The Federalist Party in the Era of Jeffersonian Democracy* (New York, 1965), 175–76; Howard A. Ohline, "Republicanism and Slavery: Origins of the Three-Fifths Clause in the United States Constitution," *William and Mary Quarterly* 28 (Oct. 1971): 563–84.

20. John Quincy Adams to Ellis Gray Loring, 19 Nov. 1839, James Freeman Clarke Papers, HL.

21. Webster quoted in Maurice G. Baxter, *Daniel Webster and the Supreme Court* (Amherst, 1966), 209–10. On *Prigg* see Wiecek, *Sources of Antislavery Constitutionalism,* 157, and Paul Finkleman, "*Prigg* v. *Pennsylvania* and Northern State Courts: Anti-Slavery Use of a Pro-Slavery Decision," *Civil War History* 25 (Sept. 1979): 5–35.

22. Salmon P. Chase to unknown, 5 Jan. 1851, and Chase to Lewis Tappan, 18 Mar. 1847, Salmon P. Chase Papers, LC.

23. Sumner quoted in Ronald B. Jager, "Charles Sumner, the Constitution, and the Civil Rights Act of 1875," *New England Quarterly* 42 (Sept. 1969): 365n; Garrison quoted in Ronald G. Walters, *The Antislavery Appeal: American Abolitionism after 1830* (Baltimore, 1976), 137; Salmon P. Chase to Edwin M. Stanton, 9 Jan. 1849, copy, Edwin M. Stanton Papers, LC. See also Charles Sumner to George William Curtis, 30 Dec. 1871, Curtis Papers, HL; and David Donald, *Charles Sumner and the Rights of Man* (New York, 1970), 427.

24. [Garrison], *Selections,* 126; Lewis Tappan to Wendell Phillips, 11 May 1837, Wendell Phillips Papers, HL.

25. Salmon P. Chase to Charles D. Cleveland, 22 Oct. 1841, and Chase to Lewis Tappan, 26 May 1842, Chase Papers, LC; Chase to Charles Sumner, 18 Nov. 1850, Charles Sumner Papers, HL.

26. James G. Birney to Salmon P. Chase, 2 Feb. 1842, Chase Papers, LC.

27. Salmon P. Chase to Lewis Tappan, 3 Apr. 1844, Chase Papers, LC.

28. Thaddeus Stevens, *Speech of Thaddeus Stevens, of Pennsylvania, on the California Question. Made in the House of Representatives, Night Session, June 10, 1850* (N.p., [1850?]); [Salmon P. Chase], *How the South Rejected Compromise in the Peace Conference of 1861: Speech of Mr. Chase, of Ohio. Published from the Notes of a Member* (New York, [1863?]); Theodore Parker to Charles Sumner, 14 July 1856, Sumner Papers, HL. For Wright's views, see Wiecek, *Sources of Antislavery Constitutionalism,* 198.

29. Salmon P. Chase to Gerrit Smith, 24 July, 9 Aug. 1852, and 15 Feb. 1856, Chase Papers, LC.

30. The passages quoted in the following discussion of the freedom national doctrine are found in [Salmon P. Chase], *Union and Freedom, without*

Compromise; Speech of Mr. Chase, of Ohio, on Mr. Clay's Compromise Resolution (Washington, D.C., [1850?]).

Chapter 3

1. For discussions of the instrumental uses of law in the early nineteenth century, see Harold M. Hyman and William M. Wiecek, *Equal Justice under Law: Constitutional Development, 1835–1875* (New York, 1982), 20–54; Jamil Zainaldin, *Law in Antebellum Society: Legal Change and Economic Expansion* (New York, 1983), 52–75; and Stanley I. Kutler, *Privilege and Creative Destruction: The Charles River Bridge Case* (New York, 1971), esp. 155–71. The relationship between instrumental uses of law, the rise of legal formalism, and developing middle-class social goals is treated in Morton J. Horwitz, *The Transformation of American Law, 1780–1860* (Cambridge, Mass.: 1977), esp. 18, 207–10, 258, 266. The relationship between political organization and the distribution of economic benefits is treated in Richard L. McCormick, "The Party Period and Public Policy: An Exploratory Hypothesis," *Journal of American History* 66 (Sept. 1979): 270–98.

2. Garrison quoted in Ronald G. Walters, *The Antislavery Appeal: American Abolitionism after 1830* (Baltimore, 1976), 26. The Garrisonian constitutional position is discussed in Aileen S. Kraditor, *Means and Ends in American Abolitionism: Garrison and His Critics on Strategy and Tactics, 1834–1850,* Vintage ed. (New York, 1969), 178–224; and William M. Wiecek, *The Sources of Antislavery Constitutionalism in America, 1790–1848* (Ithaca, 1977), 202–87.

3. Lawrence J. Friedman, "The Gerrit Smith Circle: Abolitionism in the Burned-Over District," *Civil War History* 26 (June 1980): 18–38; Lewis Tappan to Lysander Spooner, 3, 15 Nov. 1855, letterbook copies, Lewis Tappan Papers, LC; John A. Alexander, "The Ideas of Lysander Spooner," *New England Quarterly* 23 (1950): 200–217; Lysander Spooner, "The Unconstitutionality of Slavery," in *The Collected Works of Lysander Spooner,* 6 vols. (Weston, Mass., 1971), 4:7–277.

4. Richard H. Sewell, *Ballots for Freedom: Antislavery Politics in the United States, 1837–1860* (New York, 1976), 3–79; Betty Fladeland, *James Gillespie Birney: Slaveholder to Abolitionist,* Greenwood Press ed. (New York, 1969), 148–49.

5. Horwitz, *Transformation of American Law,* 207–10 and passim; Perry Miller, *The Life of the Mind in America from the Revolution to the Civil War* (New York, 1965), 105–9, 179, 186–206. The tension the antislavery constitutional debate produced for northern jurists is the subject of Robert M. Cover, *Justice Accused: Antislavery and Judicial Process* (New Haven, 1975).

6. Spooner later argued that the Civil War had been fought not to end slavery but to compel individuals to submit to the national government. It was his view (shared by Gerrit Smith) that individuals retained the liberty to withdraw from the obligations and constraints of the Constitution. Therefore, only those who consented to be governed could be traitors. See Alexander, "Ideas

of Spooner," 200–217. See also Whitney R. Cross, *The Burned-Over District: The Social and Intellectual History of Enthusiastic Religion in Western New York, 1800–1850* (Ithaca, 1950), 287–357.

7. Alvan Stewart, manuscript entry, dated Philadelphia, 6 May 1844, in "Antislavery Album or Contributions from Friends of Freedom," Western Anti-Slavery Society Papers, LC. See also Sewell, *Ballots for Freedom*, 50–51; and Wiecek, *Sources of Antislavery Constitutionalism*, 254–55.

8. Luther R. Marsh, ed., *Writings and Speeches of Alvan Stewart, on Slavery* (New York, 1860), 255–56; Francis Hawley to Joseph R. Hawley, 2 June 1845, Joseph R. Hawley Papers, LC.

9. Wendell Phillips, *The Constitution a Pro-Slavery Compact*, 3d ed. (New York, 1856); Phillips, *Review of Lysander Spooner on the Unconstitutionality of Slavery* (Boston, 1847); Miller, *Life of the Mind*, 179.

10. Lewis Tappan to Lysander Spooner, 15 Nov. 1855, letterbook copy, Tappan Papers, LC; Alexander, "Ideas of Lysander Spooner," 200–217.

11. Phillips, *Review of Spooner*, 4, 11; Marsh, ed., *Writings and Speeches of Alvan Stewart*, 256.

12. Phillips, *Review of Spooner*, 11, 15, 17, 20, 23.

13. David Dudley Field to Charles Sumner, 7 Mar. 1848, Charles Sumner Papers, HL; Horwitz, *Transformation of American Law*, 266.

14. Adin Ballou to Wendell Phillips, 24 Mar. 1847, Wendell Phillips Papers, HL.

15. Pierpont quoted in Wiecek, *Sources of Antislavery Constitutionalism*, 204; Wendell Phillips to Charles Sumner, 17 Feb. 1845, Sumner Papers, HL.

16. Salmon P. Chase to Gerrit Smith, 3 May 1850, Salmon P. Chase Papers, LC; Chase to Thaddeus Stevens, 18 Apr. 1842, Thaddeus Stevens Papers, LC.

17. Gamaliel Bailey to Wendell Phillips, 3 June 1843, Phillips Papers, HL.

18. J. Miller McKim to Wendell Phillips, 25 Jan. 1845, Phillips Papers, HL. The relationship between abolitionism and middle-class desires for self-control and self-improvement are treated in Lewis Perry, *Childhood, Marriage and Reform: Henry Clarke Wright, 1797–1870* (Chicago, 1980), 266–67 and passim.

19. See, for example, clipping of Henry Wilson's speech enclosed in Henry Wilson to E. A. Stanbury, 31 Jan. 1851, Henry Wilson Papers, LC; Sewell, *Ballots for Freedom*, 127, 286–88.

20. Phillips to Sumner, 3 Sept. 1852 and 7 Mar. 1853, Sumner Papers, HL; Sumner to Phillips, 4 Feb. 1855 and n.d., Phillips Papers, HL.

21. L. P. Noble to Charles Sumner, 1 July 1854, Sumner Papers, HL; William Goodell to George Washington Julian, 18 June 1857, Joshua R. Giddings–George Washington Julian Papers, LC; Beriah Green to Wendell Phillips, 29 Dec. 1859, and James G. Birney et al. to Phillips, July 1838, Phillips Papers, HL.

22. *Congressional Globe*, 27th Cong., 2d sess., 429. Popular interest in Adams's argument increased with the outbreak of the Civil War, and the speech appeared in pamphlet form. See John Quincy Adams, *The Abolition of Slavery the Right of the Government under the War Power* (Boston, 1861).

23. William Goodell to Elihu B. Washburne, 20 Mar. 1858, Elihu B. Washburne Papers, LC; Gerrit Smith to Salmon P. Chase, 8 June 1859, Chase Papers, LC; Francis Hawley to Joseph R. Hawley, 2 June 1845, Hawley Papers, LC.

24. Marsh, ed., *Writings and Speeches of Alvan Stewart*, 129–54, 420.

25. For Gerrit Smith's agrarian views, see Ralph V. Harlow, *Gerrit Smith: Philanthropist and Reformer* (New York, 1939), 181–242; Cross, *Burned-Over District*, 326–27; Gerrit Smith, *Land Reform: Speech of Gerrit Smith, Made in Syracuse, January 20, 1848, on Land Reform* (Syracuse, 1849).

26. For an analysis of Seward's "higher law" speech see Glyndon G. Van Deusen, *William Henry Seward* (New York, 1967), 122–24, 201–3.

27. Lewis Tappan to William Slade, 30 Dec. 1856; Tappan to John G. Fee, 10 July 1855; Tappan to Salmon P. Chase, 23 June 1852; Tappan to Samuel Lewis, 23 June 1852; Tappan to Francis Gillette et al., 5 Dec. 1839; Tappan to Gerrit Smith, 5 Dec. 1848, letterbook copies, Tappan Papers, LC; Tappan to Charles Sumner, 5 Apr. 1848, Sumner Papers, HL.

28. Jay quoted in Bayard Tuckerman, *William Jay and the Constitutional Movement for the Abolition of Slavery* (New York, 1893), 118–19; William Jay to Lewis Tappan, 5 Oct. 1844, Tappan Papers, LC.

29. Jay quoted in Tuckerman, *Jay*, 43–45; Lewis Tappan to William Jay, 11 Oct. 1844, letterbook copy, Tappan Papers, LC.

30. Jay's comments on disunion are quoted in Kraditor, *Means and Ends*, 205. See also Lewis Tappan to William Jay, Mar. 1843, letterbook copy, Tappan Papers, LC; Tuckerman, *Jay*, 118–21.

31. William Jay to Charles Sumner, 16 Dec. 1850 and 21 Feb. 1850, also John Jay to Charles Sumner, 4 Jan. 1850, Sumner Papers, HL.

32. Wendell Phillips's marginal comments in Thomas Wentworth Higginson to Phillips, 2 Mar. 1853, Phillips Papers, HL; Lewis Tappan to Salmon P. Chase, 23 June 1852, letterbook copy, Tappan Papers, LC; [Salmon P. Chase], *Speech of Hon. Salmon P. Chase, Delivered at the Republican Mass Meeting in Cincinnati, August 21, 1855; Together with Extracts from His Speeches in the Senate on Kindred Subjects* (Columbus, 1855).

33. Chase, *Speech in Cincinnati*.

Chapter 4

1. Harold Schwartz, *Samuel Gridley Howe, Social Reformer, 1801–1876* (Cambridge, Mass., 1956), 7–39; *Dictionary of American Biography*, 2:294; Perry Miller, ed., *Margaret Fuller, American Romantic: A Selection from Her Writings and Correspondence* (Ithaca, 1963), xiv–xvi; Steven Rowan and James Neal Primm, eds., *Germans for a Free Missouri: Translations from the St. Louis Radical Press, 1857–1862* (Columbia, Mo., 1983), 241, 139–42.

2. [William Lloyd Garrison], *Selections from the Writings and Speeches of William Lloyd Garrison*, New American Library ed. (New York, 1969), 125–26.

3. Jonathan A. Glickstein, "'Poverty Is Not Slavery': American Abolitionists

and the Competitive Labor Market," in Lewis Perry and Michael Fellman, eds., *Antislavery Reconsidered: New Perspectives on the Abolitionists* (Baton Rouge, 1979), 195-218; Phyllis F. Field, *The Politics of Race in New York: The Struggle for Black Suffrage in the Civil War Era* (Ithaca, 1982), 75, 111; Lee Benson, *The Concept of Jacksonian Democracy: New York as a Test Case* (Princeton, 1961), 224–26, 237, 240–42; George M. Fredrickson, *The Black Image in the White Mind: The Debate on Afro-American Character and Destiny, 1817–1914* (New York, 1971), 61–66, 90–95.

4. On the relationship between antislavery reform and middle-class economic and political goals, see Paul E. Johnson, *A Shopkeeper's Millennium: Society and Revivals in Rochester, New York, 1815–1837* (New York, 1978), 5–8, 15–61; Ronald G. Walters, *The Antislavery Appeal: American Abolitionism after 1830* (Baltimore, 1976), 111–28; and David Brion Davis, *The Problem of Slavery in the Age of Revolution, 1770–1823* (Ithaca, 1975), esp. 264, 362, 403.

5. Lewis Tappan to Joshua R. Giddings, 1 Feb. 1840, Joshua R. Giddings–George Washington Julian Papers, LC; Theodore Sedgwick to Charles Sumner, 9 June 1844, Charles Sumner Papers, HL.

6. See Peter Temin, *The Jacksonian Economy* (New York, 1969), 172–77.

7. Historians who have searched for consistent themes of political thought in the Democratic and Whig parties have concentrated their attention on liberals who embraced this utilitarian critique of slavery. Thus, each of the individuals whom Marvin Meyers selected to illustrate the Jacksonian "persuasion"—Theodore Sedgwick (d. 1839), William Leggett, and Robert Rantoul, Jr.—opposed slavery as an obstacle to progress. The same antislavery conviction pervaded the entrepreneurial, evangelical, and modernizing aspects of what Daniel Walker Howe delineated as Whig "political culture." See Meyers, *The Jacksonian Persuasion: Politics and Belief* (Stanford, 1957), 163–233; and Howe, *The Political Culture of the American Whigs* (Chicago, 1979), 43–68, 108–22, 167–209.

8. Theodore Sedgwick, *Public and Private Economy: Part I* (New York, 1836), 2, 31, 131, 141; Theodore Sedgwick to Horace Mann, 1 Dec. 1838, Horace Mann Papers, MHS; Joseph Dorfman, *The Economic Mind in American Civilization, 1606–1865*, 2 vols. (New York, 1946), 2:650–52.

9. Sedgwick, *Public and Private Economy*, 62, 95–113.

10. Ibid., 95–113, 225–26; Meyers, *Jacksonian Persuasion*, 184.

11. Sedgwick, *Public and Private Economy*, 2, 15–17, 22–25, 31–41, 70, 131, 141, 148; Wendell Phillips, *Speeches, Lectures, and Letters*, Negro Universities Press ed. (New York, 1968), 503–4.

12. Sedgwick, *Public and Private Economy*, 246–64.

13. William Elder, *A Memoir of Henry C. Carey. Read before the Historical Society of Pennsylvania, Philadelphia, January 5, 1880* (Philadelphia, 1880), 27–28; Dorfman, *Economic Mind*, 2:789–805; Eric Foner, *Free Soil, Free Labor, Free Men: The Ideology of the Republican Party before the Civil War* (New York, 1970), 36–37.

14. Henry C. Carey, *Principles of Political Economy, Part the Fourth: Of the Causes Which Retard Improvement in the Political Condition of Man* (Philadelphia, 1840), 200–202, 204, 207.

15. Henry C. Carey to Charles Sumner, 4 May, 24 July 1852, 20, 25 Nov. and 1, 3 Dec. 1847, Sumner Papers, HL.

16. Henry C. Carey, *Principles of Political Economy, Part the Second: Of the Causes Which Retard Increase in the Production of Wealth, and Improvement in the Physical and Moral Condition of Man* (Philadelphia, 1838), 32, 194, 383.

17. Elder, *Memoir of Carey*, 27–28.

18. Henry C. Carey, *American Civil War, Correspondence with Mr. H. C. Carey, of Philadelphia* (N.p., 1861), 15.

19. Leavitt's most successful reading primers were *Easy Lessons in Reading; For the Use of the Younger Classes in Common Schools* (Keene, N.H., 1823), and *Selections for Reading and Speaking, for the Higher Classes in Common Schools* (Boston, 1847). Both volumes appeared in several editions. For Leavitt's views on free trade, see *Memorial of Joshua Leavitt, Setting Forth Importance of an Equitable and Adequate Market for American Wheat, Accompanied with Statistical Tables* (Albany, [1841?]); also Leavitt to Salmon P. Chase, 16 June 1868, Chase Papers, LC.

20. Joshua Leavitt, *The Moral and Social Benefits of Cheap Postage* (New York, 1849), 10–11.

21. Julian P. Bretz first drew attention to Leavitt's role in the development of economic arguments against slavery in his pioneering essay, "The Economic Background of the Liberty Party," *American Historical Review* 34 (Jan. 1929): 250, 255–56.

22. Joshua Leavitt, *The Financial Power of Slavery: The Substance of an Address Delivered in Ohio, in September, 1840, by Joshua Leavitt, of New York* (N.p., [1841?]), 1, 4; Louis Filler, *The Crusade against Slavery, 1830–1860* (New York, 1960), 24–25.

23. Leavitt, *Financial Power*, 1–3.

24. Joshua Leavitt, *Alarming Disclosures: Political Power of Slavery. Substance of Several Speeches by Rev. Joshua Leavitt in the Ohio Anti-Slavery Convention, and at Public Meetings in That State, in Oct. 1840, and Published in the "Emancipator"* (N.p., 1840), 3–7, 13–14; Leavitt, *Financial Power*, 2, 4.

25. Alvan Stewart, *The Causes of Hard Times* (Boston, 1840), 1–4; Walters, *Antislavery Appeal*, 125.

26. See Alan Dawley, *Class and Community: The Industrial Revolution in Lynn* (Cambridge, Mass., 1976), 64–65, 73–74; and Johnson, *Shopkeeper's Millennium*, 55–61.

27. Walters, *Antislavery Appeal*, 16–17.

28. Victor Ullman, *Martin R. Delany: The Beginnings of Black Nationalism* (Boston, 1971), 28–29, 269–98; *Dictionary of American Biography*, 3:68.

29. William Elder to Salmon P. Chase, 3 July, 5 Sept. 1844, Salmon P. Chase Papers, HSP.

30. Elder to Chase, 5 Jan. 1845, ibid.

31. Elder, *Third Parties*, 1–28.

32. Ibid.

33. Ibid., 12–13.

34. Ibid., 14.

35. [Garrison], *Selections*, 125–26; Eric Foner, *Politics and Ideology in the Age*

of the Civil War (New York, 1980), 57–76, argues to the contrary that artisans identified with the plight of the slave but not with the abolitionists' "view of economic relations."

36. Elder, *Third Parties*, 13.

37. Ibid., 4–6, 22–88.

38. Ibid., 14–17.

39. Elder, *Memoir of Carey*, 17–18, 21, 263–64; William Elder, *Questions of The Day: Economic and Social* (Philadelphia, 1871), 86–87.

40. William Elder, *Conversations on the Principal Subjects of Political Economy* (Philadelphia, 1882), 261–62. Elder dedicated this volume to Alexander Hamilton, Henry C. Carey, and Stephen Colwell, whom he characterized as "The Political Economists of the New World for the New Time." Elder, *Memoir of Carey*, 17–18, 21, 263–64; Elder, *Questions of the Day*, 86–87.

41. Timothy L. Smith, *Revivalism and Social Reform: American Protestantism on the Eve of the Civil War,* Harper Torchbooks ed. (New York, 1965), 160, 181; *Dictionary of American Biography*, 9:217–18.

42. C. S. Griffin, *Their Brothers' Keepers: Moral Stewardship in the United States* (New Brunswick, N.J., 1960), esp. 23–60. For the impact of Calvinism across the upper North and the disruptive role of the "ultraists" see Lois Kimball Mathews, *The Expansion of New England: The Spread of New England Settlement to the Mississippi River, 1620–1825* (Boston, 1909); and Rev. Stephen Peet, *Presbyterian and Congregational Churches and Ministers in Wisconsin: Including an Account of the Organization of the Convention and the Plan of Union* (Milwaukee, 1851).

43. Quoted in Smith, *Revivalism and Social Reform*, 182, 187.

44. Henry C. Carey, *A Memoir of Stephen Colwell: Read before the American Philosophical Society, Friday November 17, 1871* (Philadelphia, 1871), 4–35; *Dictionary of American Biography*, 2:327; Stephen Colwell, *The South: A Letter from a Friend in the North. With Special Reference to the Effects of Disunion upon Slavery* (Philadelphia, 1856), 4, 41; Willie Lee Rose, *Rehearsal for Reconstruction: The Port Royal Experiment,* Vintage ed. (New York, 1967), 76.

45. Stephen Colwell, *The Position of Christianity in the United States, in Its Relations with Our Political Institutions and Specially with Reference to Religious Instruction in the Public Schools,* Arno Press ed. (New York, 1972); Colwell, *New Themes for Protestant Clergy: Creeds without Charity, Theology without Humanity, Protestantism without Christianity: With Notes by the Editor on the Literature of Charity, Population, Pauperism, Political Economy, and Protestantism* (Philadelphia, 1851).

46. Colwell, *New Themes for Protestant Clergy*, 125, 168, 359–63.

47. Stephen Colwell, *The Five Cotton States and New York; or, Remarks upon the Social and·Economical Aspects of the Southern Political Crisis* (N.p., Jan. 1861), 6, 51, 62–64; Field, *Politics of Race in New York*, 75, 111, 220–30; Michael F. Holt, *Forging a Majority: The Formation of the Republican Party in Pittsburgh, 1848–1860* (New Haven, 1969), 311; Ronald P. Formisano, *The Birth of Mass Political Parties: Michigan, 1827–1861* (Princeton, 1971), 323–34.

Chapter 5

1. Calhoun quoted in William W. Freehling, *Prelude to Civil War: The Nullification Controversy in South Carolina, 1816–1834* (New York, 1965), 257.

2. Wendell Phillips, *Speeches, Lectures, and Letters,* Negro Universities Press ed. (New York, 1968), 580–81.

3. Austin Willey, *The History of the Antislavery Cause in State and Nation* (Portland, Me., 1886), 493. See also William Birney, *James G. Birney and His Times: The Genesis of the Republican Party with Some Account of Abolition Movements in the South before 1828* (New York, 1890), 5, 41.

4. Phillips, notes for a lecture on Chartism, n.d., Wendell Phillips Papers, HL.

5. As Geoffrey Blodgett observes of liberal reformers in the late nineteenth century, this cautious response to mass politics intended to replace narrow self-interest with the abstract interests of the state ("A New Look at the American Gilded Age," *Historical Reflections* 1 [Winter 1974]: 241; and Blodgett, "The Mugwump Reputation, 1870 to the Present," *Journal of American History* 66 [Mar. 1980]: 880–81). On the relationship between popular political participation and the distribution of economic benefits, see Richard L. McCormick, "The Party Period and Public Policy: An Exploratory Hypothesis," *Journal of American History* 66 (Sept. 1979): 279–98.

6. On the relationship between "ethno-cultural" political bonds and antislavery reform see Phyllis F. Field, *The Politics of Race in New York: The Struggle for Black Suffrage in the Civil War Era* (Ithaca, 1982), 220–30; Michael F. Holt, *The Political Crisis of the 1850s* (New York, 1978), 178–81; and Eric Foner, *Free Soil, Free Labor, Free Men: The Ideology of the Republican Party before the Civil War* (New York, 1970), 226–30, 260.

7. William Jay to Charles Sumner, 16 Dec. 1850, Sumner Papers, HL; Ronald L. Walters, *The Antislavery Appeal: American Abolitionism after 1830* (Baltimore, 1976), 113–14.

8. Kinley J. Brauer, *Cotton versus Conscience: Massachusetts Whig Politics and Southwestern Expansion, 1843–1848* (Lexington, 1967), esp. 74–76; Allan Nevins, *The Emergence of Lincoln,* Vol. 2, *Prologue to the Civil War, 1859–1861* (New York, 1950), 23, 91, 105.

9. Holt, *Political Crisis of the 1850s,* 191; Field, *Politics of Race,* 113, 145–46.

10. Lewis Tappan to Seth M. Gates, 31 Jan. 1840, letterbook copy, Lewis Tappan Papers, LC; Tappan to Joshua R. Giddings, 1 Feb. 1840, Joshua R. Giddings–George Washington Julian Papers, LC; Richard H. Sewell, *Ballots for Freedom: Antislavery Politics in the United States, 1837–1860* (New York, 1976), 48, 64.

11. Salmon P. Chase to Charles D. Cleveland, 29 Aug. 1840, Salmon P. Chase Papers, HSP.

12. James G. Birney, diary, 3 Mar. 1840, James G. Birney Papers, LC.

13. Salmon P. Chase to Charles D. Cleveland, 22 Oct. 1841, Salmon P. Chase Papers, LC; Chase to Joshua R. Giddings, 21 Jan. 1842, Giddings-Julian Papers, LC; Chase to Charles Sumner, 13 Apr. 1850, Charles Sumner Papers, HL; Chase to Gerrit Smith, 13 Sept. 1851, Chase Papers, LC.

14. Chase to Charles Sumner, 13 Apr. 1850, Sumner Papers, HL; and Chase quoted in David Franklin Hughes, "Salmon P. Chase: Chief Justice" (Ph.D. dissertation, Princeton University, 1963), 23.

15. Chase to Joshua R. Giddings, 21 Jan., 15 Feb. 1842, Giddings-Julian Papers, LC.

16. Wilson quoted in Richard H. Abbott, *Cobbler in Congress: The Life of Henry Wilson, 1812–1875* (Lexington, 1972), 37; see also 21, 38–40.

17. James G. Birney, diary, 19 Apr. 1842, Birney Papers, LC; Birney to Salmon P. Chase, 2 Feb. 1842, Chase Papers, LC; see also Julian P. Bretz, "The Economic Background of the Liberty Party," *American Historical Review* 34 (Jan. 1929): 250–64.

18. Chase to Joshua R. Giddings, 9 Feb. 1843, Giddings-Julian Papers, LC; Lewis Tappan to William Jay, Mar. 1843, letterbook copy, Tappan Papers, LC.

19. James Brewer Stewart, *Joshua R. Giddings and the Tactics of Radical Politics* (Cleveland, 1970), 40, 62–78; John Quincy Adams, *The Jubilee of the Constitution: A Discourse Delivered at the Request of the New York Historical Society, in the City of New York, on Tuesday, the 30th of April, 1839; Being the Fiftieth Anniversary of the Inauguration of George Washington as President of the United States, on Thursday, the 30th of April, 1789* (New York, 1839), esp. 11, 16, 128.

20. Claude M. Fuess, *Daniel Webster*, 2 vols. (Boston, 1930), 2 : 113. Joshua R. Giddings, *Pacificus: The Rights and Privileges of the Several States in Regard to Slavery; Being a Series of Essays, Published in the Western Reserve Chronicle, (Ohio), After the Election of 1842. By a Whig of Ohio* (N.p., n.d.), 1. Stewart, *Giddings*, 46–47, 73–76. Stewart notes that the censure vote passed "with the entire Democratic party and almost all Southern Whigs casting their vote for the measure."

21. Giddings, *Pacificus*, 13, 14.

22. Ibid., 9.

23. Ibid.

24. Joshua R. Giddings to Jacob M. Howard, 4, 13 Nov. 1844, and David Lee Child to Howard, 7 Oct. 1844, Howard Papers, Detroit Public Library; Elizur Wright, Jr., to Salmon P. Chase, 3 Feb. 1844, Chase Papers, LC. See also Howard's autobiographic sketch in the Charles Lanman Papers, Detroit Public Library.

25. Richard H. Sewell, *John P. Hale and the Politics of Abolition* (Cambridge, Mass., 1965), 82.

26. Amos Tuck, autobiographical sketch, probably written in 1850, 83–104; Tuck to his son, 24 Sept. 1879, Amos Tuck Papers, Dartmouth College Library.

27. Joshua R. Giddings to John P. Hale, 25 July 1846, John P. Hale Papers, Dartmouth College Library.

28. Salmon P. Chase to Joshua R. Giddings, 9 Feb. 1843, Giddings-Julian Papers, LC.

29. Albert Gallatin Riddle, "The Election of Salmon P. Chase to the Senate, February 22, 1849," *Republic* 4 (1875): 183. Like Giddings, Riddle remained loyal to the national Whig party until 1848 and favored Giddings over Chase for the Senate. His critical portrait of Chase in 1875 was followed by favorable

biographies of James A. Garfield (1880) and Benjamin F. Wade (1886). On Riddle's involvement in the senatorial election, see Stewart, *Giddings*, 202; and Chase to Riddle, 24 Feb. 1849, Chase Papers, LC. For Riddle's entire career see *Dictionary of American Biography*, 8:591.

30. George Washington Julian, review of T. C. Smith, *The Liberty and Free Soil Parties in the Northwest* (New York, 1897), in the *American Historical Review* 4 (Oct. 1898–July 1899): 180–81; John G. Sproat, *"The Best Men": Liberal Reformers in the Gilded Age* (New York, 1968), 48–49.

31. Salmon P. Chase to Eli Nichols, 9 Nov. 1848, letterbook copy, Chase Papers, LC.

32. Salmon P. Chase to his wife, 25 Dec. 1848, Chase Papers, LC. See also Chase to Stanley Matthews, 24, 29 Jan. 1849, in Annie A. Nunns, ed., "Some Letters of Salmon P. Chase, 1848–1865," *American Historical Review* 34 (1929): 543, 548.

33. Salmon P. Chase to his wife, 20 Dec. 1848, Chase Papers, LC; Chase to Edwin M. Stanton, 9 Jan. 1848, copy, Edwin M. Stanton Papers, LC; Joshua R. Giddings to Charles Sumner, 11 Feb. 1847, Sumner Papers, HL; Joseph M. Root to Chase, 5 Apr. 1848, and Chase to Eli Nichols, 9 Nov. 1848, letterbook copy, Chase Papers, LC; Chase to Stanley Matthews, 29 Jan. 1849, in Nunns, ed., "Letters of Chase," 547; Foner, *Free Soil*, 137, 166; Stewart, *Giddings*, 104; Reinhard H. Luthin, "Salmon P. Chase's Political Career before the Civil War," *Mississippi Valley Historical Review* 29 (Mar. 1943): 524; Eugene H. Roseboom, "Salmon P. Chase and the Know Nothings," *Mississippi Valley Historical Review* 25 (Dec. 1938): 340.

34. Riddle, "Election of Chase," 179–83; S. P. Chase to A. G. Riddle, 24 Feb. 1849, typescript copy, Chase Papers, LC; T. Noble to S. P. Chase, 24 Feb. 1849, in Nunns, ed., "Letters of Chase," 545; Stewart, *Giddings*, 202; Sewell, *Ballots for Freedom*, 208; Frederick J. Blue, "The Ohio Free Soilers and the Problem of Factionalism," *Ohio History* 76 (Winter 1967): 23.

35. Norton S. Townshend, "Salmon P. Chase," *Ohio Archaeological and Historical Society Quarterly* 1 (Sept. 1887): 111–26; Riddle, "Election of Chase," 179–83. Neither the Whigs nor the Democrats could organize the House without antislavery support. To gain a majority, the Whigs needed all the Free Soil votes; the Democrats needed but two. See Riddle, "Election of Chase," 179–83; and Chase to his wife, 20, 30 Dec. 1848, Chase Papers, LC.

36. S. P. Chase to Stanley Matthews, 18 Jan. 1849, in Nunns, ed., "Letters of Chase," 539; Stanley Matthews to Chase, 11 Jan. 1849, and Chase to E. S. Hamlin, 16 Jan. 1849, Chase Papers, LC.

37. Stanley Matthews to Chase, 20, 26 Jan. 1849, and Chase to E. S. Hamlin, 20 Jan. 1849, Chase Papers, LC.

38. Giddings to Sumner, 29 Oct. 1849, Sumner Papers, HL; Riddle, "Election of Chase," 179, 182–83; Chase to Stanley Matthews, 18 Jan. 1849, in Nunns, ed., "Letters of Chase," 539.

Chapter 6

1. This view of the radical impact of antislavery reform is developed in Margaret Shortreed, "The Antislavery Radicals: From Crusade to Revolution, 1840–1868," *Past and Present* 16 (Nov. 1959): 65–89, an essay that anticipated much of the revisionist writing of the 1960s. Indispensable studies of the interaction of antislavery reform and politics are James M. McPherson, *The Struggle for Equality: Abolitionists and the Negro in the Civil War and Reconstruction* (New York, 1964); David Montgomery, *Beyond Equality: Labor and the Radical Republicans, 1862–1872* (New York, 1967); Eric Foner, *Free Soil, Free Labor, Free Men: The Ideology of the Republican Party before the Civil War* (New York, 1970); and Richard H. Sewell, *Ballots for Freedom: Antislavery Politics in the United States, 1837–1860* (New York, 1976).

2. William H. Seward, *California, Union, and Freedom: Speech of William H. Seward, on the Admission of California, Delivered in the Senate of the United States, March 11, 1850* (Washington, D.C., 1850); Glyndon G. Van Deusen, *William Henry Seward* (New York, 1967), 121–28.

3. The antislavery character of northern Whiggery is stressed in James Brewer Stewart, "Abolitionists, Insurgents, and Third Parties: Sectionalism and Partisan Politics in Northern Whiggery, 1836–1844," in Alan M. Kraut, ed., *Crusaders and Compromisers: Essays on the Relationship of the Antislavery Struggle to the Antebellum Party System* (Westport, Conn., 1983), 25–43. On ethnic and religious distinctions in the new Republican party see Michael F. Holt, *Forging a Majority: The Formation of the Republican Party in Pittsburgh, 1848–1860* (New Haven, 1969); and Ronald P. Formisano, *The Birth of Mass Political Parties: Michigan, 1827–1861* (Princeton, 1971).

4. Wendell Phillips, *Speeches, Lectures, and Letters*, Negro Universities Press ed. (New York, 1968), 529.

5. Samuel May to Francis W. Bird, 16 Apr. 1885, Francis W. Bird Papers, HL. On the survival of the Democracy during the Civil War, see Joel H. Silbey, *A Respectable Minority: The Democratic Party in the Civil War Era, 1860–1868* (New York, 1977), esp. 158–76. Suggestive on the nature and effect of the party system is Samuel P. Hays, "Political Parties and the Community-Society Continuum," in William Nisbet Chambers and Walter Dean Burnham, eds., *The American Party Systems*, 2d ed. (New York, 1975), 152–81, esp. 161.

6. Chase to Butler, 14 Dec. 1862, Benjamin F. Butler Papers, LC, as quoted in Louis S. Gerteis, "Salmon P. Chase, Radicalism, and the Politics of Emancipation, 1861–1864," *Journal of American History* 60 (June 1973): 52.

7. Salmon P. Chase to Edward S. Hamlin, 2, 17 Jan., 2 Feb. 1850, Salmon P. Chase Papers, LC; Chase to Charles Sumner, 26 Nov. 1846, Charles Sumner Papers, HL; Sumner to Chase, 24 Jan. 1850, Chase Papers, LC; Victor B. Howard, "The Illinois Republican Party: The Party Becomes Conservative, 1855–1856," *Illinois State Historical Society Journal* 64 (Autumn 1971): 288n; Gamaliel Bailey to Joshua R. Giddings, 29 Sept. 1849, Joshua R. Giddings–George Washington Julian Papers, LC.

8. Salmon P. Chase to Edward S. Hamlin, 22 Jan. 1850; Charles Sumner to Chase, 24 Jan. 1850, Chase Papers, LC.

9. Salmon P. Chase to Edward S. Hamlin, 2, 28 Feb., 16 Mar. and 16 Apr. 1850, Chase Papers, LC.

10. Salmon P. Chase to unknown, 29 Sept. 1850, and Chase to [John F. Morse?], 3 Dec. 1850, Chase Papers, LC; James Brewer Stewart, *Joshua R. Giddings and the Tactics of Radical Politics* (Cleveland, 1970), 117; Alston Ellis, "Samuel Lewis, Progressive Educator in the Early History of Ohio," *Ohio Archaeological and Historical Society Publications* 21 (Jan. 1916): 71–87; Joseph G. Rayback, "The Liberty Party Leaders of Ohio: Exponents of Antislavery Coalition," *Ohio Archaeological and Historical Quarterly* 57 (1948): 170; *Dictionary of American Biography*, 6:223–24; Samuel Lewis to Joshua R. Giddings, 20 Mar. 1849, Giddings-Julian Papers, LC; Lewis Tappan to Samuel Lewis, 23 June 1852, letterbook copy, Lewis Tappan Papers, LC; Edward S. Hamlin to Salmon P. Chase, 1 July 1850, and Edward L. Pierce's manuscript biography of Salmon P. Chase, Chase Papers, LC.

Although Lewis joined with Giddings in the September 1851 Cleveland convention that adopted Liberty League resolutions on the unconstitutionality of slavery, by 1852 he and Giddings were willing to return to what Chase insisted were the Democratic principles of 1848. Both Lewis and Giddings supported the Pittsburgh "Free Democratic" platform of 1852.

11. Charles Sumner to Salmon P. Chase, 12 Mar., 1 Oct. 1847, 16 Nov. 1848, and James A. Briggs to Chase, 15 Sept. 1848, Chase Papers, LC; Thomas Corwin to Charles Sumner, 25 Oct. 1847, and Joshua R. Giddings to Sumner, 21 Feb. 1847, Sumner Papers, HL. See also Hans L. Trefousse, *Benjamin Franklin Wade, Radical Republican from Ohio* (New York, 1963), 64–67; and Sewell, *Ballots for Freedom*, 141–42.

The antislavery enthusiasm for Corwin resulted largely from wishful thinking among antislavery Whigs. Corwin had no intention of tarnishing his credentials with the national Whig party. Writing to the Indiana Whig leader Caleb B. Smith in May 1848, Corwin declared that "I will go for any Whig South, North, East or West who is most certain of success, rather than take any Democrat named yet, on the subject of Slavery, its extension &c." John C. Calhoun or Zachary Taylor, he thought, would be every bit as "good for the north, as any Democrat in the whole party, from Mason & Dixon's line to Canada." Daniel Webster, as secretary of state in Fillmore's administration, thought Corwin was sufficiently hostile to antislavery agitation in the Whig party to be willing to use his patronage powers as treasury secretary to punish the *Boston Atlas* for its support of antislavery Congressman Horace Mann. See Daniel Webster to Thomas Corwin, 13 Nov. 1850, Thomas Corwin Papers, LC; Thomas Corwin to Caleb B. Smith, 10 May 1848, Caleb B. Smith Papers, LC.

12. Salmon P. Chase to Edward S. Hamlin, 9 Dec. 1850, Chase Papers, LC. Chase was quick to add, however, that if the Democracy could not be brought to Giddings's side, Hamlin should encourage the Free Democrats to put forward a candidate of their own. Chase suggested Hamlin himself as well as Leicester King, Jacob Brinkerhoff, and Milton Sutliff among others.

13. Salmon P. Chase to [John F. Morse], 12 Dec. 1850, Chase Papers, LC; Chase to Stanley Matthews, 13 Dec. 1850, in Annie A. Nunns, ed., "Some

Letters of Salmon P. Chase, 1848–1865," *American Historical Review* 34 (1929): 536–55.

14. Salmon P. Chase to [John F. Morse], 12 Dec. and Chase to his wife, 16 Jan. 1851, Chase Papers, LC; Trefousse, *Wade*, 64–67.

15. Joshua R. Giddings to Charles Sumner, 17 Mar. 1851, and Salmon P. Chase to Charles Sumner, 28 Apr. 1851, Sumner Papers, HL.

16. Salmon P. Chase to Joshua R. Giddings, 9 Sept. 1851, Chase Papers, LC.

17. Salmon P. Chase to Edward S. Hamlin, 27 May 1850, 5 Dec. 1851, 10 Mar., 28 June, 19 July 1852; and Chase to unknown, 13 Aug. 1852, Chase Papers, LC. Joshua R. Giddings to George Washington Julian, 30 June 1852, Giddings-Julian Papers, LC; Lewis Tappan to Giddings, 17 June 1852, letterbook copy, Tappan Papers, LC.

18. On the importance of race in maintaining Whig and Democratic party loyalties in New York, see Phyllis F. Field, *The Politics of Race in New York: The Struggle for Black Suffrage in the Civil War Era* (Ithaca, 1982), 19–79; William H. Seward to Salmon P. Chase, 26 Dec. 1846, 20 Jan. 1847, 12 June 1848, Chase Papers, LC. Lewis Tappan's distrust of Seward as governor seems to have been overcome by the "higher law" speech. See Lewis Tappan to Seth M. Gates, 10 Mar. 1840, and Tappan to Gamaliel Bailey, 20 Mar. 1850, letterbook copies, Lewis Tappan Papers, LC.

19. William H. Seward to Salmon P. Chase, 22 Jan. 1846 and 12 June 1848, Chase Papers, LC; Seward to Charles Sumner, 9 Nov. 1852, Sumner Papers, HL.

20. Sewell, *Ballots for Freedom*, 224–29.

21. Salmon P. Chase to Benjamin F. Butler, 26 July 1849, letterbook copy, Chase Papers, LC.

22. Ibid.

23. The *Cleveland True Democrat*—successor to the *True American*—was edited by John Vaughan and James A. Briggs, both of whom had recently denounced Chase's Free Soil–Democratic coalition. The *Boston Republican*—successor to the *Boston Whig*—was edited by Charles Francis Adams, William S. Robinson, and Henry Wilson. Only Wilson favored cooperation with the Democracy.

24. Charles Sumner to Salmon P. Chase, 18 Sept. 1849, Chase Papers, LC.

25. Salmon P. Chase to Charles Sumner, 15, 19 Sept. 1849, Sumner Papers, HL.

26. Gamaliel Bailey to Charles Sumner, 23 Sept. 1849, Sumner Papers, HL; Bailey to Joshua R. Giddings, 19 Sept. 1849, Giddings-Julian Papers, LC.

27. Henry B. Stanton to Salmon P. Chase, 1 Oct. 1849, Chase Papers, LC; Sewell, *Ballots for Freedom*, 214.

28. Elizur Wright, Jr., to Salmon P. Chase, 30 Jan. 1845, Chase Papers, LC.

29. Stephen C. Phillips et al. to S. P. Chase, 25 June 1845, Chase Papers, LC.

30. Charles Sumner to Salmon P. Chase, 12 Dec. 1846, Chase Papers, LC.

31. Charles Sumner to Salmon P. Chase, 12 Dec. 1846 and 7 Feb. 1848, Chase Papers, LC; Thomas G. Cary to Sumner, 1 Aug. 1847, and John A. Andrew to Sumner, 29 Oct. 1846, Sumner Papers, HL; David Donald, *Charles Sumner and the Coming of the Civil War* (New York, 1960), 183–89.

32. Horace Mann to Charles Sumner, 9 Jan. 1850, Sumner Papers, HL; Amos Tuck, autobiographical sketch, 102–3, Amos Tuck Papers, Dartmouth College Library.

33. Theodore Parker to Henry Wilson, 15 Feb. 1855, Henry Wilson Papers, LC. For similarly condescending expressions of concern, see A. G. Browne to Charles Sumner, 17 Apr. 1855, Sumner Papers, HL.

34. Richard H. Abbott, *Cobbler in Congress: The Life of Henry Wilson, 1812–1875* (Lexington, 1972), 23, 47; Donald, *Sumner and the Coming of the Civil War,* 178–79. John B. Alley had been apprenticed for five years as a shoemaker before he launched his own shoe manufacturing firm in Lynn, Massachusetts. In 1847, at the age of thirty, Alley moved to Boston, where he established a successful hide and leather house and took a leading role in antislavery politics. See *Biographical Directory of American Congresses, 1774–1961* (Washington, D.C., 1961), 474.

35. S. C. Phillips to Charles Sumner, 9 Jan. 1851, Sumner Papers, HL; Abbott, *Cobbler in Congress,* 38–40; Martin B. Duberman, *Charles Francis Adams, 1807–1886* (Boston, 1961), 172–74.

36. S. C. Phillips to Charles Sumner, 15 Jan. 1851, Sumner Papers, HL; Samuel Gridley Howe to Horace Mann, n.d. [April 1851], Samuel Gridley Howe Papers, HL; Duberman, *Adams,* 174, 199; S. C. Phillips's biographical sketches in *National Cyclopedia of American Biography,* 62 vols. (1891–1984), 11:489–90, and *Biographical Directory of the American Congresses,* 1455.

37. Samuel Gridley Howe to Horace Mann, n.d. [April 1851], Howe Papers, HL.

38. In this discussion of the proposed constitutional reforms of 1853, I have relied on Samuel Shapiro, "The Conservative Dilemma; The Massachusetts Constitutional Convention of 1853," *New England Quarterly* 33 (June 1960): 207–24.

39. Abbott, *Cobbler in Congress,* 40–50.

40. Salmon P. Chase to Edward S. Hamlin, 2 Apr. 1851, and Chase to Benjamin F. Butler, 26 July 1849, letterbook copy, Chase Papers, LC.

41. Sewell, *Ballots for Freedom,* 248–49.

42. Henry Wilson to Charles Sumner, 3 Feb. and 23 June 1852, Sumner Papers, HL; Donald, *Sumner and the Coming of the Civil War,* 220. For assessments of pro-Scott sentiment among Conscience Whigs, see James W. Stone to Charles Sumner, 29 May, 6, 8 June, 1852, Sumner Papers, HL; and George G. Fogg to John P. Hale, 3 Aug. 1852, copy, John P. Hale Papers, Dartmouth College Library.

43. Salmon P. Chase to Edward S. Hamlin, 19 July 1852, Chase Papers, LC; R. H. Dana to Charles Sumner, 11 Aug. 1852, Sumner Papers, HL; [S. P. Chase], *The Radical Democracy of New York and the Independent Democracy: Letter from Senator Chase, of Ohio, to Hon. B. F. Butler, of New York,* (N.p., 1852).

Chapter 7

1. Charles Sumner to Amasa Walker, 26 Apr. 1854, Amasa Walker Papers, MHS.

2. Wendell Phillips, *Speeches, Lectures, and Letters,* Negro Universities Press ed. (New York, 1968), 260.

3. Historians disagree concerning the relative importance of antislavery doctrine and nativist sentiment in the emerging Republican party. Richard H. Sewell, *Ballots for Freedom: Antislavery Politics in the United States, 1837–1860* (New York, 1976), 265–89, and Eric Foner, *Free Soil, Free Labor, Free Men: The Ideology of the Republican Party before the Civil War* (New York, 1970), 226–60, emphasize the centrality of antislavery doctrine. Joel Silbey, *A Respectable Minority: The Democratic Party in the Civil War Era, 1860–1868* (New York, 1977), 3–29, summarizes the findings of those students of political behavior (including himself) who judge "ethno-cultural" identities to be at the heart of party alignments. Michael F. Holt, *The Political Crisis of the 1850s* (New York, 1978), pursues a middle course. Of particular importance for the following discussion of reformist reactions to nativism is the evidence presented by Holt and others which traces the roots of nativism to native workingmen. In addition to Holt, as cited above, see Holt, "The Politics of Impatience: The Origins of Know Nothingism," *Journal of American History* 60 (Sept. 1973): 309–31; Jean Gould Hales, "'Co-Laborers in the Cause': Women in the Ante-Bellum Nativist Movement," *Civil War History* 25 (June 1979): 119–38; Hales, "The Shaping of Nativist Sentiment, 1848–1860" (Ph.D. dissertation, Stanford University, 1973), esp. 1–25, 403–61; Steven Joseph Ross, "Workers on the Edge: Work, Leisure, and Politics in Industrializing Cincinnati, 1830–1860" (Ph.D. dissertation, Princeton University, 1980), 332–51. See also the recent discussions of nativism in William E. Gienapp, "Nativism and the Creation of a Republican Majority in the North before the Civil War," *Journal of American History* 72 (Dec. 1985): 529–59; Dale Baum, *The Civil War Party System: The Case of Massachusetts, 1848–1876* (Chapel Hill, 1984), 24–54; and Sean Wilentz, *Chants Democratic: New York City and the Rise of the American Working Class, 1788–1850* (New York, 1984), 266–70.

4. William H. Seward to Charles Sumner, 9 Nov. 1852, 13 Sept. 1854, 22 Oct. 1855, and William Jay to Sumner, 10 Aug. 1855, Charles Sumner Papers, HL.

5. John McLean to Caleb B. Smith, 6 May 1848; Thomas Corwin to Smith, 10 May 1848; and Schuyler Colfax to Smith, 19 Oct. 1859, Caleb B. Smith Papers, LC; Joshua R. Giddings to Charles Sumner, 22 Dec. 1848, Sumner Papers, HL; *Dictionary of American Biography,* 9:244–45.

6. Gamaliel Bailey to George Washington Julian, 16 Mar. 1849; Caleb B. Smith to Julian, 13 Feb. 1859; and Smith to Julian, 2 Jan. 1861, Joshua R. Giddings–George Washington Julian Papers, LC; Joseph Medill to Elihu B. Washburne, 13 Jan. 1862, Elihu B. Washburne Papers, LC.

7. Edward Magdol, *Owen Lovejoy: Abolitionist in Congress* (New Brunswick, N.J., 1967), 59–62, 79–81; Zebina Eastman, "History of the Anti-Slavery Agitation, and the Growth of the Liberty and Republican Parties in the State of Illinois," in Rufus Blanchard, *Discovery and Conquests of the North-West, with the History of Chicago* (Wheaton, Ill., 1881).

8. Zebina Eastman to Elihu B. Washburne, 18 Sept. 1852, Washburne Papers, LC; Henry Wilson to Charles Sumner, 2 July 1854, Sumner Papers, HL.

9. William H. Seward to Charles Sumner, 19 May 1853; Edward L. Pierce to Sumner, 4 May 1858; Schouler to Sumner, 27 Sept. 1869 and n.d. 1847, Sumner Papers, HL; Denison to S. P. Chase, 1 Jan. 1859, and E. L. Pierce to Chase, 31 May 1859, Salmon P. Chase Papers, LC; Reinhard H. Luthin, "Salmon P. Chase's Political Career before the Civil War," *Mississippi Valley Historical Review* 29 (Mar. 1943): 523–25; Eugene H. Roseboom, "Salmon P. Chase and the Know Nothings," *Mississippi Valley Historical Review* 25 (Dec. 1938): 338; Frank O. Gatell, *John Gorham Palfrey and the New England Conscience* (Cambridge, Mass., 1963), 145, 190; Kinley J. Brauer, *Cotton versus Conscience: Massachusetts Whig Politics and Southwestern Expansion, 1843–1848* (Lexington, 1967), 221n.

10. Gilbert Osofsky, "Abolitionists, Irish Immigrants, and the Dilemma of Romantic Nationalism," *American Historical Review* 80 (Oct. 1975): 889–912.

11. "Letter of Daniel O'Connell on American Slavery," 11 Oct. 1843, in [Salmon P. Chase et al.], *Liberty or Slavery? Daniel O'Connell on American Slavery: Reply to O'Connell by Hon. S. P. Chase* [Cincinnati, 1863], 8. O'Connell's letter to the Cincinnati Irish Repeal Association and Chase's reply were reprinted to consolidate Unionist support following the issuance of the Emancipation Proclamation.

12. "Letter of Hon. S. P. Chase in Reply to Daniel O'Connell," 30 Nov. 1843, in [Chase et al.], *Liberty or Slavery?* 14.

13. Garrison quoted in Osofsky, "Abolitionists," 900, 906.

14. Bailey quoted in Sewell, *Ballots for Freedom*, 268.

15. Stephen C. Phillips to Charles Sumner, 15 Nov. 1854, Sumner Papers, HL.

16. Salmon P. Chase to Edward S. Hamlin, 21 Nov. 1854 and 22 Jan. 1855, Chase Papers, LC.

17. Salmon P. Chase to Charles Sumner, 16 July 1858, Sumner Papers, HL.

18. Salmon P. Chase to Edward S. Hamlin, 9 Feb. 1855, Chase Papers, LC; Sewell, *Ballots for Freedom*, 272; *Biographical Directory of the American Congresses*, 655.

19. Lewis D. Campbell to Salmon P. Chase, 28 May 1855, Chase Papers, LC.

20. Salmon P. Chase to Lewis D. Campbell, 29 May 1855, and Edward L. Pierce to Chase, 4 June 1855, Chase Papers, LC.

21. Salmon P. Chase to Elihu B. Washburne, 18 June 1859, Washburne Papers, LC; Chase to Charles Sumner, 19 June 1855, and Lewis D. Campbell to Sumner, 16 Oct. 1855, Sumner Papers, HL; Chase to [David Heaton et al.], 23 Oct. 1855, and Campbell to Chase, 6 Aug. 1855 and 4 July 1856, Chase Papers, LC; Roseboom, "Chase and the Know Nothings," 343n, 337–50.

22. Salmon P. Chase to Sydney Howard Gay, 14 Mar. 1854, Sydney Howard Gay Collection, Columbia University; Edward L. Pierce to Charles Sumner, 10 May 1857, Sumner Papers, HL.

23. Gamaliel Bailey to Salmon P. Chase, 25 June, 27 Nov. 1855, Salmon P. Chase Papers, HSP; William H. Seward to Charles Sumner, 9 Nov. 1855, Sumner Papers, HL.

24. George Washington Julian to E. A. Stansbury, 15 Sept. 1857, Giddings-Julian Papers, LC.

25. Francis W. Bird to Charles Sumner, 15 Apr. 1854 and 8 June 1857, Sumner Papers, HL; Edward L. Pierce to Salmon P. Chase, 3 Aug. 1857, Chase Papers, LC.

26. Salmon P. Chase to Edward S. Hamlin, 22 Jan. 1855, Chase Papers, LC; Hamlin quoted in Roseboom, "Chase and the Know Nothings," 337. See also James Brewer Stewart, *Joshua R. Giddings and the Tactics of Radical Politics* (Cleveland, 1970), 117; and E. S. Hamlin, "Salmon Portland Chase," *International Review* 2 (Sept. 1875): 662—91.

27. Adams quoted in Martin B. Duberman, *Charles Francis Adams, 1807—1886* (Boston, 1961), 177; Kevin Sweeney, "Rum, Romanism, Representation, and Reform: Coalition Politics in Massachusetts, 1847—1853," *Civil War History* 22 (June 1976): 116—37; Francis W. Bird to Sumner, 15 Apr. 1854 and 8 June 1857; and Edward L. Pierce to Sumner, 31 May 1859, Sumner Papers, HL; see also Richard H. Abbott, *Cobbler in Congress: The Life of Henry Wilson, 1812—1875* (Lexington, 1972), 16, 38—40, 75; Brauer, *Cotton versus Conscience*, 24; Henry Wilson to Sumner, 1 Sept. 1853; J. W. Stone to Sumner, 6 June 1852; Albert G. Browne to Charles Sumner, 3 Jan. 1855, Sumner Papers, HL.

28. Salmon P. Chase to John P. Bigelow, 23 Sept. 1854, John P. Bigelow Papers, HL; Chase to Nettie, 24 Dec. 1866, Chase Papers, LC.

29. James W. Stone to Charles Sumner, 3 Feb. 1855, Sumner Papers, HL; Samuel Gridley Howe to Charles Sumner, 9 Feb. 1855, Samuel Gridley Howe Papers, HL; Ichabod Codding to his wife, 14 Apr. 1855, Ichabod Codding Papers, microfilm copy, Illinois Historical Society; Duberman, *Adams,* 200—201; Salmon P. Chase to [N. S. Townshend?], 2 May 1849, Chase Papers, HSP; Gamaliel Bailey to Joshua R. Giddings, 29 Sept. 1849, and John C. Vaughan to Charles Sumner, 15 Sept. 1851, Sumner Papers, HL; Chase to Edward S. Hamlin, 2 Feb. 1851, Chase Papers, LC.

30. Duberman, *Adams,* 213.

31. Garrison quoted in Osofsky, "Abolitionists," 907.

32. William Elder to Salmon P. Chase, 14 Jan. 1845, Chase Papers, HSP.

33. Theodore Parker to Wendell Phillips, 14 May 1859, Wendell Phillips Papers, HL; see also Eugene D. Genovese, *Roll, Jordan, Roll: The World the Slaves Made* (New York, 1976), 298.

34. George William Curtis to Charles Eliot Norton, 19 Aug. 1861, George William Curtis Papers, HL.

35. *New York Independent* quoted in Phyllis F. Field, *The Politics of Race in New York: The Struggle for Black Suffrage in the Civil War Era* (Ithaca, 1982), 123; Jacob M. Howard to Sumner, 22 June 1865, Sumner Papers, HL.

36. David A. Wells to Charles Sumner, 14 Apr. [1872], Sumner Papers, HL.

Chapter 8

1. Wendell Phillips, "Washington and the West, Speech of Wendell Phillips, Esq. at the Tremont Temple, Thursday Evening April 17, 1862," clipping in the Amasa Walker Papers, MHS.

2. Of the most radical defender of slavery, Eugene Genovese writes: "George Fitzhugh asked a question. If it was true, as proslavery spokesmen confidently asserted, that the Negro slave fared better, materially and spiritually, than the free white workers and peasants of the Western world, then how could capitalism be reconciled with Christian morality? If this assertion was true, did not justice and conscience require that all labor be enslaved for its own happiness and protection?" (Genovese, *The World the Slaveholders Made: Two Essays in Interpretation,* Vintage Books ed. [New York, 1969], 126).

3. Stephen Colwell, *The Five Cotton States and New York; or, Remarks upon the Social and Economical Aspects of the Southern Political Crisis* (N.p., Jan. 1861), 6.

4. *Dictionary of American Biography,* 10:338–39; Richard H. Abbott, *Cobbler in Congress: The Life of Henry Wilson, 1812–1875* (Lexington, 1972), 37; Richard H. Sewell, *Ballots for Freedom: Antislavery Politics in the United States, 1837–1860* (New York, 1976), 9, 26; John G. Sproat, *"The Best Men": Liberal Reformers in the Gilded Age* (New York, 1968), 184; J. Dresno, Jr., to Amasa Walker, 27 Jan. 1848; William Warren to Amasa Walker, 31 Jan. 1848; and "Mr. Walker's Speech at the Massachusetts State Antimasonic Convention . . . ," clipping, Walker Papers, MHS; Amasa Walker to Charles Sumner, 12 June, 20 Dec. 1854, Charles Sumner Papers, HL.

5. Amasa Walker, *Address of the Free Soil Members of the Legislature to Their Constituents,* broadside, 24 Apr. 1849, Walker Papers, MHS.

6. Ibid.

7. *New York Independent,* 5 Sept. 1861, 10 Aug. [1862?], clippings in Walker Papers, MHS.

8. Amasa Walker, *The Science of Wealth: A Manual of Political Economy, Embracing the Laws of Trade Currency and Finance. Condensed and Arranged for Popular Reading and Use as a Textbook,* 7th ed. (Philadelphia, 1872) [the first edition appeared in 1866], 34–35, 50, 76, 284–85, 427–28; George M. Fredrickson, *The Inner Civil War: Northern Intellectuals and the Crisis of the Union* (New York, 1965), 202, 223; Burton J. Bledstein, *The Culture of Professionalism: The Middle Class and the Development of Higher Education in America* (New York, 1976), 53–55.

9. George Opdyke, *A Treatise on Political Economy* (New York, 1851), 151, 339.

10. Elizur Wright, Jr., to Salmon P. Chase, 3 Feb. 1861, Chase Papers, LC.

11. Daniel R. Goodloe, *Inquiry into the Causes Which Have Retarded the Accumulation of Wealth and Increase of Population in the Southern States: In Which the Question of Slavery Is Considered in a Politico-Economical Point of View. By a Carolinian* (Washington, D.C., 1846), 8; Goodloe, "Resources and Industrial Condition of the Southern States," in *Report of the Commissioner of Agriculture for the Year 1865* (Washington, D.C., 1866), 118; Goodloe to Charles Sumner, 6 May 1865, Sumner Papers, HL.

12. Goodloe, "Resources and Industrial Condition," 119, 122; Goodloe, *The South and the North: Being a Reply to a Lecture on the North and the South, by Ellwood Fisher, Delivered before the Young Men's Mercantile Library Association of Cincinnati, January 16, 1849. By a Carolinian* (Washington, D.C., 1849), 6, 14; Goodloe, *Inquiry,* 18.

13. Robert W. Fogel and Stanley L. Engerman, *Time on the Cross: The Eco-*

nomics of American Negro Slavery (Boston, 1974), 70. Fogel and Engerman conclude that "on average, slaveowners earned about 10 percent on the market price of their bondmen," that "rates of return were approximately the same for investments in males and females," and that "they were also approximately the same across geographical regions." See also Goodloe, "Resources and Industrial Condition," 122; Ulrich B. Phillips, *American Negro Slavery: A Survey of the Supply, Employment and Control of Negro Labor as Determined by the Plantation Regime*, Louisiana State University Press ed., intro. by Eugene D. Genovese (Baton Rouge, 1966), 349–52, 401.

14. Goodloe, *Inquiry*, 10, 18; Goodloe, "Resources and Industrial Condition," 119, 121, 122.

15. Goodloe to Charles Sumner, 22 June 1870, Sumner Papers, HL; Goodloe, *Inquiry*, 115.

16. See Arthur M. Schlesinger, Sr.'s, introduction to Frederick Law Olmsted, *The Cotton Kingdom: A Traveller's Observations on Cotton and Slavery in the American Slave States* (New York, 1962), ix–lvi; and Lawrence N. Powell's introduction to the Schlesinger edition (New York, 1984), ix–xxxiii.

17. Charles Capen McLaughlin, ed., *The Papers of Frederick Law Olmsted*, Vol. 1, *The Formative Years, 1822 to 1852* (Baltimore, 1977), 3–46.

18. Frederick Law Olmsted to Frederick Kingsbury, 23 Sept. 1847, and Olmsted to Charles Loring Brace, 4 July 1848, in McLaughlin, ed., *Olmsted Papers*, 1:303, 320; Fredrickson, *Inner Civil War*, 101.

19. Frederick Law Olmsted to Frederick Kingsbury, 23 Sept. 1847, McLaughlin, ed., *Olmsted Papers*, 1:303; George William Curtis to Charles Eliot Norton, 3 Aug. 1860, George William Curtis Papers, HL. See also Harvey Wish's introduction to *Frederick Law Olmsted: The Slave States* (New York, 1959), 7–37.

20. On Goodloe's role as editor, see Schlesinger's introduction to Olmsted, *Cotton Kingdom*, xxviii–xxxiv; McLaughlin, ed., *Olmsted Papers*, 1:24; and Charles E. Beveridge and Charles Capen McLaughlin, eds., *The Papers of Frederick Law Olmsted*, Vol. 2, *Slavery and the South, 1852 to 1857* (Baltimore, 1981), 35.

21. Olmsted, *Cotton Kingdom*, 444, 446, 478.

22. Ibid., 454–57.

23. Ibid., 454–55. In Beveridge and McLaughlin, eds., *Olmsted Papers*, 2:465, 470, the editors identify the plantation as that of Meredith Calhoun, located in the Red River district of Louisiana and visited by Olmsted in March 1853. In his letter to the *Times*, Olmsted wrote of the second whipping that "I must say, however, that the girl did not seem to suffer the intense pain that I should have supposed she would." This remark is omitted from the account in *A Journey in the Back Country* and *The Cotton Kingdom*. The presence of the "young gentleman of fifteen," described in later accounts, is not mentioned in the *Times* article. See Beveridge and McLaughlin, eds., *Olmsted Papers*, 2:215–30.

24. Olmsted, *Cotton Kingdom*, 445, 456–57, 475.

25. Kinley J. Brauer, *Cotton versus Conscience: Massachusetts Whig Politics and Southwestern Expansion, 1843–1848* (Lexington, 1967), 159–60.

26. Frederick Douglass, *Narrative of the Life of Frederick Douglass, an American*

Slave. Written by Himself (Boston, 1845), xxi.

27. It was an image as well of what Barrington Moore, Jr., delineated as the Prussian road to industrial capitalism. See *Social Origins of Dictatorship and Democracy: Lord and Peasant in the Making of the Modern World* (Boston, 1966), 115, 121; and Genovese, *World Slaveholders Made*, 226–27.

28. James S. Pike to Salmon P. Chase, 27 Feb. 1858, Chase Papers, HSP; Olmsted, *Cotton Kingdom*, 584; Ronald G. Walters, *The Antislavery Appeal: American Abolitionism after 1830* (Baltimore, 1976), 113–14. See also Eric Foner, *Free Soil, Free Labor, Free Men: The Ideology of the Republican Party before the Civil War* (New York, 1970), 21–23.

29. Glyndon G. Van Deusen, *William Henry Seward* (New York, 1967), 205–6.

30. Records of the Board of Commissioners for the Emancipation of Slaves in the District of Columbia, 1862–67, Record Group 217, National Archives; Chase to William Greenleaf Eliot, 31 Mar. 1862, William Greenleaf Eliot Papers, Missouri Historical Society; Michael J. Kurtz, "Emancipation in the Federal City," *Civil War History* 24 (Sept. 1978): 250–67.

31. Salmon P. Chase to Gerrit Smith, 3 May 1850, Salmon P. Chase Papers, LC.

32. Salmon P. Chase to [John F. Morse?], 3 Dec. 1850, Chase Papers, LC.

33. Salmon P. Chase to E. S. Hamlin, 15 Jan. 1851, Chase Papers, LC; Chase to Charles Sumner, 26 Feb. 1851, Sumner Papers, HL; Chase to unknown, 1 Apr. 1851, Autography File, HL.

34. Frederick Law Olmsted, *A Journey in the Back Country* (New York, 1860), viii–ix.

35. Quoted in Arthur Zilversmit, *The First Emancipation: The Abolition of Slavery in the North* (Chicago, 1967), 87.

36. Quoted in Alice D. Adams, *The Neglected Period of Anti-Slavery in America, 1808–1831* (Boston, 1908), 172–74.

37. Parker Pillsbury to Wendell Phillips, 21 Apr. 1864, Wendell Phillips Papers, HL; see also John L. Thomas, "Romantic Reform in America," *American Quarterly* 17 (Winter 1965): 656–81.

38. Theodore Sedgwick, *The Practicability of the Abolition of Slavery: A Lecture at the Lyceum in Stockbridge, Massachusetts, February, 1831* (New York, 1831), 24–25, 38, 43–48.

39. [William Lloyd Garrison], *Selections from the Writings and Speeches of William Lloyd Garrison*, New American Library ed. (New York, 1969), 69.

40. Joshua Leavitt, *Alarming Disclosures: Political Power of Slavery. Substance of Several Speeches by Rev. Joshua Leavitt in the Ohio Anti-Slavery Convention, and at Public Meetings in That State, in Oct. 1840, and Published in the "Emancipator"* (N.p., 1840), 3–5, 13–41.

41. Salmon P. Chase, *The Address of the Southern and Western Liberty Convention to the People of the United States* (Cincinnati, 1845).

42. Eli Thayer to Horace Greeley, 2 Feb. 1855, Horace Greeley Papers, New York Public Library; George Winston Smith, "Ante-Bellum Attempts of Northern Business Interests to 'Redeem' the Upper South," *Journal of Southern History* 11 (May 1945): 191–92.

Chapter 9

1. George M. Fredrickson, *The Inner Civil War: Northern Intellectuals and the Crisis of the Union* (New York, 1965), 202–5; Francis Walker is quoted on 223. Concerning the relationship between the domestic sphere of middle-class family life and middle-class involvement in social welfare and missionary activities in the mid- and late nineteenth century, see Mary P. Ryan, *Cradle of the Middle Class: The Family in Oneida County, New York, 1790–1865* (Cambridge, Mass., 1981), 210–50; and Jane Unter, *The Gospel of Gentility: American Women Missionaries in Turn-of-the-Century China* (New Haven, 1984), esp. xiii–xvii.

2. The reference here is to early nineteenth-century doctrines of agrarianism and communitarianism, the best discussions of which appear in Arthur Bestor, *Backwoods Utopias: The Sectarian Origins and the Owenite Phase of Communitarian Socialism in America, 1663–1829,* 2d ed. (Philadelphia, 1970), esp. 202–29; and Whitney R. Cross, *The Burned-Over District: The Social and Intellectual History of Enthusiastic Religion in Western New York, 1800–1850* (Ithaca, 1950), 322–40. As Cross observed in the context of Gerrit Smith's advocacy of agrarianism, "the historians of land policy have paid insufficient attention to the ideological aspects of their subject to realize the possible connection in people's minds between rent wars and homesteading theories." For a recent discussion of land reform in the context of the New York City workingmen's movement, see Sean Wilentz, *Chants Democratic: New York City and the Rise of the American Working Class, 1788–1850* (New York, 1984), 335–43.

On Amasa and Francis Walker, see Fredrickson, *Inner Civil War,* 223; and Amasa Walker, *The Science of Wealth: A Manual of Political Economy, Embracing the Laws of Currency and Finance. Condensed and Arranged for Popular Reading and Use as a Textbook,* 7th ed. (Philadelphia, 1872), 34–35, 76, 309, 430–49.

3. William Lloyd Garrison to Wendell Phillips, 19 Apr. 1861, Wendell Phillips Papers, HL; Lydia Maria Child to Charles Sumner, 16 July 1861, Charles Sumner Papers, HL; Wendell Phillips, *Speeches, Lectures, and Letters,* Negro Universities Press ed. (New York, 1968), 348; [William Lloyd Garrison], *Selections from the Writings and Speeches of William Lloyd Garrison,* New American Library ed. (New York, 1969), 46.

4. Child quoted in James M. McPherson, *The Struggle for Equality: Abolitionists and the Negro in the Civil War and Reconstruction* (Princeton, 1964), 91; George William Curtis to Charles Eliot Norton, 19 Aug. 1861, 1 Mar. 1862, and 6 Feb. 1863, George William Curtis Papers, HL; Edward L. Pierce, "The Contraband of Fortress Monroe," *Atlantic,* 8 (1861): 640. A railroad lawyer closely associated politically with Massachusetts's Senator Charles Sumner, Pierce would shortly be chosen by Secretary of the Treasury Salmon P. Chase to direct the administration of contraband labor at Port Royal, South Carolina. See Salmon P. Chase to Edward L. Pierce, 2 Aug. 1862, James Freeman Clarke Papers, HL; and Louis S. Gerteis, *From Contraband to Freedman: Federal Policy toward Southern Blacks, 1861–1865* (Westport, Conn., 1973), 51–53. See also Fredrickson, *Inner Civil War,* 209; Eric Foner, *Free Soil, Free Labor, Free Men: The Ideology of the Republican Party before the Civil War* (New York, 1970), 309; and *Dictionary of American Biography,* 2:614–16.

5. Lydia Maria Child to Sarah Shaw, 11 Aug. 1865, in Milton Meltzer and Patricia G. Holland, eds., *Lydia Maria Child: Selected Letters, 1817–1880* (Amherst, 1982), 457; Child, *The Freedmen's Book* (Boston, 1865), iii; [Child], *Letters of Lydia Maria Child with a Biographical Introduction by John G. Whittier and an Appendix by Wendell Phillips* (Boston, 1883), viix. Child's abolitionist career and her advocacy of expanded female rights and responsibilities are discussed in Blanche Glassman Hersh, *The Slavery of Sex: Feminist Abolitionists in America* (Urbana, 1978). On Child's importance in the developing cult of domesticity, see Ann Douglas, *The Feminization of American Culture* (New York 1977), 56–57; Steven Mintz, *A Prism of Expectations: The Family in Victorian Culture* (New York, 1983), 84–86; and Ellen K. Rothman, *Hands and Hearts: A History of Courtship in America* (New York, 1984), 65. In northern missionary work among the freedmen, female teachers primarily carried out the work of moral uplift while male superintendents instructed the freedmen in the rigors and presumed rewards of free labor. See Henry Lee Swint, *The Northern Teacher in the South, 1862–1870* (Nashville, 1941); and Willie Lee Rose, *Rehearsal for Reconstruction: The Port Royal Experiment* (New York, 1964).

6. [Lydia Maria Child], *The Mother's Book. By Mrs. Child* (Boston, 1831), v, 4, 9.

7. Lydia Maria Child to Lucy Searle, 5 June 1861, and Child to Sarah Shaw, 31 July and 25 Aug. 1877, in Meltzer and Holland, eds., *Selected Letters*, 383, 543–44; [Child], *Letters*, xx.

8. Norman Ware, *The Industrial Worker, 1840–1860*, Quadrangle books ed. (Chicago, 1944), 136; David Montgomery, *Beyond Equality: Labor and the Radical Republicans, 1862–1872*, Vintage Books ed. (New York, 1967), 296–334; John G. Sproat, *"The Best Men": Liberal Reformers in the Gilded Age* (New York, 1968), 211–12.

9. Lydia Maria Child to George Washington Julian, 12 July 1871, in Meltzer and Holland, eds., *Selected Letters*, 500; Child to Charles Sumner, 4 July 1870, Charles Sumner Papers, HL.

10. John A. Andrew to Charles Sumner, 10 Dec. 1862, Sumner Papers, HL.

11. Daniel R. Goodloe, "Resources and Industrial Condition of the Southern States," in *Report of the Commissioner of Agriculture for the Year 1865* (Washington, D.C., 1866), 102–3, 188–89, 126.

12. W. H. Furness to Charles Sumner, 24 Nov. 1867, Sumner Papers, HL.

13. Although the decline in Jamaican sugar production (which Child and other reformers noted) is not in doubt, the freedmen's responses to emancipation (which was the reformers' central concern) continues to demand close scholarly scrutiny. On one hand, the transition to freedom in the Caribbean witnessed the rise of peasantries, rooted to some extent in preemancipation slave cultivation of provision plots and expanded in the postemancipation setting wherever land-labor ratios permitted the growth of self-sufficient agriculture. In this setting, labor's flight from the plantations in Jamaica has been viewed as an expression of the freedmen's preference for self-sufficiency over dependent wage labor on white-owned plantations. On the other hand, the freedmen's departure from the plantations does not seem to have followed immediately upon emancipation. It certainly increased in the wake of a sharp decline in sugar prices in the 1840s and a correspondingly sharp drop in

wages that followed. This development, when combined with the planters' practice of deducting wages for rent (on one plantation rents amounted to nearly 15 percent of wages in the 1830s) and the seasonal pattern of employment, which replaced the rhythm of intense labor and relative leisure characteristic of slavery, could easily have made peasant cultivation not simply a choice by the freedmen but, for increasing numbers, a necessity as well.

For discussions of changing patterns of labor and production in the postemancipation Caribbean, see Stanley Engerman and David Eltis, "Economic Aspects of the Abolition Debate," in Christine Bolt and Seymour Drescher, eds., *Anti-Slavery, Religion, and Reform: Essays in Memory of Roger Anstey* (Kent, England, 1980), esp. 285–86; Sidney W. Mintz, "Slavery and the Rise of Peasantries," *Historical Reflections* 6 (Summer 1979): 213–42; Michael Craton, *Searching for the Invisible Man: Slaves and Plantation Life in Jamaica* (Cambridge, Mass., 1978), 175–93; and Douglas Hall, "The Flight from the Estates Reconsidered: The British West Indies, 1838–42," *Journal of Caribbean History* 10–11 (1978): 7–24.

14. Lydia Maria Child, *The Right Way the Safe Way, Proved by Emancipation in the British West Indies, and Elsewhere* (New York, 1862), 55, 64, 69, 70, 78; Child, *The Evils of Slavery, and the Cure of Slavery. The First Proved by the Opinions of Southerners Themselves, the Last Shown by Historical Evidence* (Newburyport, Mass., 1836), 17.

15. John Jay, *The Progress and Results of Emancipation in the English West Indies: A Lecture Delivered before the Philomathian Society of the City of New York* (New York, 1842), 18–19, 38.

16. Salmon P. Chase to unknown, 13 Dec. 1850, Salmon P. Chase Papers, HSP. Many of the same ambiguities expressed by American antislavery reformers characterized British abolitionist assessments of emancipation in the West Indies. See David Eltis, "Abolitionist Perceptions of Post-Emancipation Society," in James Walvin, ed., *Slavery and British Society, 1776–1846* (London, 1982), 201–6; and Howard Temperley, "Abolition and the National Interest," in Jack Hayward, ed., *Out of Slavery: Abolition and After* (London, 1985), 86–107.

17. Thomas Carlyle, *Occasional Discourse on the Negro Question* (London, [1849]). The optimism of antislavery reformers concerning West Indian emancipation is emphasized in James M. McPherson, "Was West Indian Emancipation a Success? The Abolitionist Debate during the American Civil War," *Caribbean Studies* 4 (July 1964): 28–34.

18. John Bigelow, *Jamaica in 1850: Or, The Effects of Sixteen Years of Freedom in a Slave Colony* (New York, 1851), i–ii, 74–75, 111.

19. Bigelow, *Jamaica in 1850*, 115–19, 138, 148–49; Carlyle, *Occasional Discourse*.

20. Richard Hildreth, *The "Ruin" of Jamaica* (New York, [1855?]), 1–12.

21. Frederick Law Olmsted, *The Cotton Kingdom: A Traveller's Observation on Cotton and Slavery in the American Slave States*, ed., with intro. by Arthur M. Schlesinger (New York, 1962), 257.

22. Olmsted, *Cotton Kingdom*, 259, 262–64, 266. See also William Fogel and Stanley L. Engerman, *Time on the Cross: The Economics of American Negro Slavery*

(New York, 1974), 179–81.

23. Salmon P. Chase to Edward L. Pierce, 27 Feb. 1862, Salmon P. Chase Papers, LC.

24. Thomas W. Conway, *Report Read before the Chamber of Commerce of the State of New York, on the Introduction of Capital and Men, from the Northern States and from Europe, into the Southern States of the Union* (New York, 1866), 10. Conway served as wartime superintendent of free labor in the military Department of the Gulf and as assistant commissioner of the Freedmen's Bureau in Louisiana. See also Conway to Charles Sumner, 22 Nov. 1865, Sumner Papers, HL; and Conway to Salmon P. Chase, 24 May 1868, and 26 Sept. 1870, Chase Papers, LC.

25. Edwin M. Stanton to [Covode], 29 May 1865, and, [Covode], unsigned and undated draft of a report to Edwin M. Stanton, John Covode Papers, LC; John Jay to Charles Sumner, 4 Jan. 1862 and 12 Jan. 1863, Sumner Papers, HL. On the freedmen's withdrawal of labor from staple crop production, see also Willie Lee Rose, *Rehearsal for Reconstruction: The Port Royal Experiment*, Vintage books ed. (New York, 1967), 79–82, 174, 203–4, 302–4; and, Steven Hahn, "Hunting, Fishing, and Foraging: Common Rights and Class Relations in the Postbellum South," *Radical History Review* 26 (Oct. 1982): 43–45.

26. Elizur Wright to John P. Hale, 12 Dec. 1860, John P. Hale Papers, Dartmouth College Library; Wright to Salmon P. Chase, 3 Feb. 1844, Chase Papers, LC. Lydia Maria Child to Francis Shaw, 26 Oct. 1879, in Meltzer and Holland, eds., *Selected Letters*, 559.

27. Joshua Leavitt to Salmon P. Chase, 27 Feb. 1862, Chase Papers, LC; Francis W. Bird, testimony, American Freedmen's Inquiry Commission Records, Adjutant General's Office, Record Group 94, National Archives; John Murray Forbes to Charles Sumner, 17 Jan. 1863, and John Jay to Sumner, 4 Jan. 1862 and 12 Jan. 1863, Sumner Papers, HL; Rose, *Rehearsal for Reconstruction*, 226. For similar proposals, see William H. Brisbane to Chase, 4 Jan. 1862 and 12 Jan. 1863, and Eli Thayer to Chase, 16, 17 Oct. 1861, Chase Papers, LC.

28. Professor J. C. Zachos to Salmon P. Chase, 9 Dec. 1862, Chase Papers, LC; John A. Andrew to Chase, 3 Jan. 1863, Chase Papers, HSP; M. C. Meigs to Charles Sumner, 16, 17 Sept. 1865, Sumner Papers, HL.

29. Francis P. Blair to Charles Sumner, 25 Oct. 1863, Sumner Papers, HL; John C. Underwood to Charles Sumner, Mar. 1865, and Benjamin F. Butler to Sumner, 5 Feb. 1863, Sumner papers, HL; Salmon P. Chase to Edward L. Pierce, 2 Aug. 1862, Clarke Papers, HL; *Dictionary of American Biography*, 10:113–14. See also Blair's antebellum opinions on Negro colonization and the commercial and territorial expansion of the United States: *Colonization and Commerce* (Washington, D.C., 1859), and *The Destiny of the Races of this Continent* (Washington, D.C., 1859).

30. Elizur Wright to Charles Sumner, 6 Mar. 1865, Sumner Papers, HL; Wright to Salmon P. Chase, 3 Feb., 7 Mar., and 4 May 1861 and 13 Nov. 1862, Chase Papers, LC; *Boston Commonwealth*, 14 June, typed copy of a clipping, Elizur Wright Papers, LC.

31. Thaddeus Stevens, *Reconstruction: Speech of the Hon. Thaddeus Stevens,*

Delivered in the City of Lancaster, September 7th, 1865 (Lancaster, Pa., 1865), 5; Sumner quoted in Allan G. Bogue, *The Earnest Men: Republicans of the Civil War Senate* (Ithaca, 1981), 230.

32. [George W. Julian], *Speeches on Political Questions by George W. Julian, with an Introduction by L. Maria Child* (New York, 1872), 50–51, 54–55, 57.

33. John Murray Forbes to Charles Sumner, 10 Aug. 1872, Sumner Papers, HL. Concerning the limited authority of the Freedmen's Bureau in the redistribution of land, see Edward L. Pierce to Charles Sumner, 18 Apr. 1864; Frank G. Shaw to Sumner, 21 Apr. 1864; and Thomas D. Eliot to Sumner, 26 July 1864, Sumner Papers, HL. On the fate of federal land reform, see Louis S. Gerteis, "Salmon P. Chase, Radicalism, and the Politics of Emancipation, 1861–1864," *Journal of American History* 60 (June 1973): 42–62.

34. Julian, *Speeches on Political Questions*, 178–79; Julian, *Political Recollections, 1840–1872* (Chicago, 1884), 277–80; Julian quoted in George Winston Smith, "Some Northern Wartime Attitudes toward the Post–Civil War South," *Journal of Southern History* 10 (Aug. 1944): 267–68; Lydia Maria Child to George Washington Julian, 27 Mar. 1864, Joshua R. Giddings–George Washington Julian Papers, LC.

35. Lydia Maria Child to Abigail Foster, 28 Mar. 1869, in Meltzer and Holland, eds., *Selected Letters*, 486; Edward Atkinson to Charles Sumner, 8 July 1867, Sumner Papers, HL; Salmon P. Chase to Edward L. Pierce, 2 Aug. 1862, Clarke Papers, HL; Rose, *Rehearsal for Reconstruction*, 297–310.

36. A. Mot to Salmon P. Chase, 10 July 1867, Chase Papers, LC; "Letter from Fernandina, Fla.," 18 May 1865, clipping in Edward L. Pierce, Freedmen's Scrapbook, 1864–65, Sumner Papers, HL; Reverend Mansfield French to Chase, 7 Feb. 1867, Chase Papers, LC. The collapse of plantation agriculture and the rise of a black peasantry in the low country is discussed in Eric Foner, *Nothing but Freedom: Emancipation and Its Legacy* (Baton Rouge, 1983), 108–10.

37. Goodloe, "Resources and Industrial Condition," 103, 118.

38. John Murray Forbes to Salmon P. Chase, 15 Aug. 1862, Chase Papers, LC.

39. John Murray Forbes to Charles Sumner, 10 Aug. 1872, Sumner Papers, HL. The work of the inquiry commission is discussed in John G. Sproat, "Blueprint for Radical Reconstruction," *Journal of Southern History* 23 (1957): 25–44; Charles Storey to Henry Wilson, 26 Apr. 1862, Henry Wilson Papers, LC; Samuel Gridley Howe, fragment of letter to [Charles Sumner], n.d.; and Howe to Sumner, 8 Jan. 1864, Samuel Gridley Howe Papers, HL.

Chapter 10

1. Salmon P. Chase, diary, 29 July 1872, Salmon P. Chase Papers, HSP.

2. General John W. Phelps to Charles Sumner, 23 Jan. 1865, and 21, 30 Dec. 1864, Charles Sumner Papers, HL; Phelps to Thaddeus Stevens, 13 Feb. 1866, Thaddeus Stevens Papers, LC; Louis S. Gerteis, *From Contraband to Freedman:*

Federal Policy toward Southern Blacks, 1861–1865 (Westport, Conn., 1973), 68–71.

3. William Lloyd Garrison to Charles Sumner, 14 Dec. 1865, Sumner Papers, HL; Garrison to George Washington Julian, 11 Feb. 1866, Joshua R. Giddings–George Washington Julian Papers, LC; Edwin M. Stanton to Horace Greeley, 5 Dec. 1866, letter marked "not sent," Edwin M. Stanton Papers, LC.

4. Francis Gillette to Charles Sumner, 8 Mar. 1870, John Murray Forbes to Sumner, 10 Aug. 1872, and Lydia Maria Child to Sumner, 8 May 1868, Sumner Papers, HL; Child to Lucy Osgood, 13 Apr. 1865, in Milton Meltzer and Patricia G. Holland, eds., *Lydia Maria Child: Selected Letters, 1817–1880* (Amherst, 1982), 452.

5. John Jay to Charles Sumner, 18 Nov. 1863, Sumner Papers, HL; Salmon P. Chase to H. Vallette, 5 Apr. 1864, Salmon P. Chase Papers, LC.

6. John A. Andrew to Charles Sumner, 21 Nov. 1865, Sumner Papers, HL.

7. Samuel Gridley Howe to Charles Sumner, 15 Jan. [1860], 16 Apr. 1861, and 19 Aug. [1861]; and Howe to Martin F. Conway, 10 Dec. [1860] and 6 Apr. [1861], Samuel Gridley Howe Papers, HL.

8. Elizur Wright, draft of letter to Salmon P. Chase, n.d., Elizur Wright Papers, LC; George William Curtis to Charles Eliot Norton, 6 Apr. 1864, 15 Oct. 1865, and 11 July 1869, George William Curtis Papers, HL; Norton to Edward L. Pierce, 24 Mar. 1866, Sumner Papers, HL.

9. Joseph R. Hawley to Charles Sumner, 23 Mar. 1870, Sumner Papers, HL; Hawley, "Declaration of . . . Political Sentiments," 11 July 1849, Joseph R. Hawley Papers, LC; W. McKee Evans, *Ballots and Fence Rails: Reconstruction on the Lower Cape Fear* (New York, 1966), 46, 248; Alexander H. Stephens to Henry Wilson, 15 Sept. 1865, Henry Wilson Papers, LC.

10. John Greenleaf Whittier to Charles Sumner, 21 Mar. 1871, Sumner Papers, HL; Whittier to Miles L. Norton et al., 3 Sept. 1872, in John B. Pickard, ed., *The Letters of John Greenleaf Whittier*, 3 vols. (Boston, 1975), 3 : 274–76; Horace Greeley to George Washington Julian, 7 Mar. 1870, Giddings-Julian Papers, LC.

11. As C. Vann Woodward concluded in *Reunion and Reaction: The Compromise of 1877 and the End of Reconstruction* (Boston, 1951), 246, "the South became a bulwark instead of a menace to the new order." For recent discussions of the same point, see Barbara Jeanne Fields, "The Advent of Capitalist Agriculture: The New South in a Bourgeois World," in Thavolia Glymph and John J. Kushma, eds., *Essays on Postbellum Southern Economy* (College Station, Texas, 1985), 73–94; and Elizabeth Fox-Genovese and Eugene D. Genovese, *Fruits of Merchant Capital: Slavery and Bourgeois Property in the Rise and Expansion of Capitalism* (New York, 1983), esp. 398.

12. Daniel R. Goodloe to Charles Sumner, 17 Mar., 11 May 1868, and 11 Sept. 1865, Sumner Papers, HL; Otto H. Olsen, *Carpetbagger's Crusade: The Life of Albion Winegar Tourgée* (Baltimore, 1965), 67.

13. Cassius M. Clay to Henry Wilson, 17 Mar. 1871, Wilson Papers, LC.

14. Salmon P. Chase to Edwin M. Stanton, 20 May 1865, Stanton Papers, LC; [Chase], "An Amendment on Reconstruction," Vol. 12, Misc., 747–48,

Chase Papers, LC; Chase to Stanley Matthews, 14 Apr. 1865, in Annie A. Nunns, ed., "Some Letters of Salmon P. Chase, 1848–1865," *American Historical Review* 34 (1929): 554; [Chase], *U.L.A. "Going Home to Vote." Authentic Speeches of S. P. Chase, Secretary of the Treasury, during His Visit to Ohio, with His Speeches at Indianapolis, and at the Mass Meeting in Baltimore, October, 1863* (Washington, D.C., 1863), 10–20; Otto H. Olsen, "Southern Reconstruction and the Question of Self-Determination," in George M. Fredrickson, ed., *A Nation Divided: Essays on the Civil War and Reconstruction* (Minneapolis, 1975), 113–41.

15. Salmon P. Chase to Gerrit Smith, 30 Feb. 1868 and 31 May 1866, Chase Papers, LC; [Chase], *Letter From Chief Justice Chase to a Committee of Colored Men* (N.p., 1865); Gerrit Smith, *No Treason in Civil War: Speech of Gerrit Smith, at Cooper Institute, New-York, June 8, 1865* (New York, 1865); Chase to Gerrit Smith, 25 June 1867, Chase Papers, LC.

16. Salmon P. Chase to William [M?] Byrd, 3 Apr. 1869, letterbook copy; Chase to H. W. Hilliard, 27 Apr. 1868; Chase to John D. Van Buren, [5?] Apr. 1868; and Chase to Van Buren, copy of letter, 3 July 1868, Chase Papers, LC.

17. Carl Schurz to Charles Sumner, 30 Sept. 1871, Sumner Papers, HL.

18. John Jay to Charles Sumner, 5 Jan. [1864], Sumner Papers, HL; Theodore Tilton to Wendell Phillips, 26 Jan. 1865, Wendell Phillips Papers, HL; Amos Tuck to Thaddeus Stevens, 26 Jan. 1866, Stevens Papers, LC.

19. Moorfield Storey to Charles Sumner, 15 May 1873, Sumner Papers, HL.

20. Edward Atkinson to Charles Sumner, 11 Apr. 1867, 25 Feb., 10, 22 June, 1868, Sumner Papers, HL; Francis W. Bird to Sumner, 6, 8 Mar. [1867], Sumner Papers, HL.

21. Lydia Maria Child to Charles Sumner, 4 July 1870; Amasa Walker to Sumner, 13 July 1868; John B. Alley to Sumner, 19 Nov. 1868; Edward Atkinson to Sumner, 11 Feb. and 4 Dec. 1868; T. P. Chandler to Sumner, 27 Nov. 1868; and Samuel Hooper to Sumner, 24 Sept. 1869, Sumner Papers, HL; Elizur Wright to George S. Boutwell, 28 Mar. 1869, Wright Papers, LC; John G. Sproat, *"The Best Men": Liberal Reformers in the Gilded Age* (New York, 1968), 170–203.

22. Austin Willey to Charles Sumner, 23 Jan. 1871; James M. Stone to Sumner, 11 Mar. 1871, Sumner Papers, HL.

23. Elizur Wright to Charles Sumner, 13 July 1872; William S. Robinson to Sumner, 14 Mar., 24 Apr. and 1 May 1871, Sumner Papers, HL.

24. D. W. Alvord to Charles Sumner, 18 Aug. 1868 and 8 Jan. 1871, Sumner Papers, HL; Alvord to Francis W. Bird, 18 May 1858, Francis W. Bird Papers, HL.

25. [Charles Sumner], *Charles Sumner: His Complete Works*, 20 vols., Negro Universities Press ed. (New York, 1969), 20:83–171, 177, 189–90.

26. [Sumner], *Works*, 20:177; Salmon P. Chase to Charles Sumner, 2 Aug. 1872, and Wendell Phillips to Sumner, 4 Aug. 1872, Sumner Papers, HL. See also Lawrence Grossman, *The Democratic Party and the Negro: Northern and National Politics, 1868–1872* (Urbana, 1976), esp. 4–6.

27. William Lloyd Garrison to Charles Sumner, 28 Mar., 22 Nov. 1871,

Sumner Papers, HL; Patrick W. Riddleberger, "The Break in the Radical Ranks: Liberal vs Stalwarts in the Election of 1872," *Journal of Negro History* 44 (Apr. 1959): 143.

28. Gerrit Smith to Charles Sumner, 13 Nov. 1868, 20 Dec. 1870, Sumner Papers, HL; Salmon P. Chase to Gerrit Smith, 28 Feb. 1868, Chase Papers, LC; Earle Dudley Ross, *The Liberal Republican Movement,* University of Washington Press ed. (Seattle, 1970), 117.

29. Gerrit Smith to Charles Sumner, 8, 31 Aug. and 8 Oct. 1871, Sumner Papers, HL.

30. Edward Atkinson to Charles Sumner, 19 Feb. 1868, 8 Apr. and 1 June 1872, Sumner Papers, HL; James M. McPherson, "Grant or Greeley? The Abolitionist Dilemma in the Election of 1872," *American Historical Review* 71 (Oct. 1965): 43–61.

31. George Washington Julian to A. L. Robinson, 12 Nov. 1872, Giddings-Julian Papers, LC; Hiram Barney to Charles Sumner, 10, 24 Apr., 6 June 1872, Sumner Papers, HL; Samuel May to Francis W. Bird, 16 Apr. 1885, Bird Papers, HL.

32. Elizur Wright to George F. Hoar, draft of letter, 30 Nov. 1884; R. G. Ingersoll to Wright, 19 Aug. 1879; L. D. Bailey to Wright, 19 Oct. 1880; and Judge D. D. McKoon [secretary of the People's party] to Wright, 24 Aug. 1881, Wright Papers, LC; Sproat, *"Best Men,"* 132–33.

33. Salmon P. Chase, Memorandum, "Miscellaneous Thoughts," Chase Papers, HSP.

34. Wendell Phillips, *Speeches, Lectures, and Letters,* Negro University Press ed. (New York, 1968), 496; Hiram Barney to Charles Sumner, 6 June 1872, Sumner Papers, HL; see also Sproat, *"Best Men,"* 194, 205–42.

35. Sallie Holley to Zebina Eastman, 8 June 1874, Zebina Eastman Collection, Chicago Historical Society; Holley to Wendell Phillips, 14 Mar. 1874, Phillips Papers, HL.

36. Concerning the biography of her father, see Sallie Holley's letters to Elizur Wright from 20 July 1876 to 20 July 1885 in the Wright Papers, LC; and Elizur Wright, *Myron Holley; and What He Did for Liberty and True Religion* (Boston, 1882). On Sallie Holley as a second-generation abolitionist, see James M. McPherson, *The Abolitionist Legacy: From Reconstruction to the NAACP* (Princeton, 1975), 30, 156, 400.

Bibliography of Primary Sources

Manuscript Collections

Boston, Massachusetts
  Massachusetts Historical Society
    Horace Mann Papers
    Amasa Walker Papers
Cambridge, Massachusetts
  Harvard University, Houghton
      Library
    Autograph File
    John Prescott Bigelow Papers
    Francis W. Bird Papers
    James Freeman Clarke Papers
    George William Curtis Papers
    Samuel Gridley and Julia Ward
      Howe Papers
    Wendell Phillips Papers
    Charles Sumner Papers
Chicago, Illinois
  Chicago Historical Society
    Zebina Eastman Collection
Detroit, Michigan
  Detroit Public Library
    Jacob M. Howard Papers
    Charles Lanman Papers
Hanover, New Hampshire
  Dartmouth College Library
    John P. Hale Papers
    Amos Tuck Papers
New York, New York
  Columbia University Library
    Sydney Howard Gay Collection
Philadelphia, Pennsylvania
  Historical Society of Pennsylvania
    Salmon P. Chase Papers
Springfield, Illinois

Illinois Historical Society
  Ichabod Codding Papers
St. Louis, Missouri
  Missouri Historical Society
    William Greenleaf Eliot Papers
Washington, D.C.
  Library of Congress
    James G. Birney Papers
    Benjamin F. Butler Papers
    Salmon P. Chase Papers
    Thomas Corwin Papers
    John Covode Papers
    Joshua R. Giddings–George
      Washington Julian Papers
    Joseph R. Hawley Papers
    Caleb Blood Smith Papers
    Edwin M. Stanton Papers
    Thaddeus Stevens Papers
    Lewis Tappan Papers
    Elihu B. Washburne Papers
    Western Anti-Slavery Society
      Papers
    Henry Wilson Papers
    Elizur Wright Papers
  National Archives
    American Freedmen's Inquiry
      Commission Records, Adju-
      tant General's Office, Record
      Group 94
    Records of the Board of Com-
      missioners for the Emancipa-
      tion of Slaves in the District of
      Columbia, 1862–67, Record
      Group 217.

Printed Material

Adams, John Quincy. *The Abolition of Slavery the Right of the Government under the War Power.* Boston, 1861.
————. *The Jubilee of the Constitution: A Discourse Delivered at the Request of the New York Historical Society, in the City of New York, on Tuesday, the 30th of April, 1839; Being the Fiftieth Anniversary of the Inauguration of George Washington as President of the United States, on Thursday, the 30th of April, 1789.* New York, 1839.
Annals of Congress. 1st Cong., 2d sess.
Annals of Congress. 5th Cong., 2d sess.
Annals of Congress. 15th Cong., 2d sess.
The Antelope. 10 Wheaton, 105–6 (1825).
Belknap, Jeremy. "Queries Respecting the Slavery and Emancipation of Negroes in Massachusetts." *Collections of the Massachusetts Historical Society,* 1st ser., 4 (1795): 191–211.
Bigelow, John. *Jamaica in 1850: Or, the Effects of Sixteen Years of Freedom in a Slave Colony.* New York, 1851.
James G. Birney v. The State of Ohio. 8 Ohio Reports, 230–39 (1837).
Birney, William. *James G. Birney and His Times: The Genesis of the Republican Party with Some Account of Abolition Movements in the South before 1828.* New York, 1890.
Blair, Francis P., Jr. *Colonization and Commerce.* Washington, D.C., 1859.
————. *The Destiny of the Races of this Continent.* Washington, D.C., 1859.
Blassingame, John W., ed. *The Frederick Douglass Papers, Series One: Speeches, Debates, and Interviews.* Volume 1, *1841–46.* New Haven, 1979.
————. *The Frederick Douglass Papers, Series One: Speeches, Debates, and Interviews.* Volume 2, *1847–54.* New Haven, 1982.
Boyd, Julian P., ed. *The Papers of Thomas Jefferson.* 20 vols. Princeton, 1950–82.
Carey, Henry C. *American Civil War, Correspondence with Mr. H. C. Carey, of Philadelphia.* N.p., 1861.
————. *A Memoir of Stephen Colwell: Read before the American Philosophical Society, Friday November 17, 1871.* Philadelphia, 1871.
————. *Principles of Political Economy, Part the Second: Of the Causes Which Retard Increase in the Production of Wealth, and Improvement in the Physical and Moral Condition of Man.* Philadelphia, 1838.
————. *Principles of Political Economy, Part the Fourth: Of the Causes Which Retard the Improvement in the Political Condition of Man.* Philadelphia, 1840.
Carlyle, Thomas. *Occasional Discourse on the Negro Question.* London, [1849].
Catterall, Helen Tunnicliff, ed. *Judicial Cases Concerning American Slavery and the Negro.* 5 vols. Washington, D.C., 1926–37.
Chase, Salmon P. *The Address of the Southern and Western Liberty Convention to the People of the United States.* Cincinnati, 1845.
————. *How the South Rejected Compromise in the Peace Conference of 1861.*

Speech of Mr. Chase, of Ohio. Published from the Notes of a Member. New York, [1863?].

———, et al. *Liberty or Slavery? Daniel O'Connell on American Slavery: Reply to O'Connell by Hon. S. P. Chase.* [Cincinnati?], 1863.

———. "Life and Character of Henry Brougham." *North American Review* 33 (1831): 227–61.

———. *The Radical Democracy of New York and the Independent Democracy: Letter from Senator Chase, of Ohio, to Hon. B. F. Butler, of New York.* N.p., 1852.

———. *A Sketch of the History of Ohio* in *Statutes of Ohio and the Laws of the Northwest Territory.* Cincinnati, 1833.

———. *Speech of Hon. Salmon P. Chase, Delivered at the Republican Mass Meeting in Cincinnati, August 21, 1855; Together with Extracts from His Speeches in the Senate on Kindred Subjects.* Columbus, 1855.

———. *Speech of Salmon P. Chase, in the Case of the Colored Woman, Matilda, Who Was Brought before the Court of Common Pleas of Hamilton County, Ohio, by Writ of Habeas Corpus; March 11, 1837.* Cincinnati, 1837.

———. U.L.A. *"Going Home to Vote." Authentic Speeches of S. P. Chase, Secretary of the Treasury, during His Visit to Ohio, with His Speeches at Indianapolis, and at the Mass Meeting in Baltimore, October, 1863.* Washington, D.C., 1863.

———. *Union and Freedom, without Compromise: Speech of Mr. Chase, of Ohio, on Mr. Clay's Compromise Resolutions.* Washington, D.C., [1850].

Child, Lydia Maria. *The Evils of Slavery, and the Cure of Slavery. The First Proved by the Opinions of Southerners Themselves, the Last Shown by Historical Evidence.* Newburyport, Mass., 1836.

———. *The Freedmen's Book.* Boston, 1865.

———. *Letters of Lydia Maria Child with a Biographical Introduction by John G. Whittier and an Appendix by Wendell Phillips.* Boston, 1883.

———. *The Mother's Book. By Mrs. Child.* Boston, 1831.

———. *The Right Way the Safe Way, Proved by Emancipation in the British West Indies, and Elsewhere.* New York, 1862.

Cobb, Thomas R. R. *An Inquiry into the Law of Negro Slavery in the United States of America. To Which is Prefixed, An Historical Sketch of Slavery.* Negro Universities Press ed. New York, 1968.

Colwell, Stephen. *The Five Cotton States and New York; or, Remarks upon the Social and Economical Aspects of the Southern Political Crisis.* N.p., Jan. 1861.

———. *New Themes for Protestant Clergy: Creeds without Charity, Theology without Humanity, Protestantism without Christianity: With Notes by the Editor on the Literature of Charity, Population, Pauperism, Political Economy, and Protestantism.* Philadelphia, 1851.

———. *The Position of Christianity in the United States in Its Relations with Our Political Institutions and Specially with Reference to Religious Instruction in the Public Schools.* Arno Press ed. New York, 1972.

———. *The South: A Letter from a Friend in the North. With Special Reference to the Effects of Disunion upon Slavery.* Philadelphia, 1856.

Congressional Globe. 27th Cong., 2d sess.

Conway, Thomas W. *Report Read before the Chamber of Commerce of the State of New York, on the Introduction of Capital and Men, from the Northern States and from Europe, into the Southern States of the Union.* New York, 1866.

[Douglass, Frederick]. *Life and Times of Frederick Douglass Written by Himself: His Early Life as a Slave, His Escape from Bondage, and His Complete History.* Collier Books ed. London, 1962.

————. *Narrative of the Life of Frederick Douglass, an American Slave. Written by Himself.* Boston, 1845.

Eastman, Zebina. "History of the Anti-Slavery Agitation, and the Growth of the Liberty and Republican Parties in the State of Illinois." In Rufus Blanchard, *Discovery and Conquests of the North-West, with the History of Chicago.* Wheaton, Ill., 1881.

Elder, William. *Conversations on the Principal Subjects of Political Economy.* Philadelphia, 1882.

————. *A Memoir of Henry C. Carey. Read before the Historical Society of Pennsylvania, January 5, 1880.* Philadelphia, 1880.

————. *Questions of the Day: Economic and Social.* Philadelphia, 1871.

————. *Third Parties: "The Duties of Anti-Slavery Voters."* Philadelphia, 1851.

[Garrison, William Lloyd]. *Selections from the Writings and Speeches of William Lloyd Garrison.* New American Library ed. New York, 1969.

Giddings, Joshua R. *Pacificus: The Rights and Privileges of the Several States in Regard to Slavery: Being a Series of Essays, Published in the Western Reserve Chronicle, (Ohio,) After the Election of 1842. By a Whig of Ohio.* N.p., n.d.

Goodloe, Daniel R. *Inquiry into the Causes Which Have Retarded the Accumulation of Wealth and Increase of Population in the Southern States: In Which the Question of Slavery Is Considered in a Politico-Economical Point of View. By a Carolinian.* Washington, D.C., 1846.

————. "Resources and Industrial Condition of the Southern States." In *Report of the Commissioner of Agriculture for the Year 1865.* Washington, D.C., 1866.

————. *The South and the North: Being a Reply to a Lecture on the North and the South, by Ellwood Fisher, Delivered before the Young Men's Mercantile Library Association of Cincinnati, January 16, 1849. By a Carolinian.* Washington, D.C., 1849.

Hamlin, E. S. "Salmon Portland Chase." *International Review* 2 (September 1875): 662–91.

Hildreth, Richard. *Despotism in America: An Inquiry into the Nature, Results, and Legal Basis of the Slave-Holding System in the United States.* Boston, 1854.

————. *The "Ruin" of Jamaica.* New York, [1855?].

Jay, John. *The Progress and Results of Emancipation in the English West Indies: A Lecture Delivered before the Philomathian Society of the City of New York.* New York, 1842.

Julian, George Washington. *Political Recollections, 1840–1872.* Chicago, 1884.

————. Review of T. C. Smith, *The Liberty and Free Soil Parties in the Northwest.* New York, 1897. *American Historical Review* 4 (October 1898–July 1899): 180–81.

———. *Speeches on Political Questions by George W. Julian, with an Introduction by L. Maria Child.* New York, 1872.

Leavitt, Joshua. *Alarming Disclosures: Political Power of Slavery. Substance of Several Speeches by Rev. Joshua Leavitt in the Ohio Anti-Slavery Convention, and at Public Meetings in That State, in Oct. 1840, and Published in the "Emancipator."* N.p., 1840.

———. *Easy Lessons in Reading; For the Use of the Younger Classes in Common Schools.* Keene, N.H., 1823.

———. *The Financial Power of Slavery: The Substance of an Address Delivered in Ohio, in September, 1840, by Joshua Leavitt, of New York.* N.p., [1841?].

———. *Memorial of Joshua Leavitt, Setting Forth Importance of an Equitable and Adequate Market for American Wheat, Accompanied with Statistical Tables.* Albany, [1841?].

———. *The Moral and Social Benefits of Cheap Postage.* New York, 1849.

———. *Selections for Reading and Speaking, for the Higher Classes in Common Schools.* Boston, 1847.

Marsh, Luther R., ed. *Writings and Speeches of Alvan Stewart, on Slavery.* New York, 1860.

McLaughlin, Charles Capen, ed. *The Papers of Frederick Law Olmsted.* Volume 1, *The Formative Years, 1822 to 1852.* Baltimore, 1972.

———. *The Papers of Frederick Law Olmsted.* Volume 2, *Slavery and the South, 1852 to 1857.* Baltimore, 1981.

Meltzer, Milton, and Holland, Patricia G., eds. *Lydia Maria Child: Selected Letters, 1817–1880.* Amherst, 1982.

Mifflin, Warner. *A Serious Expostulation with the Members of the House of Representatives of the United States.* Philadelphia, 1793.

Nunns, Annie A., ed. "Some Letters of Salmon P. Chase, 1848–1865." *American Historical Review* 34 (1929): 536–55.

Olmsted, Frederick Law. *The Cotton Kingdom: A Traveller's Observations on Cotton and Slavery in the American Slave States.* New York, 1962.

———. *A Journey in the Back Country.* New York, 1860.

Opdyke, George. *A Treatise on Political Economy.* New York, 1851.

Padover, Saul K., ed. *The Complete Jefferson: Containing His Major Writings, Published and Unpublished, Except His Letters.* Books for Libraries Press ed. Freeport, N.Y., 1969.

Parrish, John. *Remarks on the Slavery of the Black People; Addressed to the Citizens of the United States, Particularly to Those Who Are in Legislative or Executive Stations in the General or State Governments; and also to Such Individuals as Hold Them in Bondage.* Philadelphia, 1806.

Peet, Rev. Stephen. *Presbyterian and Congregational Churches and Ministers in Wisconsin: Including an Account of the Organization of the Convention and the Plan of Union.* Milwaukee, 1851.

Phillips, Wendell. *The Constitution a Pro-Slavery Compact.* 3d ed. New York, 1856.

———. *Review of Lysander Spooner on the Unconstitutionality of Slavery.* Boston, 1847.

————. *Speeches, Lectures, and Letters.* Negro Universities Press ed. New York, 1968.

Pierce, Edward L. "The Contraband of Fortress Monroe." *Atlantic* 8 (1861): 626–40.

Riddle, Albert Gallatin. "The Election of Salmon P. Chase to the Senate, February 22, 1849." *Republic* 4 (1875): 180–88.

Ripley, C. Peter, ed. *The Black Abolitionist Papers.* Vol. 1, *The British Isles, 1830–1865.* Chapel Hill, 1985.

Sedgwick, Theodore. *The Practicability of the Abolition of Slavery: A Lecture at the Lyceum in Stockbridge, Massachusetts, February, 1831.* New York, 1831.

————. *Public and Private Economy: Part I.* New York, 1836.

Seward, William H. *California, Union, and Freedom: Speech of William H. Seward, on the Admission of California, Delivered in the Senate of the United States, March 11, 1850.* Washington, D.C., 1850.

Sharp, Granville. *Letter from Granville Sharp, Esq. of London, to the Maryland Society for Promoting the Abolition of Slavery, and the Relief of Free Negroes and Others, Unlawfully Held in Bondage.* Baltimore, 1793.

Smith, Gerrit. *Land Reform: Speech of Gerrit Smith, Made in Syracuse, January 20, 1848, on Land Reform.* Syracuse, 1849.

————. *No Treason in Civil War: Speech of Gerrit Smith, at Cooper Institute, New-York, June 8, 1865.* New York, 1865.

Smith, Theodore Clarke. *The Liberty and Free Soil Parties in the Northwest.* New York, 1897.

[Spooner, Lysander]. *The Collected Works of Lysander Spooner.* 6 vols. Weston, Mass., 1971.

Stevens, Thaddeus. *Reconstruction: Speech of the Hon. Thaddeus Stevens, Delivered in the City of Lancaster, September 7th, 1865.* Lancaster, Pa., 1865.

————. *Speech of Thaddeus Stevens, of Pennsylvania, on the California Question. Made in the House of Representatives, Night Session, June 10, 1850.* N.p., [1850?].

Stewart, Alvan. *The Causes of Hard Times.* Boston, 1840.

Stuart, Charles. *A Memoir of Granville Sharp.* New York, 1836.

[Sumner, Charles]. *Charles Sumner: His Complete Works.* 20 vols. Negro Universities Press ed. New York, 1969.

Tuckerman, Bayard. *William Jay and the Constitutional Movement for the Abolition of Slavery.* New York, 1893.

Walker, Amasa. *Address of the Free Soil Members of the Legislature to Their Constituents.* Broadside. N.p., 1849.

————. *The Science of Wealth: A Manual of Political Economy, Embracing the Laws of Trade Currency and Finance. Condensed and Arranged for Popular Reading and Use as a Textbook.* 7th ed. Philadelphia, 1872.

Washburn, Emory. "Extinction of Slavery in Massachusetts." In *Proceedings of the Massachusetts Historical Society, 1855–1858.* Boston, 1859: 188–203.

Webster, Daniel, et al. *A Memorial to the Congress of the United States on the Subject of Restraining the Increase of Slavery in New States to Be Admitted into the Union.* Boston, 1819. Reprinted in *The Nebraska Question.* Boston, 1854.

Willey, Austin. *The History of the Antislavery Cause in State and Nation.* Portland, Me., 1886.
Wright, Elizur. *Myron Holley; and What He Did for Liberty and True Religion.* Boston, 1882.

Index